Contents

Acknowledgements		vii
Introduction		ix
The Secret History of a London Wedding	*Vogue* 1929	1
The Shooting Party	*Vogue* 1929	6
At a Point-to-Point	*The Lady* 1930	10
In Covent Garden Now	*The Lady* 1930	14
Faringdon House	*House & Garden* 1948	18
Paris Column	*Sunday Times* 1949–53	23
Britain Revisited	*Sunday Times* 1950	76
Chic – English, French and American	*Atlantic Monthly* 1951	81
Rome is only a Village	*Sunday Times* 1952	85
The Mystery of the Missing Arsenic	*Picture Post* 1953	88
The English Aristocracy	*Encounter* 1955	92
Wicked Thoughts in Greece	*Sunday Times* 1955	106
A Queen of France	*Sunday Times* 1955	111
Channel-Crossing	*The New Statesman & Nation* 1956	115
A Heart of Stone	*The New Statesman & Nation* 1956	118
In Defence of Louis XV	*Sunday Times* 1956	120

Portrait of a French Country House

Sunday Times 1961   123

Reading for Pleasure

The Times 1961   133

Blor

Sunday Times 1962   136

The Other Island

The Water Beetle 1962   146

A Bad Time

The Water Beetle 1962   152

The Last to be Broken on the Wheel

New York Times 1963   165

The Sun King

Spectator 1964   168

Paris Diary

The New Statesman 1966   173

My friend Evelyn Waugh

Arts et Loisirs 1966   177

Garden of Delights

Sunday Times 1967   180

Tam & Fritz: Carlyle and Frederick the Great

History Today 1968   183

Views

The Listener 1968   197

France, May 1968: A Revolution Diary Parts I & II

Spectator 1968   202

A
Talent to
Annoy

By the same author

NOVELS

Highland Fling
Christmas Pudding
Wigs on the Green
Pigeon Pie
The Pursuit of Love
Love in a Cold Climate
The Blessing
Don't Tell Alfred

NON-FICTION

Madame de Pompadour
Voltaire in Love
The Sun King
Frederick the Great
The Water Beetle (essays)

EDITED

The Ladies of Alderley
The Stanleys of Alderley
Noblesse Oblige

A Talent to Annoy

Essays, Articles and Reviews 1929–1968

by Nancy Mitford

EDITED BY CHARLOTTE MOSLEY

HAMISH HAMILTON: LONDON

First published in Great Britain 1986
by Hamish Hamilton Ltd
27 Wrights Lane London W8 5TZ

British Library Cataloguing in Publication Data

Mitford, Nancy
  A talent to annoy: essays, articles &
  reviews, 1929–1968.
  I. Title   II. Mosley, Charlotte
  828′.91208   PR6025.I88

  ISBN 0-241-11916-2

Typeset by Rowland Phototypesetting Ltd, Bury St Edmunds, Suffolk
Printed and bound in Great Britain by
Billing & Sons Ltd, Worcester

Acknowledgements

The editor would like to thank The Duchess of Devonshire for permission to quote from Nancy Mitford's letters, Lady Selina Hastings for her help in gathering material, and A. D. Peters & Co. Ltd for permission to use the material.

The editor acknowledges the following publications in which Nancy Mitford's articles were first printed:

Arts et Loisirs: 'My Friend Evelyn Waugh'. The Condé Nast Publications Ltd: 'The Shooting Party', 'Faringdon House' and 'The Secret History of a London Wedding' (© the Condé Nast Publications Ltd 1929). *Encounter:* 'The English Aristocracy'. *History Today:* 'Carlyle and Frederick the Great'. *The Lady:* 'At a Point-to-Point' and 'In Covent Garden Now'. *The Listener:* 'Views'. *The New Statesman:* 'Channel-Crossing'; 'A Heart of Stone' and 'Paris Diary'. The *Spectator:* 'The Sun King' and 'France, May 1968: 'A Revolution Diary'. The *Sunday Times:* 'Paris Column'; 'Britain Revisited'; 'Rome is only a Village'; 'Wicked Thoughts in Greece'; 'A Queen of France'; 'In Defence of Louis XV'; 'Portrait of a French Country House'; 'Blor'; 'A Garden of Delights'. *The Times:* 'Reading for Pleasure'.

'The Mystery of the Missing Arsenic' first appeared in *Picture Post.* 'The Other Island' and 'A Bad Time' were first published in *The Water Beetle.*

'Chic – English, French and American' appeared under the title 'What is Chic?' in the *Atlantic Monthly* © 1951 the Atlantic Monthly Company, Boston.

The Review of 'Voltaire and the Calas Case' was first printed in *The New York Times* © 1963 by the New York Times Company. Reprinted by permission.

The extracts from Evelyn Waugh's letters are reprinted by kind permission of Auberon Waugh.

Introduction

It is for her romantic novels and historical biographies that Nancy Mitford is most widely known and loved. She is less famous today – and was less loved at the time – for her journalism. In this she was able to exercise to the full her delight in teasing, something she could only do indirectly in her books. But, although the purpose of her articles was often to tease, Nancy was no less assiduous in her research and took no fewer pains in their writing than she did in her biographies and novels. She wrote to her sister, Diana Mosley, about the weekly column commissioned by the *Sunday Times*: 'The fact is these articles which look like nothing at all take me ages of fussing and rewriting if they are to succeed' and to Evelyn Waugh: 'They take me for ever, 8 hours a day for a month.'

Nancy frequently complained (not entirely with justification as she attended at least one good school and was well-taught at home) of her lack of any formal education, and it is true, like many girls of her generation, she never went to a university. But a feeling of being under-educated may have worked in her favour, certainly as regards her journalism; she became very well-read in the subjects that interested her and kept a keen and inquiring mind throughout her life, looking on education as an open-ended process. Unlike many people who long to learn, Nancy had no desire to teach. This lack of any didactic purpose or pomposity, together with the idiosyncracy of her point of view, give Nancy's articles an immediacy which is unfettered by ideology or theory and which leaves her journalism as fresh, funny and readable as when it was first published. Her talents were recognised by her friend and literary adviser, Evelyn Waugh, who wrote: 'It is your métier.'

Nancy Mitford was born in 1904, the eldest of seven children of Lord and Lady Redesdale. A rich vein of literary talent ran through both sides of the family and was inherited by Nancy and three of her sisters. Their paternal grandfather, Bertram Mitford, was the author of several books, in particular of *Tales of Old Japan*; a best-seller in its day, it remains still in print. Their maternal grandfather, Thomas Gibson Bowles, was a journalist and founder of a weekly news magazine, *Vanity Fair*, and of the still-popular weekly *The Lady*. This talent for writing manifests itself not only in published books, but also in the vast correspondence that was carried on between members of the family and their friends over several generations. Nancy herself was a brilliant and prolific letter-writer. Her letters were written above all to amuse (and are not, therefore, always reliable as regards the exact truth); they were also exercises in observation and as such often led on naturally to her articles.

Nancy's first journalism consisted of snippets of anonymous gossip written in her early twenties to earn money. Contrary to what people might have thought, this was the only time during her career as a journalist that she did provide newspapers with gossip; later on she was always very discreet in what she wrote for publication. When the *Sunday Times* tried to persuade her to become a kind of Paris William Hickey, she refused and gave up her regular column in the paper.

The desire for financial independence spurred Nancy's early writing. Her first signed articles were occasional pieces for English and American glossy magazines until 1929 when she became a regular contributor to *The Lady*. From this time on, until the onset of her fatal illness in 1968, Nancy wrote frequent articles and reviews for a wide range of newspapers and magazines. A short selection of her journalism was published in 1966 in *The Water Beetle*, which Nancy herself edited. The present collection, while by no means exhaustive, covers a wider time span and aims to reflect the full range of her interests and concerns. These remained fairly constant throughout her life: history, France, clothes, the theatre, travel, the incongruous and language. A fascination with this last initially drew her to the subject of U and Non-U and inspired her to write the article for which she is most famous: 'The English Aristocracy'. Although it is true that the subject provided an irresistible opportunity for 'an anthology of teases', it also reflected a real linguistic interest which reoccurs regularly in her articles.

Nancy's journalism enabled her to pursue and combine her interests in a less formal and structured way than that required by her books. It allowed her to cover a wider variety of topics, sometimes ephemeral or exotic. The research her articles entailed was also a good training for the excellent biographies which she wrote during the last part of her career. Her creativity as a novelist may have been waning, but her sharp sense of personalities and their idiosyncrasies had not deserted her and it combined successfully with the reporter's skill she had developed through her journalism. The traits and insights which make *Madame de Pompadour*, *The Sun King* and *Frederick the Great* perennial favourites can all be seen in the pieces she wrote for newspapers and magazines.

C.M.

The Secret History of a London Wedding

Nancy Mitford to Mark Ogilvie-Grant March 26, 1929

'I'm making such a lot of money with articles – £22 since Christmas and more owing to me so I'm saving it up to be married but Evelyn Waugh says don't save it, dress better and catch a better man. Evelyn is always so full of sound common sense.'

'Nancy Mitford's sister, Diana, was married to Bryan Guinness on January 30, 1929. Nancy was one of the bridesmaids.'

It is in Sheridan's *Critic* that the heroine goes mad in white satin with flowers in her hair, while the confidante goes mad in white linen with straw in hers. Every heroine, even in 1929, has her confidante, and when the heroine is arranging her wedding it is the confidante who sees more of what goes on behind the scenes than anyone else.

The first time that the confidante hears of Mr D. is probably during the London season. The heroine meets him continually, spends a large part of her mornings telephoning to him, and her entire evenings dancing with him. One day Mr D. is seen lunching with the heroine's father at the Marlborough Club, shortly afterwards there is an announcement in *The Times*, and Mr D. becomes the hero, which surprises nobody, and least of all the confidante.

It is now that this good creature is in her element. Her advice is asked, though seldom taken, on every question which crops up. She reads with great interest all the letters of congratulations that pour in by every post for weeks. The heroine definitely enjoys the first fifty or sixty very much indeed, after that she says with a sigh 'How too kind people are,' and in a few days she is heard cursing in the most ungrateful and unladylike manner every time a letter arrives. The same applies to the wedding presents. 'Who gives quickly gives twice,' says the proverb, and in this case it is certainly true. When she is first engaged the heroine goes into raptures over any little thing that arrives, while three days before the wedding she refuses to take any interest in an immensely valuable diamond brooch that arrives hot from Bond Street.

The heroine and the confidante quickly learn to discriminate between a present and the average wedding present. A present is a thing which one might be given at any time, and which one would always receive rapturously, like Burton's *Arabian Nights*, an antique topaz necklace, a book plate, a Louis XIV clock, shoe buckles, a life subscription to the Embassy, books from the Nonesuch Press, and so on.

The average wedding present is a horror, such as a little silver ash tray, a blotter covered in chintz, a screen to go round the telephone, made of reproductions of Dutch pictures, every variety of really hideous electric fittings, a silver soup tureen that might have come out of an ogre's castle, a beaten brass tray, and cut glass and bubble glass so dreadful that it has to be seen to be believed. All these horrors pour in at every hour of the day, leavened from time to time by a real present, and the worst of it is that they are mostly expensive things, but only given as a sort of duty and chosen with no care or taste.

'The glass will be the easiest to deal with,' murmurs the confidante, 'that only needs a good kick.'

'Perhaps we may be burgled,' says the hero, who is busy making a list, 'and get rid of some of the silver that way.'

The hero, at this important period of his life, steadies his nerves by making endless lists, with which his pockets fairly bulge. Lists of wedding presents, lists of bridesmaids, of relatives, hymn tunes, acquaintances, ushers, chauffeurs, invitations, churches, everything has its list. No list when once made is ever read again, as by the time it is really wanted it is always lost.

The choice of a church is not a very difficult matter. The heroine talks, in a way which deceives no one, of a nice quiet country wedding, or, if it must be London, of St Ethelburga the Virgin, St Mary the Wardrobe, the crypt of the House of Commons, and the chapel of the Tower of London, but the lot eventually falls, as everyone knows it must, upon the fashionable Gothic of St Margaret's, Westminster.

Choosing a wedding dress is not so easy. Whether to have it of satin, tulle or velvet is a problem, but an even greater one seems to be how to avoid the Victorian or the mediaeval appearance which a long skirt is apt to give. At last a perfect dress is found, off-white satin with lovely pearl embroideries, the long train of which forms part of the dress itself.

The heroine is now free to give her whole mind to her trousseau. 'All I want in the way of undies,' she explains to the confidante, who is naturally all attention, 'is a dozen sets of pink satin, which is much more chic now than crêpe de Chine, don't you think? and about a dozen pairs of pyjamas. With a few slips to wear under cotton frocks that is really enough, and by having little I can afford to have real lace on everything. As we're going to Paris for our honeymoon I shan't buy more than three evening dresses here, a black, a white, and a pink one. Then I must have an evening coat (silver, I thought, with white fox), a really good black coat and skirt, three or four jumper suits, two printed velvet dresses and one or two satin ones. With my going away dress and coat and a fur coat this will be all I shall need for London. For the country I'm getting two tweed coats and skirts, and a long fur-trimmed tweed coat with a skirt to match, several satin and woolly jumpers to wear with them, and, of course, hats, shoes, gloves and scarfs to go with everything.'

At this moment the heroine's Nanny comes in saying reproachfully, 'You don't seem to have ordered any combinations or nice warm woolly nighties,' but the heroine is busy poring over *Vogue* to find a picture for the bridesmaids' dresses, and doesn't hear.

'How many bridesmaids can I decently have?' says the heroine. The confidante has heard of someone having seventeen, but the heroine's mother thinks it vulgar to have more than ten, so the heroine compromises with eight grown-ups and four children. The bridesmaids' dresses are the next obstacle (a wedding is a sort of mental obstacle race). Luckily, in the case of this particular heroine her friends are like herself, good and beautiful, and unlike most bridesmaids in that they complain neither of the dresses themselves nor of their cost, which the thoughtful heroine arranges with the shop to be as reasonable as possible. The dresses, when finally chosen, are copied from a photograph in *Vogue* of a dress worn by Greta Garbo, and made of hundreds of yards of pearl-coloured tulle, making the bridesmaids look, as the

3

papers say, like a flight of angels. The hero, having done his part by giving each a lovely crystal necklace, the list headed 'Bridesmaids' can be thrown away. (It may here be noted that the bridesmaids are chosen for their looks, the ushers for their well-known devotion to the bride, and the best man for the air of calm superiority with which he meets all eventualities.)

The most tiresome and worrying obstacle that has to be overcome is sending out the invitations. Who to ask? 'Shall we ask X?' 'No, because that looks as though we want him to send us a present.' 'Yes, but on the other hand if we don't ask him he'll be so hurt.'

At last, after much thought, the list is made out, and written in a little red *carnet*, which is invariably lost when it is most needed. To this list are added the names of the people who have sent presents, when the heroine can remember not to lose their cards among the debris of unpacking.

Almost the worst ordeal for everyone is the present which arrives with no card, and as this is generally the kind of thing that people snatch off the mantelpiece and give to the butler to do up it is utterly impossible to trace.

Now we come to the day before the wedding. The heroine, utterly worn out, and the confidante, who is becoming hourly more insane, drag themselves from shop to shop, from writing table to telephone.

The tenants come up from the country to see the presents, which, when laid out on long trestle tables, look like a cross between a charity bazaar and the Victoria and Albert Museum, the detectives taking the place of stallholders or curators.

Last moment arrangements are made at every meal, 'Then will you put the relations' names on their pews?'

'Your car will come immediately before ours, and will be number three.'

'Do you realise we've forgotten to ask Great Aunt Agatha?'

'Well! it's too late now.'

Finally, to everyone's unspeakable relief, the heroine, having literally been pushed into her wedding dress by what appear to be the dressmakers, a wreath maker, a hairdresser and a photographer, arrives at the church, gets married, has all her make-up kissed off her face at the reception, and goes away in a shower of confetti, leaving the confidante to go mad at her leisure, with everyone round her saying, as they always do at weddings, 'How wonderfully quick they've been with the photographs; do you see, dear, they've got them here already?'

Vogue, March 6, 1929

The Shooting Party

Some Hints For The Woman Guest

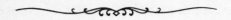

Nancy Mitford to Mark Ogilvie-Grant January 8, 1930

'I do think Mrs Settle is a stingy old thing, she only gave me £6.6.0. for my shooting party article in spite of having my name and all.'

At this time of the year invitations to shooting parties descend in showers upon members of both sexes. As a general rule, however, in spite of asseverations to the contrary ('the modern sportswoman is to be seen everywhere with dog and gun,' etc.), a woman is only asked to these entertainments on account of some man whose presence she can be relied upon to secure. Women at a shooting party are, in fact, slightly superfluous, the only object in asking them being to ensure that the men, who are essential, shall arrive safely. The wives, of course, bring their husbands; it has become a rigid habit with them to do so, much as they might prefer to leave them behind. The unmarried woman is seldom asked, unless one of the men is known to be so much under her thumb that she alone can be relied upon to produce him.

Bearing this in mind, she who receives an invitation to a shooting party should first of all ascertain if the man for whose presence she will be responsible is willing to go with her. If, on being shown the invitation, he should say 'Shoot with that swine again? No, thank you,' or 'What a pity, I have promised to go to the Lord Mayor's Banquet that night,' it is considered tactful to refuse altogether, the woman who under such circumstances accepts for herself alone being seldom asked twice.

When these preliminaries have been settled, enter the date of the shoot neatly in your engagement book. Almost immediately an invitation to a much better shoot on the same date will arrive, but, remembering from last year that although the birds are more numerous the house is colder, you will omit to show this to your husband until you have posted the answer.

At last the great day comes. As a shooting party generally covers a longer period of time than any other sort of house-party, and as the guests are chosen for their skill with the gun rather than for personal charm, it is advisable to arrive fairly late, certainly no earlier than for tea, but preferably in time to dress for dinner. You will thus make your first appearance fortified by a hot bath, and possibly, if your hostess has a thoughtful disposition, by a cocktail sent up to your bedroom.

Unless former experience has proved that this house is truly warm, it is advisable to wear a little coat over your dinner dress; chattering teeth and goose flesh do not add very materially to the feeling of good cheer which is supposed to pervade the dinner table on the first evening, and there are few houses where it is considered good form to rise during dinner and beat the breast in order to stimulate circulation. During this meal, unless your fellow-guests are well known to you, be very careful when choosing subjects for conversation. All personalities should be avoided. It is awkward to ask your neighbour if he knows where Mrs X got her money, only to find that he was married to her himself for several years and is now practically ruined by the enormous alimony which he is obliged to pay her. Your host and his immediate family may, however, safely be mentioned in terms of sickening eulogy.

Art is another topic which should be left severely alone. It is a mistake to begin a house-party on doubtful terms with another member of it, and a discussion on the respective merits of Sir Luke Fildes and Picasso might easily lead to such an estrangement. But do not be discouraged. It is tolerably safe to chatter away on such subjects as The Toll of the Road, the latest outrage perpetrated by the Bright Young People, and the Wall Street crash. You may happen to be the wife of some well-known gun, in which case you will have a perfect fund of shooting anecdotes at your finger tips which can be reeled off with little or no mental effort.

After dinner, if you find the company of the other women a little tedious (and remember that you will have a great deal of it during the next day or two) you can go to your room and spend some time repairing the damage which eating always seems to effect upon the face. You then take your embroidery and return to the drawing-room. For a woman who stays much in country houses, 'work' of some sort is indispensable. You probably never touch it at home, and most likely have only the vaguest idea of how it should be done, but if it is well begun for you at some school of needlework you can always muddle along with the background. As a barricade and as a topic of conversation it is an invaluable asset. When you are asked to go for a walk, play bridge, or do anything else that you particularly dislike, you can entrench yourself behind it. 'My dear, I *must* get on with this wretched work, it is for mother's birthday and I don't see *how* it is to be finished in time.' Should your hostess remember it from last year, and be tactless enough to say so, you answer airily, 'Oh! that was finished ages ago, I'm doing the companion chair now, it's quite different if you look into it.'

The following day you will probably be awakened by angry voices in the hall beneath your room. Pay no attention to these but quickly go to sleep again. It is a curious anomaly that, while most men pretend to like shooting, it invariably brings their worst passions to the surface, especially when they are getting ready to leave the house after breakfast. If you wish to be really tactful, stay in bed until quite twelve o'clock. No hostess wants to be bothered with her women guests in the morning unless there are some men about to amuse them. Above all, remember that you will probably be obliged to go out to lunch with the guns and spend the afternoon with them, so put on your stoutest tweeds (choosing a colour that will not shock the birds), thick shoes, and a mackintosh.

On arriving at the appointed place for lunch, which will be either, if you are lucky, a warm room in some cottage, or, more probably, a windswept haystack, you will certainly have to wait for at least an hour. This time is occupied in unpacking the lunch and gossiping. When at last the men appear, do not speak to them until they have addressed you first. If the shooting has been good they will come up to you smiling, saying something like 'Well, well, this isn't the worst part of the day is it, what? Ha, ha, what?' and conversation will then flow smoothly and cheerfully. If it has been bad, on the other hand, the tactful woman remains silent until the softening influence of food and drink has been felt.

8

After luncheon you will accompany the guns to some bleak hedgerow, where you will sit quite still for a great time, preferably in silence. If, however, you must speak, be careful at all costs to avoid remarks like 'Please don't beat poor Fido quite so hard,' or 'Oh, would you mind killing off that wounded hare? It reminds me of Aunt Florence.'

When the man with whom you are standing breaks a heavy silence by saying angrily, 'Shut up and lie down,' remember that he is most probably addressing not you, but his dog.

At the end of each drive you will be expected to wander about with your eyes fixed on the ground, pretending to look for dead birds. The fact that even if you should happen to find one no bribe would induce you to touch it will probably render your search of but small value, but it is better to appear happy and occupied for fear that your hostess should think that you are bored. It is a consolation during this time to remember that no afternoon lasts for ever and that sooner or later you will wend safely home to tea.

That evening at dinner, conversation will present no difficulties. The ice having now been thawed, you will be completely neglected by the men, who will shout at each other across the table 'That was a high bird down by King's Cover,' 'Your dog better now? I knew Ellimans would do the trick.'

'Next year I shall drive that gorse differently.'

Presently the game card will be brought in; this will cause great excitement and keep the party happy till dinner is over, especially if there has been a sweepstake on the bag.

When, after two or three days of this sort of thing, you arrive back at your home, you will appreciate the warm and friendly atmosphere and the feeling that in spite of being a woman, you do count for something there. Your writing table will seem particularly well arranged as you sit down to accept two more shooting invitations which were waiting for you in the hall on your return.

Vogue, December 11, 1929

At a Point-to-Point

Nancy Mitford to Mark Ogilvie-Grant April 11, 1930

'The Lady people have now definitely taken me on at £5.5.0. a week to write a sort of running commentary of current events. They are sending me to everything free . . . I think I shall get lots of fun out of it don't you. So to celebrate this I went out today and bought myself a *divine* coral tiara – the family think I've gone mad.'

It is well known all over the world that the English, as a nation, take their pleasures sadly. Their pleasures! Can anybody who seriously considers for a moment in what these so-called 'pleasures' consist be surprised if they are taken sadly? The truth is that Englishmen are brought up from early childhood with a warped idea of 'pleasure'. Cold and damp can be endured without complaint, if necessary; boredom, alas, must come to all; but the alliance of piercing cold with agonising boredom is hard to recognize as the final delirium of joy.

It is cold, in winter, to stand all day in a muddy field; it is surely not otherwise than boring to watch physical achievements in which one has no part. Yet that, to many Englishmen, comes under the heading of Pleasure.

It is natural, therefore, that they should take their pleasures sadly. They look sad for the very ordinary reason that they *are* sad, and no wonder! And, personally, I think that the most sadly boring way of spending a day is to go racing, and that the most sadly boring form of racing is the point-to-point.

A point-to-point is a steeplechase for amateurs, held not upon a proper race-course, but in the bleak and muddy depths of some hunting country, and largely attended by the said amateurs, their friends and relations, the gentry from a radius of about twenty miles, and quantities of those rough men who always seem to spring up like mushrooms in the neighbourhood of a horse. A colder or more maddeningly dull entertainment it would be difficult to imagine.

These and other words of warning having been poured at great length and with some repetition into The Lady's ears, she has nevertheless decided that go to a point-to-point she must. She has never done so before but, like the young calf, she knows no fear, and her purpose is fixed. While, therefore, I cannot turn her from it, I can and will give her a few words of advice in the hope of rendering her day a trifle more agreeable than it would otherwise have been. Listen, then, to me, Lady.

First of all I must warn you that nothing short of a miracle can prevent you from being desperately cold for most of the day. All the same, you will suffer less acutely if you can manage to arrive at the races fairly warm; if you can do this, the cold may not have time to penetrate your very bones. To this end, when you get up in the morning, put on all your warmest clothes. Is that clear? Not your warmest smart clothes, and not your smartest warm clothes, but your warmest clothes.

Nobody will notice what you are wearing: they will be feeling far too wretched themselves to think of that; but they may just glance at your face, and this will not be looking its prettiest if pinched and blue with cold. If you haven't a fur or leather coat, wear a mackintosh over your tweeds; it is the next best thing for keeping out the wind. If you have no Newmarket boots, and scorn the homely galosh, wear woollen stockings, socks, and your very thickest shoes.

A great help towards arriving warm is to take several hot-water bottles in the car. These can be applied to the small of the back, and are very comforting.

I will assume, Lady, that the races are taking place at a distance of some thirty miles from your home, that you will be propelled towards them in a large and comfortable motor-car, and that you will be accompanied by a party of four or five friends, one of whom is to ride in the second race. This gallant, if mistaken, youth has with him his fiancée, whose expression of utter despair contrasts painfully with the false gaiety of her demeanour and does little to enhance your enjoyment of the drive. On reaching your destination, which will be some bare field, you will pay 10s. for the privilege of entering its muddy confines and of parking your car in a neat row with several dozen others. You should now have at least

11

half an hour before the first race during which to eat your luncheon.

This meal depends for its success upon quantity more than quality. Who has not suffered from the dreary kind of picnic which consists of two excellent pâté de foie gras sandwiches per head to whet an appetite which has to be satisfied with dry biscuits or hard green apples?

See to it, therefore, that your cook provides a large if unambitious meal of meat or chicken sandwiches. Plum cake (which will be eaten at intervals during the afternoon) is always appreciated, while hot coffee and cherry-brandy are absolutely indispensable. During this interlude you will, if lucky, be entertained by a one-legged hurdler, a negro with a banjo, and several tipsters. The jockey of your party and his fiancée are unlikely to eat much, but will probably make considerable inroads upon the cherry-brandy.

It is only after luncheon that the real misery begins. You are now obliged to untuck the warm rug, cast aside the hot-water bottles, open the door of the car, and sally forth into the biting wind.

With chattering teeth and watery eyes you plough your way through deep mud to the 'paddock', a roped-off enclosure where two or three rather skittish horses are being mounted by men dressed with little or no taste in a curious assortment of colours. The scene is a dreary one, but is surrounded by a large crowd of sheltering bodies into which you insert yourself thankfully. The wind, however, assails you with redoubled vigour as you are led away by some optimist towards the bookmakers. Let me here remind you that it is in no way your duty to put money on those of your acquaintances who may be riding: your pound does them no good, and is lost to you for ever. Far better keep it to spend on flowers, books, or chocolates for them in the nursing home where they are almost certain to pass the next few weeks.

If you are apt to be upset by the sight of blood and wounds at close quarters, you should now climb to the roof of the car and watch the race from that coign of vantage. If the sight of suffering is in any way pleasurable to you, you will best be able to indulge your sadistic tendencies at the water-jump.

Your happiest moments will occur between the races, when, without appearing in any way soft or un-English, you can get back inside the car and press the hot-water bottle (tepid by now, but a furnace compared with your own temperature) to your stomach, while internally you apply such cherry-brandy as your riding friend has been kind enough to leave in the flask.

Too soon, alas, will you be forced to abandon this refuge in order to see him mount. The fiancée, whose life has now become a dreary desert, and who has just observed the motor-ambulance leaving the field with a groaning load, stands by with the wan smile of a Roman matron on her face, holding his scarf and gloves. When her beloved has left at an uncontrolled gallop for the starting-post, it is your duty to escort her to the water-jump, tactfully pretending not to notice the tears which are raining down her cheeks.

'They're off!'

Round and round they go: over the water-jump, out into the country, back again – three miles and a half in all. Bodies everywhere – loose horses galloping about. After an eternity, the race is over, and your friend is not only still living and unhurt, but has also come in sixth. Presently he swaggers up to the car and begins to explain why he didn't win, pretending that he enjoyed it enormously. You saw his face as he approached the water-jump and know better. Never mind, every one is happy now; six in the car with the windows shut makes a fairly good warmth, and all suspense is over. The fiancée looks human again, takes an interest in plum-cake, and even pretends that *she* really enjoyed it, too.

Whenever you leave, you are certain to see for the first time numbers of people whom you had been hoping to meet all day. This cannot be helped, and you will be too tired by then to do more than wave languidly in their direction.

The drive home will be rendered rather pleasant by the return of some modicum of warmth to your body; but the hot bath which greets you on your arrival will surely be the most pleasurable moment of all that day of pleasure.

The Lady, March 6, 1930

In Covent Garden Now

The Royal Opera House, Covent Garden, presents to the admirer of Victorian decoration one of the most satisfying interiors to be found in London.

So thought the Lady as she settled down into her stall to witness her first Wagner opera, *Das Rheingold*. This was, in fact, a great occasion in her life. She had always regarded herself as a cultured and not unmusical person, but, until then, had never seen any of Wagner's portentous masterpieces, and was therefore looking forward with delight to a profound aesthetic experience. She knew what happiness many people derive from the Ring, and foresaw that the time would come when she herself would be the very embodiment of the Perfect Wagnerite, touring the Continent in the wake of her favourite singers with Bayreuth as her headquarters.

Meanwhile she chattered to her companion (a well-known Wagner enthusiast) and gazed about her at as smart a gathering of people as London can produce, all, like herself, in a twitter of happy expectation. Unfortunately, she omitted to read on her programme the story of the opera. If she had done so what followed might have seemed a little less obscure.

At last the lights went down, the overture began, and the Lady prepared herself for an evening of overwhelming delight. It is true that she felt a moment's apprehension on hearing her friend murmur to himself happily, 'Now for nearly three hours without one break.' But she felt sure that this could not be the case. Is not the entr'acte well known to be an indispensable adjunct to such entertainments? Do not certain people use Covent Garden almost as a club, in which to see and be seen? The Lady, of course, would never herself descend to such practices; but it is pleasant in any case to meet friends and enemies, especially when dressed up in one's very best clothes.

The curtain slowly rose. The stage was in semi-darkness, but three women in diaphanous garments were just visible, floating about in mid-air. The Lady was forcibly reminded of something – but of what? Of course; the aquarium at the Zoo. Oh, well, probably, in fact certainly, they were meant to be under the sea, or perhaps under a river – probably the Rhine.

The Lady noticed that each of the women was supported by four strong ropes. As they hung about in the air (or water) they sang loudly. A sort of toad creeping on the rocks sang loudly, too. A charming spectacle, she thought, almost outdoing that breathless moment in Peter Pan when the grown-up actress, impersonating the 'boy who never grew up', is wafted by creaking machinery in and out of the window.

After about half an hour the Lady became just slightly impatient. The mermaids, or whatever they were, kept on floating in and out of rocks, but the recitative, she thought privately, was perhaps a little dull. However, anything might happen. They might turn out to be Valkyries and sing the song which she had heard on the gramophone; or they might even begin to spin. Somebody did light a bonfire behind one of the rocks, but it soon went out again – as, naturally, it would under the water. Finally, with screams of girlish laughter, the mermaids floated away upon their straining ropes at immense speed and the curtain went down. The Lady felt tired but happy, and waited for the lights to go on; she thought it would be delicious to move again, and perhaps even have something to drink. But the music, instead of fading away, grew louder every moment, and soon the curtain rose once more. The scene had now changed to the sort of thing which our grandmothers used to reproduce so happily in water colour; rocky crags, one of them surmounted by a castle, rose on every hand beneath an angry sky.

In the foreground sat the inevitable two figures without which no composition of the kind is complete, dressed in white with long blue cloaks. The man's face was entirely covered with russet hair. As he rose to sing the Lady's companion hissed into her ear the word 'Schorr – Schorr.'[1]

'Shaw,' she thought, 'George Bernard? Evidently not.' She recollected seeing photographs of GBS in which he presented a very different figure from the rather portly one before her. 'It's the name of the singer, I expect. Well, that's something to remember. Shaw.'

[1] Friedrich Schorr (1888–1953). Hungarian bass-baritone.

Now began, if the horrid truth must be known, a period of rather serious boredom.

The Lady began to be worn out with the loudness and dulness of the music. She felt stiff and tired and thought longingly of her bed. Presently a blonde in a green evening frock appeared from behind one of the crags. She seemed to be in some sort of trouble, and was soon followed by two lunatics dressed as Robinson Crusoe and Man Friday. Probably the blonde had escaped from a lunatic asylum and they were pursuing her.

They began a very long argument with Shaw. Once or twice it looked as though things might be livened up by a bit of a fight (Shaw had a spear in his hand), but they always ended by beginning another song and seemed too busy singing to do anything else.

The Lady kept on nearly going to sleep for what seemed like hours; but each time she awoke to find the same people still in the same positions and shouting their strange songs. Two men of the audience got up and left; the Lady envied them much. She longed to lie down on the floor and sleep. There were now some more people on the stage, a peroxide youth who appeared half-heartedly in love with the blonde in green, and another lunatic dressed as Shock-Headed Peter.

At last the blonde was removed by Robinson Crusoe in spite of the feeble efforts of the peroxide young man to retain her, and the curtain went down.

Still no entr'acte. The Lady was in a trance of leaden despair; she ached all over.

The next scene took place in the asylum, a sort of cave, very dark and depressing, and might have been quite exciting if only the action had been speeded up a little. Two lunatics teased and tortured each other, others ran about with armfuls of firewood, and one got into a dark cupboard and kept jumping out at Shaw (who appeared with Shock-Headed Peter), waving electric torches in his face. The Lady slept a little during this scene and only really came to at the beginning of the next – which brought her back again among the crags. All the same people were there: Shaw, the blonde in green, Shock-Headed Peter, Robinson Crusoe, Man Friday, and the other lunatics with their bundles of firewood.

Nature now had her way. The Lady fell into a blessed and

profound sleep from which she was only awakened by the sound of clapping. All was over.

Stunned and shattered in mind, stiff and sore in body, she tottered towards her car.

'I never knew,' she moaned from the depths of disillusionment, 'that three hours *could* go so slowly.'

The Lady, May 22, 1930

Faringdon House

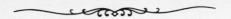

Merlingford nestled in a valley of south-westerly aspect, among orchards and old mellow farmhouses. It was a villa, built at about the same time as Alconleigh, but by a very different architect, and with a very different end in view. It was a house to live in, not to rush out from all day to kill enemies and animals. It was suitable for a bachelor, or a married couple with one, or at most two; beautiful, clever, delicate children.

Lord Merlin loved jewels; his two black whippets wore diamond necklaces designed for whiter, but not slimmer or more graceful necks than theirs. This was a neighbour-tease of long standing; there was a feeling among the local gentry that it incited the good burghers of Merlinford to dishonesty.

From *The Pursuit of Love* by Nancy Mitford

When Mr Wood of Bath built Faringdon House, about the middle of the eighteenth century, his customer was Poet Laureate Pye (generally supposed to have been the worst poet laureate England has ever had and described as 'eminently respectable in everything but his poetry' by Lord Byron who, of course, knew all about respectability). Pye ordered the house to be built and Pye paid the bill, established himself there, wrote reams of dreary long-forgotten verse in praise of his master George III, and brought up his dreary long-forgotten children beneath its roof. But I believe that Mr Wood, gifted with second sight, saw two hundred years beyond the laureate and built it specially for Lord Berners, its present occupant. For those who are lucky enough to be friends of the lord and therefore visitors to his house, he being the most hospitable of men, find it impossible to think of one without the other, so much of a piece are they, both standing four-square on English soil but both formed in all their essential proportions by European classicism.

Faringdon is a real country house for all its elegance, not one of those pretty old-maidish town houses that sometimes occur in the

18

English countryside, looking sweet but silly and exhaling an atmosphere of afternoon tea. It is plain and gray and square and solid and is as much a part of the rolling Berkshire landscape before it as of the little old market town of Faringdon to which it turns its back and which is hidden from view by the parish church and huge clumps of elm trees. Faringdon House has very little in the way of a flower garden, Lord Berners is not fond of flowers growing in beds, and considers that such things as herbaceous borders are more suitable to the half-timbered houses of Surrey stockbrokers than to a classical house which should be surrounded by a plain expanse of lawn to enhance the perfection of its line. Indoors, his house, as we shall see, is always buried in flowers but they are large brilliant tropical flowers in vases, not buttercups, the little children's dower.

A broad space of lawn runs from the house to the church – it is bordered by elm trees and, until it came down in the gale of last March, a big cedar stood there. Cedars are crashing all over England now. As the fashion for planting them only began in the eighteenth century and as their alloted span is a thousand years this seems rather inexplicable. Perhaps now that tea under the cedars, that daily sacrifice to them in fine weather, when footmen in striped waistcoats placed trays of glittering silver beneath their shade every afternoon, has become a thing of the past, they are sulkily dying of boredom. Anyhow, for the moment, Faringdon smells deliciously of burning cedar wood as a result.

At the end of the lawn, overshadowed by the trees on one side and the church on the other, and hedged with a tangle of roses and mock orange, there is a grassy walk where, head in hand on moonless nights appears the ghost of Hampden Pye. His story has been immortalized in the *Ingoldsby Legends* under the name of Hamilton Tighe. It seems that he was a sailor who married a peasant and that his uncle Admiral Pye, in the best traditions of the British Navy, sent him to the forefront of the battle so that he should be killed, which he duly was, his poor head being blown off.

So Faringdon acquired that which every respectable country house must have – a ghost. It also has, equally important, a rookery and a flock of pigeons. And such pigeons! They are Lord Berners' famous multi-coloured birds, but it is no use asking him for a setting of eggs, for the secret of their brilliant plumage lies

19

less in the breeding than in what happens to them every Easter Sunday when they are dyed and dried in the linen cupboard before being set free to flutter like a cloud of confetti between church and house to astonish the students of bird life in Berkshire. This bird motif, which is repeated over and over again inside the house, is the signature of its owner, so to speak, who prefers feathered to many other sorts of friends. As with flowers, he rather disdains the modest English sparrow, eschewing it for something gaudier.

The town, though its presence can be felt, is invisible from the house itself, but the huge walled kitchen garden, a perfect village of hothouses, lies on a southern slope overlooking it, and has a delicious view of old roofs and gardens descending the opposite slope to a little stream. This kitchen garden, I must say in passing, ministers most wonderfully to the house, producing exquisite vegetables, fruit and flowers with a perfect disregard for the slow-rolling seasons, the vagaries of the Berkshire climate, and indeed of all known rules. Mr Cyril Connolly once said that when every sort of luxury has been forever banned in England, Lord Berners will somehow manage to maintain a secret melon house.

To the north, Faringdon has a most beautiful view, enjoyed by all the principal rooms in the house. It extends, from a terrace buried in honeysuckle, for many miles over a landscape such as is beloved of all English sporting painters, from Stubbs to Cecil Alden, that is to say a patchwork of fields and hedges, dotted with elm trees. Not a house or building of any sort can be seen, not a pylon or one inch of wire, just green English grass alternating with brown English arable, mile after mile, until finally they merge into the pale but piercing blue of a far distant horizon.

Such is Faringdon House as it stands in its environment, sober and restrained, typical abode, you would say, of an English country squire. Typical, except perhaps for the coloured pigeons, the striped pink and white Italian tubs full of geraniums round the front, and what is that curious car drawn up in the drive? A smart coupé of 1904. Not quite typical, and inside not typical at all. Open the front door, there is scented warmth, there is such light, such a profusion of flowers, such a river of witty chat, accompanied by tunes, from hidden musical boxes.

We must give it to Mr Wood of Bath that he did his bit. He placed the house upon a semi-basement, which always makes for warmth and comfort, and to this basement with real eighteenth-century carelessness, he relegated both God and the cook, putting chapel and kitchen there side by side. He introduced a graceful double staircase, pillars, decorated plaster ceilings, classical chimney pieces, as many paltry details, most likely, as the poet laureate was willing to afford; the proportions of all the rooms are excellent. Upon this prettiness, this excellence, Lord Berners has superimposed his own taste and fantasy and created something so personal that it is very difficult to convey its aspect to those who have not seen for themselves.

I can remember, during the tedious or frightening but always sleepless nights of fire-watching in wartime London, that the place I longed to be in most intensely was the red bedroom at Faringdon, with its crackling fire, its Bessarabian carpet of bunchy flowers and above all its four-post bed, whence from beneath a huge fat fluffy old-fashioned quilt one can gaze out at the view, head still on pillow.

It has always been a great treat to stay at Faringdon, but during the war it was paradise to people working in London, since there they found a double relief from discomfort and from boredom.

During the war the big drawing room, with its white flock paper and priceless French and Italian furniture, was shut up in favour of the little green drawing room. This is as pretty, cozy and characteristic as a room can be, its dark olive walls providing the perfect background for a riot of tropical birds, some alive and hopping about, some stuffed in cases, some pressed, like flowers in a screen, some modelled in china, one jumping with a song out of a gold box, and hundreds between the green morocco covers of Mr Gould. Like all the rest of the house this room is buried in flowers of the brightest colours, arranged under the eye of Lord Berners himself. His ancestors, simpering or morose, hang high upon the walls and have for neighbours at eye-level a Paul Klee, one or two of Lord Berners' own Roman landscapes, and a varying selection of Impressionists and others, including Sisley, Corot, Degas, Boudin and Matisse. Mr Pye would be startled if he could see his austere little room with its sporting print view glittering like a jewel box – Mr Wood, I think, might find it very much to his taste.

There is something magic about all of Faringdon, and Lord Berners himself, in his skull cap, looks not unlike a magician, but

21

perhaps the greatest, most amazing conjuring tricks are reserved for the dining room. In this pleasant sunny white room, scattered with large silver-gilt birds and wonderful Sèvres and Dresden china, a standard of culinary perfection has been maintained through the darkest days of war. Cook or no cook, raw materials or no raw materials, a succession of utterly delicious courses would somehow waft themselves to the sideboard, and the poor Londoner, starved, or sated with Spam, would see sights and taste tastes he had long ago forgotten to believe in.

Faringdon is solid and elegant and so is Lord Berners. So great is his sense of elegance, fantasy and humour that the solid quality of his talents, and above all the immense amount of hard work he has done all his life are sometimes overlooked, though a moment's reflection would show that without great talent and hard work he could not, as he does, write and paint like a professional, in addition to shining as a composer of music (Stravinsky himself has said that the only important living English composer is Lord Berners). But one of the greatest of his achievements is the atmosphere he has created around himself at Faringdon, a house where the second best has never been and will never be allowed to encroach, either in comfort, conversation or in manners.

House and Garden, May, 1948

Paris Column

Ian Fleming arranged for Nancy to write a column from Paris for the *Sunday Times*. She contributed regularly for four years.

Evelyn Waugh to Nancy Mitford December 5, 1949

'I was delighted to read that "the most brilliant of the younger writers" has joined the staff of the *Sunday Times*." You should have said "youngest writers". We are much younger than Max Beerbohm or E. M. Forster. There are none younger than us.'

Nancy Mitford to Evelyn Waugh December 7, 1949

'You are horrid. You know quite well *I* didn't say I was the m b of the y ws – I was appalled by the whole thing, specially as the article is deadly beyond belief (Prod [Peter Rodd] says unreadable). I'd hoped to creep in on the woman's page unnoticed. Never mind I've found a lovely picture for it as I know you will admit. I have to provide my own ill*eo*stration what Cecil [Beaton] calls, it is part of the horror. Now don't let's hear any more about it please. I *must* earn money when I can. I shall never inherit any as far as I know, haven't got any except what I make, & extreme old age looms all too near. Then I shall so want a little fire & perhaps a pair of steel-rimmed specs & a molar or 2 do admit. I think of 0 else. (The article) It won't do anybody any harm, it can't be worse or more boring than the existing woman's page (which is all about welfare in Scandinavia if you want to know, ask Laura if it's not true) & if unreadable nobody is obliged to read it.'

Evelyn Waugh to Nancy Mitford February 8, 1950

'Another *very* good article in *Sunday Times*. It is your métier. You may well become one of the historic foreign correspondents.'

'The columns of the *Sunday Times* will always be open to you.'

It was a perfectly gorgeous shade of burnt orange.' If you would not expect to hear these words in the rue de Rivoli, you would be wrong, because now that the Americans have all gone home in search of central heating, the rue de Rivoli is a purely English street again, full of my compatriots wondering whether they can afford its perfectly gorgeous goods.

'No,' says Sir Stafford Cripps; 'Yes,' says the little man who gives you 800 francs for a pound note.

At the Louvre (shop, not palace), Christmas is in full mechanical swing. Every window is a puppet show, and the tunes of the Red Flag, Stille Nacht and other foreign Christmas music keep up a running river of sentimental sound. On, on, through the Palais Royal, past its sinister shops containing broken jade, torn lace or tarnished medals – nothing to tempt us here – to Paul Morihien's famous bookshop and art gallery combined, very much patronised by M. Jean Cocteau, and by all the Paris highbrows.

The object of this walk was the private view of Carmen Gandarillas's pictures, which have been introduced to Paris by M. Cocteau. 'You will be one of the many artists who, though not French, have been tenderly adopted by France.' Mlle. Gandarillas, Chilian by birth, is really a Londoner. Her pictures have an English look, green and fresh, which has charmed everybody here.

We have, as usual, a choice of centenary exhibitions, not all equally fascinating (just now there are Goethe, Chopin and a hundred years of reinforced concrete); but none of this year's anniversaries has attracted more notice than the eightieth birthday of M. André Gide, and no exhibition has been crowded with such earnest students as that, in the Bibliothèque de Sainte Geneviève, which commemorates it.

Here in glass cases, each with a queue waiting to examine it, can be seen relics of his many friendships, some with almost historical characters, such as Oscar Wilde, Francis Jammes, Paul

Valéry and Charles Louis-Philippe, while a whole case is devoted to his correspondence with M. Paul Claudel.

The two literary giants, who are nearly the same age, have run neck and neck since before the century began. When I was new to the Parisian scene I once asked: 'Do they like each other?' '*Ils s'estiment*,' was the reply.

It is said that while M. Gide favoured publication of these letters, doubts were felt as to whether M. Claudel would consent: when approached, he hummed and hawed, and finally announced that he had lost his friend's letters in the Tokyo earthquake. The alleged answer will not surprise anybody conversant with the ways of French writers: 'Happily, the Master kept copies of everything he wrote.'

English visitors here often complain to me that there are no well-dressed women in Paris. They come expecting to see Dior models all round them, and feel cheated when they don't. This is not surprising. *Les élégantes*, of whom there are dozens, and who are certainly the best-dressed women in the world, never set foot in the street, and seldom go to a restaurant.

They get into their motor-cars in the courtyards of their houses; the double doors are then thrown open by the *concierge*; there is a glimpse of black velvet and dark fur; and they are gone. The instinct of the French aristocracy drives them to live privately hidden away, and this has been so ever since the Revolution. Social life takes place almost entirely in private houses, each glittering like a miniature Wallace Collection. In these, and these alone, can be seen the lovely clothes of the big dressmakers, on the women for whom they were designed.

The rich French, like the rich Italians, keep up a standard of living which to the English is hardly a memory. The poor French, even the *petite bourgeoisie*, cannot afford to buy any new clothes at all. They spend most of what they earn on food and are admirably fed, but dowdy.

At this time of year it is possible to see what really is the fashionable line. Every autumn and spring the big houses produce quantities of clothes, but finally the trend is described by elegant Frenchwomen who know exactly what they want. The English fashion experts always like straight up-and-down little-boy clothes: they have but to see a pencil skirt to proclaim that skimpiness is back. But the pencil skirts here are worn with bulky, bloused jackets, not straight up-and-down at all. The line actually worn by French-women is very much that of the 'new look' as it was when invented by M. Dior three years ago. Skirts are rather full and rather long, waists are small and shoulders slope; there is no exaggeration.

The oracle himself, M. Dior, has said there will be no radical change for at least ten years after the initiation of the 'new look'. Women can choose the clothes that suit them, within wide limits.

The prices are more horrifying than ever. I was with an English friend when she saw an embroidered jacket. 'Darling, I must have it. I don't mind what it costs; it's an investment. You could wear it over any old skirt and still be the best-dressed person in the room.' So we asked the price, £360. Collapse of my friend.

I spoke of this to a Frenchwoman who knows about the business of *haute couture*. She said that such a jacket costs about £60 to make, that another £20 should be added for overheads, and then it would be fair to double the whole, for the *griffe*, the label of a big house. Result £160, not £360.

She thought there ought to be a buyers' strike, and said that if nobody bought any clothes for two months or so the prices would come tumbling down. But there will be no such strike, and, in fact, the houses are busier than ever.

December 11, 1949

*

There is an idea among English people that Christmas is hardly kept at all in France, where, they imagine, the New Year is everything. This may have been so in the old anti-clerical days, and may still be so among violently anti-clerical families, but on the whole it is not true.

Wherever you look at Christmas time you see Father Christmas, a Christmas tree in most houses however poor, and signs of festivity. Christmas Eve, *le Réveillon*, is celebrated by innumerable parties which break up at midnight for Mass, are resumed afterwards and then go on until any hour. There is no self-consciousness about clothes for church; the women sweep up the aisle in their ball dresses, a tulle veil on their heads, and this adds very much to the picturesque scene in huge dark cold churches crammed with people.

M. Marcel Rochas has celebrated the inauguration of his new scent, Moustache, with an exhibition of moustachio'd male portraits from the sixteenth century to our day. There was a rumour that he got to work with a burnt cork on various pictures so that they could be hung with the other moustaches, but I must say I saw no signs of this. The exhibition, which includes pictures by Renoir, Fragonard, Tintoretto, Philippe de Champaigne and Van Dyck, and portraits of Mallarmé, Vuillard, Cardinal Richelieu, Valéry, James Joyce and Christian Bérard, takes place in M. Rochas's very pretty shop and is well worth a visit.

I received, the other day, the 1950 catalogue of Etablissement Nicolas, a wine merchant with branches all over Paris. These catalogues are so beautifully produced and illustrated that bibliophiles collect them, and they are full of delicious temptation. Such lovely wines as Château Vigneau 1904, Château Smith-Haut-Lafite 1916, Bâtard Montrachet 1928, Pouilly Fumé 1929 can be bought for 10s. a bottle, while for between £1 and £1 10s. a *prestigieuse bouteille* will be specially decanted and brought *à domicile dans un panier calorifugé.* These include Mouton Rothschild 1870, Clos d'Estournel 1869 and Latour 1858. *Un très grand Porto* has a page to itself. It is Porto Imperial 1848 and costs £2 10s.

Baron Philippe de Rothschild, owner of the Mouton Rothschild vineyard, has an amusing new idea for labelling his bottles. Each label bears the words *il a été tiré de cette bouteille* so many examples of which this is number such and such, just as though it was an *édition de luxe.*

The Rothschild family is very much in the news, Baron Philippe's father, the late Baron Henri de Rothschild, having bequeathed his library to the Bibliothèque Nationale, where a selection of its 5,000 volumes is now on show. The French Press has hailed this as the most wonderful Christmas present received by France for many years.

Baron Henri de Rothschild inherited a library from his father, and began collecting himself when he was twelve. He had knowledge and taste, never bought an incomplete book or one that had been retouched and was specially fond of autographed letters. It is always fascinating to see old friends of the past revealed by their handwriting, and at this exhibition I was especially struck by that of Madame de Sévigné, untidy and hard to read; Madame de Pompadour, crystal clear, more like a twentieth- than an eighteenth-century hand; and Rabelais, neat as a governess.

The books I personally covet most in this dazzling collection are the Molière of 1734 with the original Boucher drawings, the Rousseau of 1774–83 with those of Moreau le Jeune, Madame de Pompadour's own copy of *Rodogune* containing the original Boucher drawing which she herself engraved, and the 'Fermiers Généraux' edition of La Fontaine bound for the comtesse d'Artois.

January 8, 1950

*

An Englishman who used to live in Paris wrote to me: 'Does nothing ever change there? Maison Nicolas – a story about Tristan Bernard – I had expected a new, if not a brave new world, but was taken back twenty years or more.'

Well, I have known Paris twenty years or more myself, and there is very little change that I can see. The *bouquinistes* by the river; the donkeys in the Tuileries gardens; the lace blouses, in the shop on the corner of the rue Duphot, which I coveted as a child and still covet now, but which have a curious remoteness like blouses in a dream; the falling cadence of the glazier's cry as he walks the streets with a huge pane of glass on his back; Madame Bousquet's salon on Thursday; the pink electric light bulbs at Larue, rapidly diminishing, alas, as they can no longer be replaced; the flock of goats milked in the street ('But how do they pasteurise it?' an American cried in horror); George of the Ritz bar; the outside platforms of the buses; the insides of the taxis which must, one feels, be the very same that took the troops up to the Battle of the Marne; the murderous accents of telephone girls when they say '*allo – j'écoute –*' all, all unchanged.

And one is still awoken at early dawn by the tumult and the shouting with which the contents of the *poubelles* or dustbins are collected. M. Poubelle, by the way, whose name has thus been so charmingly perpetuated, was Prefect of the Seine in the 1880s and imposed these receptacles upon the Parisian housewife to her very great and strongly expressed rage.

The plays are still mostly written by M. Guitry and M. Bernstein. Mlle Printemps and M. Jouvet are still going strong. Mme Colette and M. Cocteau are the most promising of the young writers, and when the other day, somebody asked M. Picasso who are the new painters he replied '*moi.*'

To prove how little anything does change, the *Figaro* recently gave us a whole page of articles and advertisements from a day in January, 1900. At the theatre, *Le Bossu* in rehearsal, the name of Guitry to the fore; Folies-Bergère, Casino de Paris, and Nouveau Cirque in full swing. The advertisements are of shops and restaurants quite as well known now as then; the cartoon, by Caran d'Ache, is on the subject of war in China; an article on cab-drivers complains that they never want to go where they are told, and always refuse to wait; in the Chambre des Députés a violent quarrel over the State Railways is reported. Baron Henri de Rothschild has a dramatic motor accident. His chauffeur, driving at a terrible speed down the avenue de Villiers, fails to observe an electric tramway in time to stop, so there is a head-on collision in which nobody is hurt, though the coupé suffers considerable damage.

Several people I know read this page through without any idea that it was not of today, though one remarked that he thought Caran d'Ache had died years ago, and another 'Henri de Rothschild? Do they mean Elie? I must ring up.' It shows how carelessly one reads the papers.

M. Andre Gide was once asked who is the greatest French lyrical poet. His reply, '*Victor Hugo, hélas,*' has become a classic. Recently

29

a French schoolmaster set it as the subject for an essay, and was rather startled to find that all his pupils had written '*Victor Hugo est l'as*.' But after all, this is only a modern way of saying the same thing.

I am very sorry that M. Gide's quarter of an hour on the radio has come to an end. The interlocutor, it is true, did most of the talking, M. Gide putting in an occasional '*évidemment*' or '*précisément ce que j'entendais*,' but his voice, when he did speak, was the voice of a genius, deeply impressive. In thirty-two sessions we were taken through his most important books, his conversion to Communism, the journey to Russia which put him against Communism, and the review of his general outlook on life in *Thésée*. Now I am buried in the Gide–Claudel correspondence, which shows the two men in their real greatness. Never a petty sentiment, or any jealousy or taking offence, each helping and admiring the other wholeheartedly; until its terrible ending it was the model of a literary friendship.

February 5, 1950

*

Passing by the Comédie-Française the other afternoon I saw on the posters that *Phèdre* was being given, and couldn't resist going in; I was lucky, they said at the box office, a seat had been returned. The play was well into the first act:

Juste ciel, tout mon sang dans mes veines se glace.
O désespoir – O crime – O déplorable race.

When the curtain went down on the despair, the crime, the deplorable family, and the lights went up, I was very much surprised to find myself surrounded by children, many of them quite young.

'Of course,' said a French friend afterwards. 'It must have been Thursday, the matinée classique. Don't you know that the children of well-to-do Parisians are all *abonnés* to the Français every Thursday afternoon? I first saw *Phèdre* when I was twelve, and I remember that there was an empty seat next to mine because the parents of the pretty little girl who always sat there had forbidden her to go. So you can imagine – next week I had to whisper the story of *Phèdre* to her all through *Tartuffe*.'

'But could you enjoy Racine, so young?' I asked.

'One always enjoyed everything at the Français. They used to give us two plays and a lecture, and – this was during the other war – in the entr'acte a man with a guitar came to sing about the War Loan:

Il faut vider vos poches
Pour battre les Boches
Donner son argent
C'est du cent pour sang.

'Alas,' he said, 'I used to know all the plays of Racine by heart, but now I've forgotten everything except the *cent pour sang*.' This week the children are getting Corneille's *Psyché* and *Le Cid*.

There are three exhibitions now at the Bibliothèque Nationale; the 150 drawings, all masterpieces, from the Albertina Museum in Vienna, which will be here until June, a celebration of the centenary of Pierre Loti's birth, and another of the fiftieth anniversary of Péguy's *Cahiers de la Quinzaine*.

It so happens that Pierre Loti was the first French writer I ever heard of, because when I was a child he went to stay with my grandfather in Gloucestershire, and thereafter became a family legend. My father, whose love for foreign intellectuals was modified, to say the least of it, used to tell how 'the fella wore red heels to his shoes and believed that he was Rameses II.' This seemed delightfully exotic, and so, when I was old enough to read them, did the works of Loti.

The exhibition contains the ring of Rameses II, as well as many gifts from contemporary potentates, including Abdul Hamid. Fantastic as he was, Loti must also have been rather practical; he rejoined the French navy in 1914, aged sixty-four, and was given command of a ship.

April 9, 1950

*

Some weeks ago the *Figaro* announced, rather in the manner of a weather forecast, that there would be *une pluie d'Anglais* at Easter, a prophecy which proved correct. There are said to have been 35,000 of them, and as thousands of French people went away the town seemed quite taken over by the English.

The ones I saw had perhaps got up too early and tried to do too much; by midday they were wandering about in a haze of exhaustion. 'Oh dear, we passed those hats half an hour ago,' I heard in a high wail as of people, lost in a jungle, remarking upon some fallen tree or other landmark.

Then a positive voice. 'There is no word for fair play in German, you know, and no word for self-control in French.' (What about *maîtrise de soi?*) And 'Oh! my feet' and 'Are we nearly there?' echoed on every side.

It has become very easy to spot the nationality of women by the way they dress, in a town or for travelling. Englishwomen wear short hair, long skirts and brown flat-heeled shoes; Americans short hair, short skirts and black flat-heeled shoes. The truly elegant, who are a race apart, wear shortish hair and skirts and plain patent leather court shoes; they have other distinguishing marks as well.

All important political speeches here nowadays have a 'hats off to the mothers of France' paragraph, and indeed the drive to raise the birth rate has already had stunning results. To achieve these results *familles nombreuses* are assisted in every possible way. They go straight to the heads of queues, are given special housing facilities, reduction of fares on all public transport and in the museums, and considerable sums in hard cash.

Mothers get about £3 a month for two children, and an extra £5 each for any more until the children are fifteen, or eighteen if apprenticed to a trade; these sums can be drawn irrespective of means. Rich people benefit further with a reduction of taxes, which becomes considerable when a family has reached six children. Formerly the law by which all fortunes must be equally divided among children made it important for the rich to keep their families as small as possible, since one or two big families could ruin an estate; now this policy has suddenly been reversed.

Fashionable young married couples retire to their country houses on their wedding day and are not seen again in Paris until they have hit the target of six. Frenchwomen are very strong, so this seldom takes more than about six years – less if there are twins.

There is a new fashion, too, in the announcement of these births in the *Figaro*, the equivalent of our *Times*. Instead of, as formerly, *Le duc et la duchesse de Sauveterre ont la joie d'annoncer la naissance de leur fils Sosthène*, we read, *Oriane, Odette, Marie-Ange, Palamède et Raimon de Sauveterre ont la joie d'annoncer la naissance de leur frère Sosthène*, so that everybody can see how the Sauveterres are getting on. Soon after Sosthène has been christened, the Sauveterre house in the rue du Bac is taken out of its dust sheets and furbished up, the Duchess sheds her country clothes and is smartened up, and no social occasion is hereafter complete without this lucky couple.

Marcel Aymé's *Clérambard*, a religious comedy, is extremely funny without any irreverence. The curtain goes up on the family of Clérambard in the hall of their ancestral home, the Comte, his wife, his mother-in-law and his slightly cretinous son the Vicomte, all working away as hard as they can on knitting machines. Pushed to it by the Comte, they slave day and night in order to prevent the castle, *ces vieilles pierres*, from falling into alien hands. 'It has been in our family four hundred years,' says Clérambard. 'Surely that's long enough,' sighs his weary mother-in-law.

The Comte, a violent man, sometimes leaves his own knitting machine to go and kill some dog or cat which has strayed into the park, and we see him sneaking off, when the Curé comes to pay an afternoon call on the family, to strangle his dog. The poor Curé is very much put out by this. Then there is a miracle. St Francis appears, resuscitates the dog, and leave a little book, *La Vie de St François d'Assise, éditions du Ciel*, with Clérambard, who alone has seen him.

Clérambard is now reformed, but with the violence of his character unchanged he becomes a violent and intransigeant Christian. He calls off the *mariage de convenance* which has been arranged for the Vicomte and insists that he must marry the local Mary Magdalene, a charming prostitute called La Langouste. He sells his castle, buys a caravan, and proposes henceforward to lead, with his family, the life of a preaching mendicant.

This is too much for Mme de Clérambard, who sends for an alienist to certify him, but while the doctor is there another miracle occurs, a heavenly vision seen by all except the Curé – 'I shall have to tell the Bishop I left my spectacles behind.' The others, now convinced that Clérambard is right, pack themselves into the caravan, and he drives them away to lead a holy life.

This play is causing a great deal of controversy among Roman Catholics. Some say that Aymé is the modern Anatole France, and that he has torn up the little flowers of St Francis, while others maintain that the revolutionary teaching of this Saint has never been taken literally, even by the Church. The London correspondent of *Le Monde* says one thing is sure. *Les têtes rondes*, as he calls the English, would neither like nor understand Aymé's mixture of jokes and religion. I don't know that he is right; this *tête ronde* likes it very much indeed.

May 7, 1950

*

A drive for politeness has been going on here, not unconnected perhaps with dollars and the tourist trade, and we have been enjoying a *quinzaine de l'amabilité*. This was announced on the wireless with *Mes hommages, Mesdames, Mesdemoiselles, Messieurs* instead of the usual *Bonjour. Une vague de courtoisie*, said the announcer, 'is about to spread over France.'

I always think the French are very polite; they certainly are to me, and I speak as I find; but English people do sometimes complain. The fact is that the French can also be quite shatteringly rude if they want to be for some reason, and have an uncanny sense of how most to annoy a particular person.

Perhaps they think the English mean to be rude, for the schools of manners of these two countries, each excellent in its way, are intensely dissimilar. English manners are casual, they come from natural good breeding and kindness of heart; the French school of manners was founded at Versailles by Louis XIV, one of the most polite men who ever lived, so polite that he never passed the humblest of his housemaids without a low bow, the poorest peasant woman without sweeping off his hat to her.

So manners here are really court manners, formal, leisured and intended to underline the fact that every human being has his own respectable place in society.

The French language is very polite, the frequent use of the words *Monsieur* and *Madame* making politeness easier from the beginning of a conversation than the English equivalent of 'I say,' 'please' or 'you'. Servants here speak to their employers in the third person. Letters are always properly addressed, and though the exaggerated politeness of writing to an older or in some way distinguished person, *A Madame, Madame de X* is dying out, and practised only by the very old-fashioned, there is a correct style of address for everybody.

A concierge is *Madame la concierge* and a duchess *Madame la duchesse*, a lawyer is *Maître*, a bishop is *Monseigneur* and so is a Royal Prince, postmen and policemen are *Monsieur le facteur* and *Monsieur l'agent* and the President of the Republic is *Monsieur le président*.

A whole book could be written on the endings of letters; their variations are infinite, though the foreigner can quite safely beg his correspondent to believe in his distinguished sentiments and leave it at that.

Acquaintances must be greeted, when met, and their hands shaken. If met a second time during the day they must be greeted and their hands shaken again, and so on. Little children at the lycée shake hands all round twice a day, and *députés*, as they rush up and down the corridors of the Palais Bourbon, shake hands each time they meet, saying *re* for *re-bonjour*.

I once saw two bus drivers lean out of their buses and shake hands as they drove along.

All these rules, which are cut and dried, certainly do oil the wheels of social life. It is easy to enter a room with assurance if you know that you must shake hands all round and that your hostess will introduce you to the other guests. The English way of sidling in, bestowing smiles here and there and pretending that any strange faces do not exist at all, is more difficult to carry off gracefully.

June 4, 1950

Oh, how I love Paris in July! For three days – the 13th, 14th, and 15th – the population dances in the streets after which there is an immense exodus to sea and mountains. I spend the long, hot evenings in my courtyard, which I have to myself, since all the other flats are empty. The air, after dinner, is full of swifts chasing in and out of the houses with happy shrieks, their evening game. Presently I look up from my book and the swifts have turned into flickering bats; then it becomes too dark to read, there is nothing overhead but stars, and all this time, and far into the night, Marie and the concierge keep up a steady muttering flow of gossip, sitting on the steps of the lodge.

Outside in the town many shops are shut *(Réouverture 1ᵉʳ Septembre)*, there is always room on the buses, rush hours exist no more because there is nobody left to rush and the traffic mainly consists of open GB sports motors full of young Englishmen and girls *coiffées à la princesse Elizabeth*, that is, with a handkerchief tied under their chins.

Little crowds do appear once a day, when it is time for the evening papers. They surround the news-vendors, and walk off reading as they go.

'Poor things, they are worried about Korea,' said my English companion, and I have seen it mentioned by English journalists as a proof that the French are getting rattled. But I know better. I know what is preoccupying them, because it happens to be my passion too – a passion, incidentally, that I have never been able to share with a fellow-countryman – *le Tour*.

Guermantes of the *Figaro* very truly says *le Tour de France est un fleuve d'oubli*, and in that stream of forgetfulness I swim, and the whole French nation swims, for three weeks every summer. The most exciting *Tour* that I can remember was in 1948, when Bobet, the idol of the French, and my idol too, was beaten by boils. Bobet, in his yellow jersey (mark of the leader), led the race day after thrilling day. He led it through Luxembourg and Belgium, down the West coast to the Pyrenees, he led it through *supplice des montagnes* and during a *folle étape dans le mistral*, and all the time his boils, we knew, were getting worse and worse, until one terrible morning all was over. *Son moral s'est effondré* we read, and the *maillot jaune* passed to another. *Il faut s'incliner devant cet homme-là* I heard that evening at a newsreel, and fervently agreed.

So *les rois de la route* are at it again – Bobet, Marinelli, Goldschmidt, Robic, all the old favourites (with names like a newly constituted French Cabinet), pedalling their way through lanes of cheering supporters all round France. But the English take no interest in the *Tour*. 'A bicycle race,' they say, 'how deadly.' So I expect I had better shut up.

I met a young English sculptor who lives here; I said, 'May we talk about eighteenth-century French sculpture' – thinking to have a lovely discussion on a subject that fascinates me. He replied that he didn't know there was any. I felt very much put in my place, but a mutual friend assured me that he had not meant to be sarcastic.

'He really doesn't know.'

'Nonsense,' I said. 'You can't go out in Paris without knowing – what about Coustou's horses and Coysevox's winged horses and the Bouchardon fountain?'

'But he doesn't go out. He stays at home all day, hewing forms.'

The Louis XV and Rocaille exhibition at the Orangerie contains many beautiful sculptures, arranged to their best advantage with contemporary furniture, pictures and tapestry. Many of them are portraits of people we know intimately through the genius of St Simon – the Regent, Cardinal Dubois, Chancellor Pontchartrain, the duc d'Harcourt and the duchesse de Bourgogne have lived and breathed for us in his pages and they live and breathe again here. They all have a singularly happy and well-fed look; nothing very terrible, one feels, can ever have happened to them until they were carried off by the final apoplexy. *Racontez, duchesse*, said the Regent, and fell dead at the feet of a pretty little gossip just as she was opening her pretty little mouth to recount some piece of scandal.

This exhibition might have been called 'In honour of Madame de Pompadour,' and indeed she has been given the place of honour, between the King and M. Gabriel. Nearly all the artists represented owed much to her perfect taste and profound knowledge, and she it was who prevented French *rocaille* from degenerating, as did the German rococo, into sugar-cake monstrosity. When she realised that it had gone far enough she inaugurated the classical style which we know as Louis XVI.

Perhaps the most beautiful thing in this exhibition is Pigalle's statue of the marquise as Amitié, an allegorical work which indicated to the Court that she and the King had entered upon a new phase in their relationship. She remained his closest friend and adviser until the end of her short life. Her body was carried from Versailles during a fearful storm; 'La marquise has bad weather for her journey,' said the King, as, with tears pouring down his cheeks, he watched the hearse out of sight. Etiquette did not permit him to attend her funeral.

When I came out of the Orangerie, my mind full of all these things, I ran into an exhibition of modern sculpture, a perfect forest of forms, which is going on in the Tuileries gardens. I'm bound to say I averted my eyes and fled.

July 30, 1950

*

What a terrible life the Paris concierge does lead. Since holidays with pay have been the rule, practically every Parisian goes to sea or mountains for a month in the summer. The society lady who said in August, 1914, 'But they can't have a war, there's nobody in Paris,' would almost, in August, 1950, have been speaking sober truth. But the poor concierge can't go; she can hardly go up the street to fetch a yard of bread. *La Porte*, more exacting than a small child, has to be watched night and day since, in a well-regulated house, nobody must be let in or out who has not first been scrutinised by the concierge. It is hardly surprising if they are a disagreeable race, often a little bit mad. The compensation for this slavery lies in the great power they wield over the *locataires* or tenants of the house. Police dossiers are largely compiled from their reports, and there are a thousand ways by which they can make life difficult for anybody against whom they bear a grudge.

So one propitiates the concierge with little offerings from time to time, rather as country people are supposed to propitiate the fairies – not only with offerings of money at Christmas and other appropriate seasons, but with scraps of food, coffee beans, and so on. I got mine on my side by bringing some stuff from London which cured her cat of mange. A friendly concierge adds wonder-

38

fully to the amenities of life, and nobody who has lived in a house where there is one would willingly do without her again – I think personally that even a devil is better than no concierge at all.

*

Among the births announced in the *Figaro* the other day was the following:

Cécile, François, Michelle, Monique, Odile, Henri, Ségolène, Thérèse, Zita, Gérald Colcombet sont heureux de faire part de la naissance de leurs petites soeurs, Mireille et Myriam.

Congratulations indeed to the Colcombets.

October 8, 1950

*

Four women have died during the last few months, all well over eighty, none of them French by birth, who have all been intimately connected with the social, literary and artistic life of Paris for fifty years and more. They were the Chilean Mme Errazuriz; Mme Sert, a Pole married to the famous Spanish artist and painter of murals; Countess Betka Potocka, Polish by birth and marriage; and Lady Mendl, an American married to an Englishman.

Eugenia Errazuriz, *la belle Chilienne*, came to France on her honeymoon in 1876, and only went back to her native land at the age of ninety, dying there early this year. Noted for her taste, greatly in advance of that of her contemporaries, Mme Errazuriz invented *la pauvreté*, or plain white rooms, sparsely furnished, a luxurious poverty in her case since the few pieces of furniture were quite priceless. She was one of Picasso's very earliest patrons, and nearly all the famous painters of the day painted portraits of this extraordinarily elegant person.

I would say, in parenthesis, that South American women often have the gift of elegance even more highly developed than it is in French women. It is generally agreed that the most elegant woman in Paris today is Mme Arturo Lopez, a great-niece of Mme Errazuriz.

Mme Sert, born Godespska, was elegant in another way, and somebody said, 'If Eugenia represents the age of bronze, Missia represents that of mother-of-pearl.' She was Diaghileff's great friend, always sat, glittering with jewels, in his box at the ballet, and had a salon of real importance for dancers, musicians and painters. Mme Sert helped to win the battle of the Marne. 'Send the troops up in taxi-cabs,' she said, half as a joke, to General Gallieni, thus solving a problem which had baffled the entire General Staff.

Countess Potocka, born Princess Betka Radziwill and descended from Talleyrand, whom she greatly resembled in looks, was purely *mondaine*. Until 1940 her home was Lançut, one of the largest houses in the world and a museum of treasures; like all Polish women of her class in the old régime she looked to Paris for everything that makes life agreeable, came here continually, and had quantities of friends and relations here. She died last summer in Switzerland, deeply regretted.

Elsie de Wolf, the eldest of the four, was married late in her long life to Sir Charles Mendl. She was the first interior decorator; until she appeared on the scene the arrangement of houses was haphazard, and rooms were generally crowded with superfluous objects. Lady Mendl, like Mme Errazuriz, saw that a great clean-up was needed; she commercialised this idea and made a fortune out of it. Between the wars her house in Versailles was the scene of many wonderful parties. She spent the war years in America, came back here when over ninety, and continued to lead the social life of a young woman almost to the day of her death.

December 3, 1950

*

The Paris season which came to an end with a bang, as it always does on July 14 (I mean literally a bang – fireworks) was a particularly brilliant one since the old lady was celebrating her 2,000th anniversary. But over all the fêtes, whether public or private, hung a sort of shadow, a shape of things to come, in the form of Monsieur Carlos de Beistegui's ball.

This ball, to be given tomorrow in one of the most beautiful of Venetian houses, the Palazzo Labia, has been a topic of conversation since last Christmas. I even heard a serious programme on the French radio (the equivalent of our *The Critics*) discussing it. The *entrée* of M. Lopez, they announced not without awe, will cost £50,000 and include two elephants. The £50,000 may well be true, since M. Lopez and his suite of twenty are to represent the Chinese Embassy to Venice in the eighteenth century and will sparkle with specially woven material covered with real jewels. But the elephants are a legend.

Indeed no party can ever have given rise to so many legends. We hear of a young couple who, for fear of Communism, had sold their estates and were off to South America. They have now spent all the money on their *entrée* at the ball. We hear of a certain lady who, intending to go as a Spanish Infanta, advertised for a dwarf to accompany her. She arrived home next day to find her hall filled with rich dwarfs of her acquaintance who had not been invited. We hear that the Communist mayor of Venice, sensing good propaganda for his side, had facilitated the ball in every way while his successor, a Christian Democrat, has not been so forthcoming.

No society people left Paris before the middle of August; they were too busy trying on their dresses. When finally they got away a yacht race round Italy ensued, since there is only one good mooring in Venice for a big yacht. It is to be hoped that these ships will not suffer the fate of the Spanish armada, as in that case the ball would be deprived of its most splendid *entrées*.

September 2, 1951

*

Nobody visiting Paris just now should miss the exhibition 'Napoléon et sa famille,' which is assembled in the Louis XIV Salle d'Honneur at the Invalides.

Napoleon was one of those people who become attached to familiar objects, and all his personal possessions, though rather plain and unostentatious, were of the first quality. One of the exhibits is a cashmere shawl, given him by his sister Pauline, which he wore round his waist at the Battle of the Pyramids and which served him as a bed-cover until the day of his death.

41

The Canova statue of the roi de Rome as a baby gives him his father's face, but this may have been a diplomatic misrepresentation, for it bears no resemblance to the fat, fair German child whose miniature Napoleon took with him to St Helena. How curious to reflect that after all the efforts, the painful rearrangement of his life which it cost him to produce an heir, the next Emperor of his name and dynasty should have been, not his grandson but Josephine's (Napoleon III was the son of her Beauharnais daughter, Queen Hortense.) And, indeed, considering Louis Bonaparte's state of health and the fearful aversion which he always felt for Hortense it is quite unlikely that Louis Napoleon, her third son, was a Bonaparte at all.

The Malmaison is well worth a visit now, and very easy to reach by bus. The garden is looking beautiful, and various rooms have been newly opened to the public, including Josephine's bedroom, which is arranged as a tent. There is some splendid Empire furniture by Jacob, with bronzes by Thomire, and in the coachhouse hangs Winterhalter's famous picture of the Empress Eugénie and her ladies.

These two shrines of Bonapartism are visited daily by large crowds, mostly French. I think the English hardly realise the esteem in which Napoleon is held here. We remember him as a conqueror, the French revere him for having consolidated the benefits of the Revolution and for the fact that so much in modern France is the fruit of his genius. The legal system, the departments, their boundaries and administration, the Banque de France, the Légion d'honneur, higher education, the framework of the Army, the constitution of the Institut de France, all owe their present forms to Napoleon. But his conquests have passed into history, useful only as the names of streets.

An American said to me: 'The French never stop complaining about German aggression, but all the Metro stations here are called after French victories over the Germans.' And he began enumerating: Iéna – Wagram – Austerlitz-Oberkampf – 'Stop.' I said, 'Oberkampf was a draper, he lived at Jouy-en-Josas and invented Toile de Jouy.'

42

A Frenchman who was there said rather crossly: *Au fond il n'y a que les etrangères qui connaissent les personnages du métro.*

Like survivors from a battle, the guests of the great ball are trickling back to Paris. Each has a tale of daring to recount, each gives the impression that it was a damned close-run thing and would never have done without his or her particular entrée. Victory, however, is undisputed and wherever he goes in Venice M. de Beistegui is acclaimed with cries of Viva Don Carlos – Carlos di Spagna.

September 16, 1951

*

Nothing shows the character of a town more clearly than the aspect and quantity of its bookshops. In Edinburgh they display sober tomes bound in cloth, varied by an open page illustrating a dry fly. In Oxford they are full of boys and girls reading the books. In London they are orderly, varied and prosperous. In Madrid they are conspicuous by their absence.

But no town that I have ever seen has so many bookshops to the square mile as Paris. There seem to be two or three in every street, though you can never be quite sure of finding them open; and it is by no means unusual, late in October, to be confronted with a yellowing card on the locked door: *Réouverture 1 er Septembre.*

When I first came here in 1945 it was to buy French books for the shop in which I then worked, so I have many friends among Paris booksellers. There is a little walk I am fond of which takes in a representative group of them, beginning with the Louis XV house in the rue St Honoré where M. Camille Bloch has his shop.

I think, for the general reader, M. Bloch must be one of the best booksellers in the world. His learning is immense. I have never known him recommend a book without having read it himself, and if his customer asks for a bibliography on any subject to do with French history, philosophy or literature, he can not only give it off-hand, but can usually supply many of the books there and then.

43

Leaving M. Bloch we pass by the Librairie de la Concorde where Mlle Jammet is an authority on modern English novels and has a good stock of them, cross the rue de Rivoli and make our way over the Tuileries gardens and the Pont Royal to see Mlle Jeandet in the rue de Verneuil. Her shop, which she runs single-handed, is frequented by young children and old book-worms, since the stock is a curious mixture of children's books and out-of-print modern highbrow literature. On the first Monday of every month she holds an extremely enjoyable salon, much frequented by publishers and other booksellers.

A little détour takes us to the quai Malaquais where M. Caillandre sits in a dream of old morocco. I love going to see him, and he greets me with '*voici la Parisienne.*'

Up the rue Bonaparte, full of bookshops, including the famous Divan, where we find M. Martineau, the greatest living expert on Stendhal, we turn right in the rue Jacob to have a word with Mme Barbier, who knows everything about old Paris. Then, taking the little narrow streets of St Germain-des-Prés, we make our way to the Cour de Rohan to find M. Deschamps.

The Cour de Rohan is picturesque, old and interesting beyond words. It is really a little village of seventeenth-century houses built into the wall of Paris at one of Philippe-Auguste's strong-points. Two gateways, a round tower and a well date from the twelfth century.

Many famous people have lived in this Cour, including the amiable Dr Guillotin, who loved animals and invented a humane method of slaughtering sheep. The poor man lived to see men and women herded to the machine, which, insult added to injury, was given his name.

Danton and Marat lived here; Sainte-Beuve kept a flat where he could come and work in peace; the baby Anatole France learnt to read at a dame school in the Cour.

M. Deschamps carries on the revolutionary tradition of the place. He resisted in the war and has been resisting ever since. He marches, he demonstrates, he signs and collects signatures. But his books are mostly of the nineteenth century. He loves romantic bindings, rare children's books and toys, and odd publications about Paris. There is no greater pleasure than an hour with M. Deschamps in his shop; he is very learned and a dear.

I went down to the Marais to an exhibition about the founders of Paris (a little bit dull, I thought). While there I went for a walk and was very glad to find that steps are at last being taken to save some of the old houses from falling into complete disrepair. The Hôtel de Sully (1624) has been bought by the Ville de Paris, and its façade on to the street, disfigured during the last century, is being put back into its original state. The existing tenants, all very poor by the look of it, cannot be removed, but as the leases fall in the Ville de Paris will take over the various flats. One of these still has contemporary *boiseries* with Sully's monogram and a painted cupola.

The Renaissance turret in the rue les Francs-Bourgeois is being cleaned and repaired. The beautiful Hôtel des Ambassadeurs de Hollande (1660), which has suffered less than most of its neighbours and still boasts at least four painted rooms, is empty. Rumour has it that a mysterious millionaire is the new owner; I only hope this is true and that he will soon take steps to prevent it falling, as they say here, into crumbs.

Meanwhile a very disquieting rumour is going about that the pretty old street lamps of Paris are soon to be replaced by strip lighting hung across the road. I find it hard to believe that the Parisians would allow their town to be disfigured in such a way, but they ought to ensure that they are not presented with a *fait accompli*.

Every French schoolboy knows about 'Bouquinquant' because of what Larousse calls . . . *son attitude à l'égard d'Anne d'Autriche qui prêta à de malignes interprétations*. His life has just appeared: *George Villiers, duc de Buckingham. L'énigme du monde*, by Philippe Erlanger, and is having an enormous success here.

It is amusing to see the story through French eyes. Buckingham has charmed M. Erlanger, just as he charmed his own contemporaries with his gift, by no means so rare among the English as French people are inclined to think it, of making fun and gaiety for those around him. He turned everything into a joke – too much so, indeed.

When he and Prince Charles got back from their humiliating journey to Spain, undertaken against the King's wishes, they were closeted for hours with James. The astonished courtiers heard only shrieks of laughter coming from the room. When, at his impeachment, he was described by a fellow MP, as The Beast (M. Erlanger says *les Anglais prêtent volontiers à leurs ennemis un aspect apocalyptique*) he burst into uncontrollable giggles.

Buckingham had almost everything in his favour. He was '*très gentil*,' beautiful, courageous and a lover of art, but he had no political sense whatever. Unfortunately for him and for his country this irresponsible fascinator was presented, at the age of twenty-three, with absolute power, power greater than that wielded by Cardinal Richelieu himself. His 'dear Dad and Gossip,' James I, could refuse him nothing; the heir to the throne loved him and spoilt him, if possible, even more.

It was bound to end in tears; tears is the *mot juste*. Charles sobbed all night after the assassination and never recovered from the blow; the Duchess of Buckingham tried to commit suicide on seeing her husband's dead body; Anne of Austria wept for fifteen long years. At the end of that time Richelieu presented Mazarin to her with the insolent words, '*Il vous plaira, Madame, il ressemble à M. de Buckingham.*'

October 14, 1951

*

The Hôtel Drouot celebrated its centenary the other day by holding an exhibition. There were drawings and engravings of auctions, catalogues of such famous sales as that of the duc d'Aumont, and posters, including the one which advertised Madame Thiers's pearl necklace. Madame Thiers, whose fabulous wealth never prevented her from counting halfpennies when she was at the Elysée, bequeathed this necklace to France. For some time it was exhibited at the Louvre, in the Galerie d'Apollon, where we can still see the Régent (the great diamond bought by Philippe d'Orléans from Thomas Pitt), Anne of Brittany's ruby

46

and the Saint Esprit of Louis XV. However, since pearls lying in a museum only deteriorate, it was thought better to sell it, and part of this necklace is worn today by Princess Troubetskoï.

Public auctions in France date from the occupation of the Romans. Like the casinos, they are run by the State, and they received their present charter from Napoleon. He laid it down that in a society where furniture and pictures constitute so important a part of private property the auctioneers must be properly trained civil servants.

The Hôtel Drouot is the first permanent home of these auctions. The great sales of the eighteenth century generally took place at the houses of such experts as Lopez and Gersaint. Basan, who thought the setting of a sale quite immaterial, simply used a *porte cochère* in the rue du Battoir, while permission was sometimes given for important collections to be sold in the Salon Carré at the Louvre.

The greatest sale the world has ever known was that of *les meubles et effets précieux au cidevant*, in other words, the contents of Versailles. Except for the linen, which was given to hospitals, and a few pieces of furniture which, the royal arms carefully removed, were kept for the Louvre, everything in the Palace was sold by auction. The sale, which began in 1793, and lasted one year, went on every day from 10 a.m. to 2 p.m. and from 4 p.m. to 8 p.m., in rooms formerly occupied by the princesse de Lamballe. Many of the famous cabinet-makers bought back their own creations, but were ruined by so doing, as taste was changing fast and collectors were soon to insist upon alligators, palm trees, sphinxes and other reminders of the Egyptian campaign.

Almost anything can be sold at the Hôtel Drouot, though live lions and tigers are no longer accepted. A forest of dwarf trees, Voltaire's brain, left by mistake in a chest of drawers and sold with it, fifty life-sized female wax figures in the uniforms of Crimean veterans, thirty guillotines, and the petrified corpse of a man have all been sold there during this century.

Le Journal d'une femme de cinquante ans, by the marquise de la Tour du Pin de Gouvernet, hitherto very difficult to come by, has just been reprinted. It is the most entertaining of the many memoirs written by aristocrats who survived the French Revolution. Madame de la Tour du Pin was a lady-in-waiting to Marie-Antoinette, and gives a lively description of the routine at Versailles, but her happiest years were spent, after she and her husband had emigrated, running a farm in America. She evidently had a talent for farming and really loved it and, as a result, she and her husband were more comfortable than most of the *émigrés*.

One day she was preparing a piece of mutton for dinner when she heard a deep voice behind her '*on ne saurait embrocher un gigot avec plus de majesté.*' It was M. de Talleyrand, who had just arrived in America from England. He told them the news of Robespierre's downfall – the Revolution was nearly over. Soon they heard that their property in France would be returned to them if they claimed it in person. They freed their slaves – a touching scene – and started for home, though not without some misgivings. They were never to be so happy and carefree again.

Like most of the aristocrats, they collaborated in a half-hearted way with Napoleon. The first time Madame de la Tour du Pin met him the Court was in mourning. She had no black dress, but so great was her curiosity to see him that she went (it was at a reception in Bordeaux, near her home) dressed in grey. Napoleon looked her up and down. '*Mais vous n'êtes donc pas du tout affligée par la mort du Roi de Danemark?*' He was always very nice to the la Tour du Pins, which did not prevent them from shamelessly deserting him when the time came.

Madame de la Tour du Pin, though of Irish ancestry – she was a Dillon – was a typical French woman, practical, elegant, sociable and very bossy. Talleyrand used to say that her husband was nicknamed Gouvernet.

November 11, 1951

*

I was rung up from UNO by a member of the French delegation whom I had not seen for some time. 'Come to luncheon,' I said. But he replied gloomily that he gets only two hours off, and it takes ten minutes to my house. The idea of bolting his food in 100 minutes clearly appalled him, and he said that we must eat in Passy.

Now the UN building is full of entrances and, as we could not afford to lose precious minutes looking for each other, we decided that it would be safest to meet in the Musée de l'Homme by that mournful-looking exhibit labelled *Squelette Anglais*. (There is something unmistakable about English bones. I am dressed from head to toe in Paris and yet no Frenchmen ever doubt my nationality. 'Sorree,' they say if they jostle me in a crowd.) We met sharp at one o'clock and raced to a local bistro where we happily guzzled until three minutes to three. 'You see,' he said, 'we've only just done it in the time.'

Then he took me to one of the meetings. I found the atmosphere inside that gigantic Nissen hut very unexpected – the spiritual atmosphere I mean, the actual air one breathes having the same horrible quality as tinned food. But the *climat moral* is heavy with goodness. Unfortunately, as every novelist knows, there is nothing so dull as goodness.

The delegate from Iraq was speaking about Morocco, proving his point, that the French are neglecting the native population there, with incomprehensible statistics and punctuating these with: 'I am so very anxious not to hurt the feelings of our kind hosts . . . I would much rather not say it . . . it does upset me but I feel I must . . . oh how I wish I could have left that bit out . . .' (This mousy little speech was later described in the *Figaro* as '*injurieux, mensonger, grossièrement calomnieux.*')

I stayed as long as I could in this fog of goodness but was finally driven out by the central heating, which reminded me of nothing so much as the turkish bath in *Helena*. And oh! how I longed for the Field of the Cloth of Gold, or even the Congress of Vienna. But all the same I must confess there is something rather reassuring about a visit to UNO.

There is nothing in English literary life to compare with the atmosphere of excitement, fuss and nonsense in which the big literary prizes here are awarded. The canvassing, not only of the juries but of general public opinion, is tremendous. Aspirants to the Femina, learning that the tender-hearted ladies of the jury are inclined to be influenced by their circumstances, vie with each other in protestations of poverty. One lady received the journalists in bed in her large, comfortable house; she explained that she had pneumonia. Should she win the prize she would be able to afford herself a little stove. Another told of an ancestral home crumbling to ruin, all the hunters sold, while a third had day-dreams of an inexpensive journey to Spain.

On the afternoon of the Femina award decision I got home to find a message from my publisher, M. André Bay, of Stock, asking me to go there at once, I knew this must mean that their only candidate, Mlle de Tourville, had won the prize. I arrived in the office to find all the partners looking as if they had just had an enormous baby. M. Delamain introduced me to Mlle de Tourville: 'She lunched with me, we were both perfectly calm, we even managed to eat a little. Then, imagine, my telephone went dead – the neighbours had to come and tell us!'

M. Bay said: 'I was supposed to do a broadcast, this evening with John Lehmann, but now, of course, it's out of the question. I could never concentrate on it.' M. Boutelleau's face was entirely covered with ink. The telephone pealed incessantly, champagne flowed. Mlle de Tourville looks, as somebody said, like a heroine of the Fronde. I am so glad she has won the prize, and it is well deserved; *Jabadao* is a beautiful book.

December 9, 1951

*

Back again among the cross, clever French, I found the now-famous quarrel between Jean Cocteau and François Mauriac in full swing. Mauriac fired the first shot with an open letter to Cocteau in the *Figaro Littéraire* explaining why he had walked out of Cocteau's new play *Bacchus*. He reproached Cocteau for the profanities which it contains and then proceeded to a most unfavourable analysis of his friend's character: '*Ta dureté est celle de l'insecte* . . . We have been members of the same troupe now for forty years . . . for nearly half a century I have watched you do your turn . . . very soon the tightrope on which you have danced for so long will lose itself in the shadow of death.'

Cocteau, who is sixty-three but sees himself as an eternal twenty-eight, was considerably nettled; he dipped his pen in venom and replied with the good old formula, *J'accuse* – 'I accuse you of being a judge who has a soft spot for the defendant. And I accuse you of being the former in your articles and the latter in your novels.' . . . 'At our age one can no longer have a beautiful body, but we ought to have beautiful souls. I accuse you of having neglected your soul . . . *Je t'accuse d'inculture*' (the worst thing a Frenchman can say to another).

Cocteau's case is rather weakened by the badness of his play. The critics, who are all fond of him (few men are more loved by their friends), could find nothing good to say and said nothing at all, writing about the difficulties of parking a motor on a first night, and so on.

February 3, 1952

*

Many people here choose to believe that all English residents abroad are in the pay of the Secret Service, especially writers, whose books are a cloak for more sinister, more profitable activities. Even Clémenceau was a prominent member. All political murders are committed by its agents, and they it was who administered a pill to President Deschanel, causing him to fall out of a *wagon-lit* in his pyjamas and run round the countryside quacking like a duck. (The railway worker who finally took him in said he knew at once that it was somebody very important because his feet were so clean.)

Prices of antique furniture are soaring here, and a climax was reached the other day at the Hôtel Drouot when a small unsigned Louis XV cabinet, with two legs and its marble top missing, was sold for over £800, bidding having started at £30. The sale room wags said it would have fetched much less had it been complete.

A member of one of the *grandes familles* recently inherited a roomful of nineteenth-century silver, black from years of storage, and sent it off to the Drouot to be sold more or less for the weight of the silver. About half an hour before the sale was to begin the auctioneer saw an expert looking with some interest at a table decoration consisting of a massive group of animals. The auctioneer began to feel a certain doubt. He sent for a workman and had the base unscrewed, revealing the signature of Germain, a famous eighteenth-century silversmith. The owner was informed, took the piece out of the sale and subsequently sold it, for more than £10,000, to one of the great collectors of silver who lives here.

It turned out to have been part of a *surtout de table* made for Louis XV to give to the King of Portugal. Like all the Braganza silver it had subsequently been divided up between the two brothers who ruled in Portugal and Brazil. Some of it already belonged to the aforesaid collector. He has now traced and bought the remaining pieces, the whole huge affair is re-united and has been on show at the Louvre.

The Drouot has just seen the last act in the 'drama of the rue Mouffetard.' An old house in that street was being demolished when five workmen dislodged a roll of parchment and 515 gold coins, louis, double louis and half louis, in mint condition, bearing the head of Louis XV. This treasure had been hidden in the wall by Nivelle, Counsellor and Secretary to Louis XVI, the day before the revolutionaries came and took him to the guillotine. The parchment was his will, in which he left everything to his daughter. A legal argument ensued as to whether the gold should count as treasure trove and go, according to French law, to the workmen who found it, whether it belonged to the Ville de Paris, who had bought the house, or to the eighty descendants of Mlle Nivelle. Finally the Court ordered it to be divided, half to go to the family and the other half to the workmen. The coins were sold before an enormous crowd of people and fetched more than had been expected, about £8,500 in all.

I have just run into an acquaintance coming away from chez Madame Antonia, the local sorceress. 'She wants one of HIS socks – dirty if possible,' she called out cheerfully across the street.

March 30, 1952

There is almost too much to see in Paris at the moment. But surpassing everything else is the great Italian exhibition at the Petit Palais. Here are treasures which it would take months to see in the towns and villages of their origin. Pictures, bronzes, sculptures, glass, ivory and jewels, from the third to the four-teenth century, almost every object is a masterpiece.

Then we have been given a tantalising glance, jostled in a mob of amateurs, of the Cognacq pictures before the first day's sale at the Galerie Charpentier where more than £300,000 was realised.

The fortune of the Cognacq family was made by Ernest Cognacq and his wife Louise Jay, who were both born in the 1830s and died in the 1920s. They founded what might be described as the Selfridges of Paris, the Samaritaine. Childless, friendless, almost inhuman, this couple never had a thought or performed an action which was not concerned with the aggran-disement of the 'Samar'. They and their employees worked seven days a week until the law of 1906 made one day of rest obligatory; even for Mme Cognacq's funeral her widower did not shut his shop.

Ernest Cognacq and his wife collected *objets de vertu* and left them to the Ville de Paris in the little Musée Cognacq-Jay; their shops and fortune they left to the late M. Gabriel Cognacq, their nephew. He assembled such a collection as can only be made by the true connoisseur, every picture, every object of which bears the stamp of personal taste and knowledge. He intended to leave it to the Louvre. Unluckily, during the war, the Vichy Govern-ment made him président du Conseil des Musées Nationaux in the place of the exiled M. David Weil. He loved this position, and was so furious when, at the Liberation, M. Weil was reinstated that he changed his will. However it is said that the jewel of the collection, the Cézanne still life, may yet find its way to the Louvre through the generosity of Mme Walter, who bought it for £33,000.

May 25, 1952

*

Why do French books never have an index? My St Simon in sixteen volumes and Mme de Sévigné in eight, the innumerable history books and *mémoires* on my shelves, whether in contemporary or modern editions, have not got an index between them. Now maître Maurice Garçon, member of the Académie française, has given us the fruits of long and patient historical research, in nearly 600 pages, without one. Oh! the irritation!

This book is called *Louis XVII, ou la fausse enigme*. Did the child of Louis XVI and Marie-Antoinette die in the Temple, or was he rescued and another child put in his place? This question has puzzled historians and fascinated the public ever since.

There were, in all, twenty-seven impersonators of the Dauphin, cropping up over a period of some thirty years after his death or disappearance, but only four of these are worthy of a moment's consideration. Maître Garçon a leading light of the French Bar, analyses the claims of these four men at some length and easily demolishes them, so easily that it is hard to see how anybody can have taken them seriously for a moment.

Maître Garçon has no doubt whatever that the real Dauphin died, as stated by his gaolers and doctors, in the Temple. Like his brother and sister, who died before the revolution, he was tubercular, and Marie-Antoinette never expected to rear him.

He was a poor little creature, not attractive. We know from his own mother and sister that he was lazy, dirty and a liar. Three years of solitary confinement with no education whatever would hardly have tended to correct these faults, and it was surely just as well for France that he did not live to become King at the Restoration.

June 22, 1952

*

With the temperature high in the nineties, never too high for me, the shrieks of the eight tiny children who play in my courtyard reached such a pitch that I began to long for the day when germ warfare will be within the reach of us all: 'Eight mild attacks of laryngitis – how much, please?' Now they have gone off to various beaches and I am alone in the house, rather missing them as a matter of fact, and the hot, slow, provincial summer life has begun.

I love it. Paris is no longer the capital of France, for the *Tour* is in progress, that great bicycle race which unites the French as nothing else can. The capital, which changes every night, is the town where the competitors stagger from their bicycles at the end of the day's run. The vast crowds which follow the *Tour* (twenty million people see it go by) dance in the streets all night, while Tino Rossi sings to them from an upper window. Meanwhile, in darkened rooms the cyclists themselves lie groaning on their beds, receiving the ministrations of their wives, friends, managers and doctors.

The newspapers and radio send their best reporters to follow the *Tour*, and we hear of little else while it is in progress. The 122 starters, we are told, will consume ten tons of meat, 1,500 chickens, 25,000 eggs, 16,000 petit-fours, and 2,000 lb of sugar in their coffee while the race is in progress.

That serious evening paper, *Le Monde*, had a long article analysing the character of Louison Bobet, the French cyclist, idol of the public, who has never yet won the *Tour*. Bobet, says *Le Monde*, must learn to master his nerves, or he will never bring the Maillot Jaune back to Paris. He is twenty-seven, a serious character who saves and invests for the old age now so nearly upon him; he wins the smaller races with perfect case, but when it comes to the *Tour* his nerves are too much for him. Up goes his temperature at the very thought of it.

This year his doctor refused to allow him to ride in it at all, which meant that his great rival, the Italian, Fausto Coppi, was almost sure to win. This pronouncement was made in rivers of tears – the doctor cried, Bobet cried, the radio announcer who told the news cried and we, the public, howled. It was bitterly disappointing.

Meanwhile the journalists excel themselves as usual. Coppi has been described as *le Machiavel de la Pédale*, another Italian, Bartali, is *le vieux lion toscan*, an elderly French rider *la Mistinguette de l'équipe*, and so on. Collectively the riders are *les rois de la route*. Their physical sufferings call forth positively biblical language; mountains during the heatwave were *un véritable calvaire pour les coureurs*. The whole thing is literary; indeed one radio commentator, after giving the *classement* up to date, said in a weary voice: *'Voici le fait important de la journée – le reste n'est que littérature.'*

July 20, 1952

55

I motored through the harvest fields and forests of the Ile de France to stay with friends in Champagne. They have a sporting estate with pheasant and duck shooting and a famous partridge shoot. I might just as well have been in Wiltshire.

Of course *vie de château* is the same all the world over, as are *vie de ferme* and *vie de chaumière*, but I have never seen a French house arranged so much like an English manor. There were chintzes, pitch pine, sporting prints, flowers *à la* Mrs Spry, a Crown Derby dinner service, English novels in the bedrooms, *Punch* and *The Field* on the drawing-room table, and in the garden, greatly to my disapproval as I think them so ugly, herbaceous borders and shaved lawns.

I couldn't resist telling my host and hostess that many English country houses have Toile de Jouy on the sofas, Redouté lamp-shades, Lunéville china, French novels in the bedrooms and *La Table Ronde* and *Revue de Paris* downstairs. They laughed and said that their great love of sport and gardening made them model themselves upon England, the home of these pastimes. 'We come in for a good deal of teasing, but there it is.'

In the evening we discussed those words and turns of phrase which are creeping into the French language to the despair of the purists. *'Plaît-il?'* for 'What did you say?' is one of the worst (it should be *'Comment?'*). A letter must never begin *'Chère Madame'*; either *'Madame'* or *'Chère Amie'* is correct. *'Cher Monsieur,'* however, is all right. *'On'* must never take the place of *'Nous'* – it is wrong to say *'On a diné chez X'* instead of *'Nous avons diné.'* Monte Carle for Monte Carlo is bad.

Of course abbreviations like *'sympa'* for *'sympathique'* and *'d'ac'* for *'d'accord,'* very much affected by the young, are too terrible for words; *'d'accord'* itself is a word that should be used with caution. It is quite all right when it means I agree with what you say, but must not be allowed to take the place of the affirmative. *'Aller au docteur, au coiffeur, etc.'* is wrong: it must be *'Chez le docteur,'* but on the other hand *'Chez Ritz'* and *'à revoir'* instead of *'au Ritz'* and *'au revoir'* are considered rather too precious.

Older people here complain very much that the young are murdering the French language, but all the same it is not in nearly as much danger as ours, since it is spoken only in France and is carefully watched over by the Académie française.

In their amusing book, *Mésentente Cordiale*, which has just appeared from Jarrolds, Nadia Legrand and Roland Gant deal with various aspects of French and English life which give rise to mutual misunderstanding. I should like to add a few observations of my own.

Justice: The French and English have a most profound horror of each other's judicial procedure. An English murderer would not be at all pleased to be kept in prison for months, if not years, while the Juge d'Instruction sifts every scrap of evidence; to be freely spoken of by Press and radio, long before the trial, as *l'odieux assassin, le parricide dénaturé, la Brinvilliers de la rue X*, etc.; to be taken almost daily to the alleged scene of his or her alleged crime, by far from gentle policemen, and strongly invited to confess. But a French murderer would find it just as upsetting to be brought to trial within a few weeks of his arrest, to see the evidence considered in what he would think a most perfunctory way at the trial itself and to be hurried to the gallows (considered here a most barbarous mode of execution) only three weeks after the verdict.

Servants: In France servants take a small percentage on the house books as a matter of course. I always think this is a splendid plan, as it means that the news of extra people to meals is received with radiant smiles instead of sad sighs. But French servants save the housewife's pocket in many ways. They wash everything at home, except sheets – a great consideration here since the laundries are expensive and bad – will take any amount of trouble to save francs on the household marketing, and are positively parsimonious with fuel, gas and electricity. They expect a month's holiday with board wages in the summer but never have days off or evenings out unless these happen to fit in with the family's arrangements.

Traffic: The aim of the French police is to get the traffic moving as fast as possible, to avoid blocks. The English police slow it down, to avoid accidents. I had a long talk with a *sergent de* *ville* the other day and he told me with pride: '*Ah, Madame, souvent je les fais marcher à cent kilomètres à l'heure!*'

Meat: People here have been very much upset by an account in the newspapers of the horrible, long, waterless journey undergone by the poor horses sent from the British Isles to be killed and eaten here. The French think it not only cruel but also extremely odd that a country so short of meat that whales and reindeer are sold in the butchers' shops should export perfectly good *biftek de cheval* to this land of plenty.

Death: The French hate death, the English rather welcome it for their friends and relations. I never receive a letter from home announcing a death without such a rider as 'far the best for him,' or 'such a mercy, really.' Such words would be inconceivable here: the French passionately mourn and miss their friends and would like to keep them on earth at the price of almost any suffering. I think they mind physical pain less than we do, in any case, both for themselves and for other people.

August 17, 1952

*

I suppose the town which has altered the least in my lifetime is Monte Carlo. The architecture has not been touched since its Edwardian heyday, and the old-fashioned comic-opera atmosphere still predominates. I have been staying at the Hotel de Paris, which is still, as I always remember it, the centre of life, the repository of all messages, the locale of all meetings. It is still furnished with excellent nineteenth-century copies of eighteenth-century pieces, and still has its frieze of old women waiting for the Casino to open.

The public garden, with its pretty lay-out of palm trees, flower beds and giant water lilies, is filled before luncheon with English ladies and gentlemen, in crêpe de Chine dresses, white shoes and stockings, white flannel trousers and white skins, reading yesterday's *Times*. They have never heard of the managerial revolution; they read the Court Circular and the bridge problems, and then walk happily home, to reappear later at the tables.

To all this the sea is a great blue backcloth; nobody thinks of going near it unless to lunch or dine on board a yacht, and nobody wanders about with a bathing dress or a towel under the arm.

The Casino, they say, is feeling the pinch. The great natural gamblers of the world are the English and the Russians, both more or less knocked out for the moment. The Americans have in no way taken their place, in spite of the fact that a game elegantly called craps has been introduced to make them feel at home.

In the harbours of the Riviera nice little yachts, flying the flags of such curious republics as Costa Rica and Andorra, echo to the sound of loud, cheerful English voices and the rich crackle of black-market notes. But the British flag is hardly seen in these waters any more.

From Monte Carlo I motored to Venice. The mountain road is thrilling, but the *autostrada* from Turin is a very dreary day's run. The beautiful, flat, rich, pale-green land, with its huge brick farm buildings and its vines hanging from tree to tree, is obscured by advertising posters, triumphal arches of dummy tyres, dummy bottles of mineral water the size of houses, and so on.

Venice must surely be the supreme monument of the human race. Here, as at Versailles, there is plenty of room for crowds, and indeed they are a necessary element; without their movement and gaiety it might be a little bit sad. Everybody has his own way of enjoying Venice. One of my friends – English, I need hardly say – goes off at once in search of hungry cats, which, when found, she marks on a map. The rest of her visit is spent in taking to each a daily ration; and she usually manages to smuggle home two or three particularly deserving cases in a specially constructed hat-box. Another friend has confessed that she lies a great deal on her bed reading gardening books – this is understandable, since one walks everywhere in Venice, and there are limits to human endurance.

Others wait for those hours of the day when all friends meet in the Piazza or at Harry's Bar. As for me, I like to wander about guide-book-less, ignorant and alone. Since I have no sense of direction whatever, I am rewarded by a series of surprises – the Colleoni statue or the Piazza again when I've only just left it.

It is very enjoyable and rather terrifying at night. Unlike most English people, I do not see the Italians as happy, laughing children: to me they are far more romantic and interesting, Vipers of Milan, Borgias, stilettos in the stocking and poison in the ring. As I walk along the dark canals, past black deserted doorways, with no noise but an occasional mysterious splash, I feel that anything might happen. You seldom see a lighted window or doorway in Venice; it is as though the whole population sits plotting in the dark. In fact, however, the people are out of an evening, milling harmlessly to and fro in the glare of neon-lighted shops.

Is Venice crumbling into the sea? This is the question which used to worry our grandmothers, and is even more pertinent today. Three years ago St Mark's was reported to be in imminent danger of collapse, and though much has been done to consolidate the basilica its condition is still far from reassuring. Italians love speed and noise and are convinced that without these attributes of modern life tourists would shun Venice. The wash from motor-boats racing up and down the Grand Canal is rapidly undermining the foundations of the palaces. At the same time hideous new hotels are arising at points of vantage.

The general tendency seems to be to destroy the very beauties and amenities that people go there to enjoy. Venetians resent any interference from foreigners in what they regard as their own affairs, but the future of Venice is of too great importance to allow feelings to be considered. Perhaps some protest from the foreigners whom the 'improvements' are designed to attract might make those responsible for them aware of certain mistakes that have been and are still being made.

October 12, 1952

*

The French have come back from their holidays in a serious mood. Wherever they look, at home and abroad, the situation is menacing. But all the troubles by which they are beset have had one good effect, they have united them as never since the war.

Apart from major problems, a minor but constantly irritating worry for Parisians is the traffic. Traffic blocks here are not as bad as in London, but the French mind them more. It is not their nature to sit calmly at the wheel thinking their own thoughts while the minutes go by and the lights change from red to green and back again with nothing moving.

They hoot, they shout, they struggle out of their motors and dart up the pavement to see what is happening. Sometimes this has a nice result, as when the conductor of the 48 had a *coup de foudre* for the concierge of a friend of mine during a particularly long traffic block. She now sits in the street with her knitting, rain and fine, to wave as he goes by. But on the whole it is bad for everybody's nerves.

There are various propositions on hand to solve this problem. The most horrible is that the Tuileries should be cut in two by a road leading from the rue de Castiglione to the Solférino bridge. This would entirely spoil one of the prettiest gardens in the world: the Tuileries are not large enough to support such a bisection. The *Figaro* is holding a referendum for or against – I have spent large sums buying up copies and crossing out *'oui'* on the form supplied.

November 9, 1952

*

The Salon de l'Enfance at the Grand Palais is really a gigantic children's party. While parents examine every commercial product connected with childhood, from unbreakable china to Walt Disney friezes *'pour orner gracieusement la chambre du petit,'* while they taste all the patent foods and drinks and learn how to stop their children from biting their nails (a good slap is never suggested nowadays, I notice), the children, like terrifying mice, cluster on swings, switch-backs, roundabouts and, most popular of all, in the model village complete with traffic lights, where they can drive miniature motors and scare the pedestrians just like real grown-ups.

While I was there wild cheering broke out: Louison Bobet, the bicyclist, had made an appearance. There was a veritable stampede of little feet as the loudspeaker announced that *le super-crack* was now at a certain stand. I could have stayed for hours had it not been for, not to put too fine a point on it, the smell. When I saw a canary dying (as though in a submarine) I felt it was time to leave. I must say I have had a fearful headache ever since.

December 7, 1952

A charmingly seasonable story is that of *la petite Nelly*. During the very cold weather her father was gathering moss in Fontainebleau forest for his flower shop. Little Nelly, aged three, wandered off and was seen no more.

Some four hundred people searched for her in vain, night fell, and there were seven degrees of frost. The following morning she was found sitting in a nest of leaves, laughing, singing and warming her bare feet in the sun. She was entirely covered with rime, but none the worse for her adventure. Asked why she had taken her shoes off she replied: 'I always do that before going to bed. I said my prayers, too.'

The splendid exhibition of religious art at the Galerie Charpentier, which is insured for a million pounds, is in aid of the fund to save Versailles. Versailles, happily, is now pronounced out of danger, the public having subscribed enough to stop the dry rot and mend the roof. M. Arturo Lopez has given 35,000 dollars to put Louis XIV's bedroom back to its original state. It is said that he wants to remove a Louis XV chimney-piece, which makes the authorities hum and haw a little, but whatever he does is sure to be perfection since he has enormous taste and knowledge of that period.

The adventure of the two English old maids, Miss Moberley and Miss Jourdain, who claimed to have seen the gardens of Trianon as they were in the eighteenth century, has hitherto been regarded with tolerant scepticism by the French. Now Léon Rey has written a long article, in the *Revue de Paris*, recapitulating their story, to which he adds a new point of some interest. The ladies describe having seen a sort of bandstand or kiosk, slightly Chinese in aspect. While conducting researches in the archives they concluded that what they saw must have been a sham ruin such as were so often constructed in *jardins de sentiment*.

M. Rey points out that this ruin never materialised any more than various other projects of the architect Mique, such as a hermitage with a clock. But the first folly ever built by Marie-Antoinette at Trianon was a wooden pagoda with a round stage looking very much like a bandstand. Like all the garden ornaments this used to be taken down in winter, and it soon disappeared, but M. Rey has found a contemporary print of it which he reproduces in his article.

Perhaps it is because the French never by any chance believe what they are told officially that their history seems to them so full of enigmas. We have only Shakespeare and Bacon, but they have countless unsolved mysteries. Who was the Man in the Iron Mask? Did the Dauphin die in the Temple? What happened to the duc de Choiseul-Praslin? Was Louis-Philippe Egalité's eldest child Louis-Philippe or was she Stella, Lady Newborough?

Now M. Grimod has posed the question *'Jeanne d'Arc, a-t-elle été brulée?'* in a very readable book of that title. He also affirms that she was a bastard of the house of Orléans, a theory I have often heard expounded by elderly French friends. 'How could a peasant's daughter have been invited to the King's table and allowed to carry the *fleur de lis*? That,' they scornfully say, 'would have been far more of a miracle than any voices!'

According to M. Grimod she was the daughter of la Reine Isabeau and the duc d'Orléans, that her royal origins saved her from the stake, that she lived to be about forty, married a Sieur des Armoises and may have had two sons. This theory has been demolished by maître Garçon in a very sarcastic and learned article entitled *Oui, Jeanne d'Arc a été brulée*, so we can take it or leave it.

A dinner guest leaving my house came face to face with a handsome, well-dressed man getting out of a cab: the latter asked if this was the Archevêché (residence of the Cardinal Archbishop of Paris).

'No, the Archevêché is in the rue Barbet-de-Jouy, the next street.'

'Thank you very much,' said the stranger, getting back into his cab. 'It is urgent, I am possessed of a devil.'

When I told this to Marie, my maid, she said 'Fancy bothering Monseigneur for a little thing like that. Why any priest could have arranged it for him!'

January 4, 1953

Sous la Coupole always means under the dome of the Institut de France, that beautiful building by le Vau which houses five Académies on the banks of the Seine. These are: les Académies des Inscriptions et Belles-Lettres, des Sciences, des Beaux-Arts, des Sciences morales et politiques and l'Académie française, to which no foreigner is ever elected and whose function it is to watch over the French language. (My grandmother used to say that as we have no such body in England 'Mothers must be the guardians of the English language.')

So important is this Academy that, in a country where precedence still counts for a great deal, its forty members sit higher than dukes at a dinner table. Once a week they meet, to make the dictionary, beneath a portrait of Cardinal de Richelieu on his deathbed. As the Academicians are none of them very young, and as it lowers their spirits to have their founder in such a sad state before their eyes, the picture is always covered with a green baize curtain.

There has seldom been so great a demand for places *sous la Coupole* as there was ten days ago when M. François-Poncet was received as an Academician. Exactly twenty-two years ago, Marshal Pétain, succeeding Marshal Foch, took the very same seat. According to the rules, M. François-Poncet was obliged to make an oration in praise of his predecessor, and everybody was anxious to see how he would manage in so delicate a situation.

I was lucky enough to be there and am able to state that he came out of it brilliantly. With the house almost equally divided between Pétainists and Gaullists he made it possible for each side to applaud him an equal number of times; on one or two occasions he even had them all clapping together. The Pétainists got in a good many claps at the beginning from *le vainqueur de Verdun* to *'je fais à la France le don de ma personne.'* But after *'une voix s'élève le dix-huit Juin'* it became the turn of the Gaullists. I sat between a darling old Gaullist with a goatee beard and a horrid old Pétainist in a wig. As soon as each saw how the other felt they started clapping ostentatiously across me at each other. The last word was with the old Gaullist, however, since the speech ended with a resounding quotation from General de Gaulle on the necessity of French unity.

The *Figaro*, which printed most of M. François-Poncet's speech next day, saw fit to leave out this quotation.

Somebody, though not necessarily an Academician, should compile a dictionary of all the French–English words which, as used on the other side of the Channel, mean either nothing at all or something quite different from their real sense.

Take *épergne* for instance. When the English use this word, always with a strong French accent, they mean a cluster of silver dishes dangling from a silver spray on the dining room table. It cannot be found in any French dictionary. Then we have *objet de vertu, savoir-faire, bon viveur*, which mean exactly nothing to the French but are full of meaning to us. *Blanc-mange* does not exist in France, either as a word or, thank goodness, as a pudding. *Salonnière* does not mean hostess, a *char-à-banc* is never motorised, a *brassière* is a bodice for a small child. *Pot-pourri* is a medley of tunes, not musty dried rose leaves in a bowl; a *porte-manteau* is a coat hanger and a *chiffon* is a duster; what we call chiffon is *mousseline de soie*.

Raconteur, which in England connotes wit, really means one who insists upon telling long dull stories. *Cul-de-sac* has not been used here since the eighteenth century; a street with no exit is an *impasse. Bijou* is not an adjective. Nobody has ever heard a French audience shout '*Encore!*'

English words current in France are quite as funny. A lady struggling out of a too-tight jersey was heard to say: '*Je suis 'andicappée par mon pull.*' A *Rugbyman* is a football player. In the racing and bicycling worlds we have *recordmen* and *supercracks*, in the motoring world *rallyes d'endurance*, and on the radio *speakers* and *speakerines*.

If somebody says 'Can I bring my *bull* to tea?' he means his French bulldog. *Gentleman* nearly always means burglar. *Snob*, in shop windows anyhow, means sporting, smart.

It is rather interesting that the English users of the supposed French words aim at appearing cultivated and cosmopolitan; the words are nearly all concerned with the art of living. The French users of English words, on the other hand, see themselves in a breezy, sporting open-air light. It shows what each country really admires in the other.

February 1, 1953

*

La Coupole is again very much in the news, with three elections for the Académie française just over and one more to come. These elections are seldom concluded without a great deal of canvassing, since the candidate is supposed to pay a visit to each of the forty immortals and respectfully beg for his vote. The visits are said to be terrifying and, like all canvassing, rather inconclusive. A few people promise to vote for their visitor, but most content themselves with assuring him that they will do their very best for him; nobody refuses definitely.

Marshal Juin got in without paying a single visit, but on the other hand M. Fernand Gregh, one of the new members, must have paid, in all, 640, because this is the sixteenth time in his eighty years of life that he has presented himself. The historian, M. Pierre Gaxotte, is another new member; he is a mere fifty-eight. His histories are written from a royalist point of view; according to him, the kings can hardly do wrong, and he has, in his *Siècle de Louis XV*, very convincingly rehabilitated that monarch.

The so-called *parti des ducs* in the Académie, which consists of the duc de Broglie and his younger brother the prince de Broglie, both physicists of genius, the duc de la Force, historian, and the comte d'Harcourt, the great and high-minded expert on German affairs who spent the war in a concentration camp, has been reinforced by the election of the duc de Lévis-Mirepoix. It is said that his family, through the Lévis, is related to the Virgin Mary and that, in a cousinly way, they tu-toi her in their prayers. Readers of Proust will remember that Mme Verdurin, after forty years of social climbing, arrived at a point when she only had to say to her coachman 'Go to the Lévis' for him to take her to the Mirepoix.

The Duke's inaugural speech is awaited with even more interest than was that of M. François-Poncet on Pétain, because he takes the seat of Charles Maurras. Whereas Pétain, Prince of Trimmers, has but little real prestige left, there are still certain intellectuals here who like to shelter their own squalid fascism and antisemitism behind the enormous literary renown of Maurras.

A journalist went the other day to ask the duc de Broglie whether, in his opinion, the terrible fogs and storms of this winter may be due to atomic experiments. The Duke looked at him vaguely and replied 'Are you interested in the world? I'm not, it's so small.'

March 1, 1953

*

'Called on Mr Cook from London who is at Paris with his drill plough, waiting for the weather to show its performance to the Duke of Orleans,' says Arthur Young, writing in 1787.

In this spring of 1953 Paris has been full of Mr Cooks who have come over for the Salon International de la Machine Agricole. In fact there were so many English visitors that they were specially catered for with nice cups of tea and nice English-speaking hostesses. These ladies hurried the Mrs Cooks off to the Salon des Arts Ménagers; really rather cruel, I thought, when they must have been so longing for Christian Dior.

I was amazed, at the show, by the size of the animals, which have certainly grown since the days when I used to live in the country. The cows were like elephants, the chickens like turkeys and every rabbit was a Harvey. Two old friends of my childhood, huge but recognisable, were La Wyandotte Blanche 'douce et familière, de tempérament tranquille' and La Rhode Island Rouge (sic) who is praised for 'sa précosité et sa rusticité.' Everybody, we are told, now recognises 'les grandes qualités de ces poules' which I for one had never doubted.

March 29, 1953

*

Living in a quiet little pension in a quiet little street at Versailles I feel a thousand miles from Paris. I receive my favourite English

67

daily paper two days late, and this lends a soothing quality to the news – 'Oh well, it's all over now.' I very much recommend this system to nervous characters. As for the *Figaro*, it has been able to think of nothing but its *concours d'erreurs*, a competition which it organises every year and which consists of spotting mistakes in learned articles on history, literature, architecture, sport and so on. This year there were 45,000 entries. The *lauréats* were dramatically woken up in the middle of the night by a journalist with the happy news, '*c'est du délire!*'

'Once you have lived in Versailles you will never like anything else,' says my landlady, and I think she may be right. I had no idea it was such a beautiful town. Like all French towns, it needs to be visited on foot; so much depends on a glimpse into a courtyard or up a narrow lane. The architecture has more fantasy than in Paris, and the stone and stucco are a prettier colour, not blackened by soot. I came across such a jewel of a house in the boulevard de la Reine that I thought, 'If that plate says dentist I shall go and make an appointment.' Luckily, however, it said Musée Houdon. The inside is as pretty as the outside, with *boiseries* in every room; there are a few busts by Houdon and some fine furniture.

Versailles has the most important public library in France, after the Bibliothèque Nationale, and an unspoilt eighteenth-century theatre, pale blue, white and gold, much more beautiful than Marie-Antoinette's theatre at Trianon. The park, always heavenly, is perhaps at its very best now and in November. Sometimes, in the early morning, they play the fountains so that a white ghost wavers at the end of each pale green alley. Work is in progress everywhere, happily, and great firework displays and illuminations are being planned for the summer.

Crapouillot's latest number is consecrated to *Bonnes manières: le savoir-vivre à travers les ages*, and is compiled by such experts as the duc de Lévis-Mirepoix, MM. de Fouquières, Pringué, de Vogué, etc. It is really an attempt to set down what good manners were and are before they vanish off the face of the earth. In America, it seems, if you say to a passer-by 'Excuse me, Sir, could you tell me the way to . . .' he has already gone up the street; you must say 'Hi – where's Times Square?' if you want an answer. In private houses an effusive show of cordiality takes the place of what we think of as good manners.

However, a new code will probably be evolved; people may think it better to live without manners and etiquette, but the thing can go too far. When Marie-Antoinette left Versailles for ever she said: 'There's one comfort, no more boring etiquette.' But when they came to take her to the scaffold in a cart drawn by a little white horse she was considerably annoyed; a grand duchess of Austria, she thought, should have had a carriage. Though the etiquette at Versailles kept everybody on the hop from morning to night, manners there, like all good manners, were very simple. When the duc de Croy took his little son to present him to Louis XV the child asked nervously what he would have to do. 'You know how to bow, I suppose?' said the Duke.

Crapouillot contains some useful hints for travellers to Paris today. The words *Monsieur, Madame, Majesté, etc.*, must never be abbreviated on envelopes. It is not done, in Paris, to telephone before eleven in the morning (those early peals, I have noticed, always herald an English voice). A quarter of an hour is long enough to wait for a dinner guest, after that the food will be spoilt. Cheese before or after pudding? The controversy goes on. The purists think it should be before and that there should be no bread on the table after the pudding.

The *jour*, or special day for receiving, is nearly dead, according to *Crapouillot* (though I still know of three, those of Madame Bousquet, the duchesse de la Rochefoucauld and the comtesse Jean de Polignac). It is supposed to be good manners to telephone before calling on sombody. A woman always sits on the right of a man in a motor-car, but a man does not take the edge of the pavement when walking with a woman, as in England. The wine glasses on a table are put slightly to the left, a trap for English visitors, who often find themselves drinking out of their neighbour's glass. *'Quant au placement à table'*, *Crapouillot* does not venture much information. 'If you have invited the Papal Nuncio, a royal highness and an ambassador, better consult some expert or you will find yourself in trouble.'

April 26, 1953

God helps those who help themselves; a ball was given this month at beautiful Champlâtreux, the Noailles house on the way to Chantilly, by the French nobility in aid of itself. *Entr'aide de la Noblesse Française.* Entrance 5,000 francs. No funnier, perhaps, than entertainments in aid of distressed gentlewomen, but it sounds funnier. There is no class here equivalent to our gentlefolk, nothing between the bourgeoisie and the nobility; the haute bourgeoisie is very proud of its status.

The fashion now is to give balls farther and farther away from Paris, with more and more acres of garden, park, and ornamental water lit by floodlighting. The several hours of the drive to the ball are happily occupied by the guests saying how dreadful last night's party had been; the hours of the drive back in inventing the stories which will be all over Paris next day about that evening's entertainment. As even the strongest tents have not availed to keep out the cloudbursts of this summer, the beauties in their ball dresses have been soaked to the skin night after night; luckily nobody ever catches cold when on pleasure bound.

The Coronation Ball at our Embassy is supposed to have provided an illustration of the famous *phlegme britannique*. The marquis de Cuevas's ballet was to dance in the garden at eleven; the guests, arriving from ten onwards, in pouring rain, were surprised to see no alternative arrangements for the ballet indoors. Nobody spoke of it or mentioned the weather at all. Punctually at eleven the rain stopped. Nobody said how lucky, or made any observation. The guests went into the garden, the Sylphides appeared among the trees and the whole thing was quite fairy-like.

The Embassy has had its outside walls cleaned and the beautiful honey colour of the stone, hidden in blackness for a hundred years, is now revealed. The Elysée, too, has been cleaned. Perhaps soon we shall see all the cathedrals white as when they were first built.

July 19, 1953

*

Another well-known test of middle age, like the policemen, is that the new fashions begin to look hideous. This, I think, will never

70

happen to me; in my eyes, whatever is the fashion seems entirely perfect. I am not the least surprised by M. Christian Dior's decision. The lovely young *élégantes* of Paris, who inspire him, have for some time been very anxious to see themselves in short skirts. It must be remembered that they never have; they were still in the schoolroom when the New Look burst like a bomb that autumn day some six years ago. Furthermore, photographs of their dancing grandmothers in the 1920s, in short skirts, low waists and cloche hats, seem as fascinating to them as the bustle seemed to us in those days. It may all come back, though it will not be quite the same; for this year, anyhow, talk about knees is all rubbish. Skirts are two inches shorter, a very nice little change, and I for one am in favour of it.

I overheard the following conversation, between an American and a waiter, about the strikes. The American said: 'I suppose they are the work of the Communists.' 'No, no,' said the waiter, speaking as to one whom he knew to have a bee in his bonnet, 'some Communists. But we are all in favour of them. We have a lot of grievances.' The American: 'What are they?' The waiter: 'Well, to mention one. They cut down the allowances for children at the age of five, just when the little nippers begin to want a glass of wine with their dinner.' American, in a dazed voice: 'Wine?' Waiter: 'Yes, of course. They have to disinfect their kidneys, like the rest of us, I suppose.'

August 16, 1953

*

An ever-fascinating study is that of the French and English seen through each other's eyes. I think all nations secretly regard each other as dirty in their personal habits, irreligious and morally lax; certainly this is true of Orientals and Europeans and of Europeans and Americans. I shall never forget the amazement with which the French read General Eisenhower's speech in which he said that they are a nation of atheists. They take it as a matter of course that the Americans are all atheists and that France is a Christian country.

71

But the French and English cherish a specially dotty set of ideas about each other. 'Going to England?' say French friends, 'Don't get murdered.' London, to them, is wreathed in a perpetual fog through which sex maniacs and policemen dance a sinister *pas de deux*. To the English imagination the black shadows cast by every tree and rock in France conceal a Corsican bandit, unhampered by any police force at all. The English have a touching and often misplaced faith in the excellence of French taste. The French have a touching and possibly exaggerated belief in the civic virtues of the English.

All conversations here about political economy, and nobody talks of much else just now, end on a note of exasperated admiration for the English, who are supposed to pay their taxes regularly, cheerfully and without any fuss. Having recently spent a month in England I am not quite sure that this is true. Tax evasion is the great topic of the day, there. The dodges employed are no doubt quite legal, but they certainly take up an enormous amount of man-hours which might be better occupied. A jargon has grown up, unknown when I lived in England – 'Expenses account – covenant – showing a loss' – incomprehensible to me until explained. Some kind friend sent me beautiful flowers; another kind friend reduced the charming thought by saying: 'Oh, that comes out of his expenses account.' So unromantic.

It seems that everybody who can do so runs some little side line – a farm for preference – in order to 'show a loss.' Old gentlemen, of great apparent respectability, give dinner parties to celebrate the fact that they have lived five years too long and thus done the Government out of millions in death duties. All these people still round on the French, whenever they think of them, for not paying their taxes. The French peasants, who wring a hard living from the land, in primitive conditions, come in for a special scolding. The English stockbroker, happily showing a loss on his model farm in Surrey, is outraged to think that some old woman in Auvergne, crippled by a life of toil on the stony mountainside, may have a few gold coins in her stocking. But the great joke is that the old woman herself is quite of the same opinion. The flesh is weak, but she truly wishes in her better moments that she could resemble those sublime English who love paying their taxes.

In fact the direct taxes here are high and collected with a good deal of severity (ten per cent increase for every month of non-payment). But the tax collectors are merciful to certain categories of earners. Writers, journalists, artists, musicians and so on are thought to deserve well of their country, to which they bring prestige and large sums in foreign currency. To enable them to save up for their old age, or the day when, because of illness or sadness, they are no longer capable of performing their creative work, they are allowed thirty per cent of their earnings tax free. This seems fair. If the State prevents the artist from saving then it should surely engage to provide him with a pretty room, a little fire to sit by and an occasional bottle of whisky out of bond when he can no longer work. It is cruel to force him to turn out second- and third-class stuff, when past the retiring age of any other profession and then allow him to die of want.

September 13, 1953

*

'We can't help loving our defeats,' said the courtiers of Louis XV during the Seven Years' War, 'they give rise to such excellent jokes.' The French never can help loving anything which makes them laugh; if there have been so far no amusing books about the defeat of 1940 and the German occupation it is because these events did not seem funny to the ordinary Frenchman.

A funny book on the subject could be written only by a cynical collaborator. Now collaborators, unfortunately, are very seldom cynical. I have yet to hear one say, 'Yes, well, I did collaborate, so what of it? The result was I always had plenty to eat, received an extra ration of coal and had no German soldiers billeted in my château, only delightful officers who used to take my children out riding.' Many collaborators are charming, cultivated men whose company at any time, except, of course, during a crisis, would be a pleasure indeed. But instead of happily chatting about Madame de Lafayette, or prehistoric paintings in the Dordogne, they still feel obliged to make excuses for their behaviour, which they alone are unable to forget.

They go droning on about the war and its causes. 'How much better not to have had it at all' is the burden of their song, 'since it

73

has settled nothing.' They ignore the fact that if we had not fought when we did Hitler would have got the atom bomb. That would have settled something – we should all by now be yawning under the sway of the most boring tyrant in history. Table talk night after night on the Third Programme and Paris Inter would not have been the least of our burdens.

The great excitement at Hyères this summer has been the young man and the milk can. A young man arrived in his small sailing boat, cluthing a milk can and asking to be taken to the nearest doctor. Somebody said, 'Would you like to leave your milk can here?' 'Certainly not. My thumb is in it.' And so it was.

He had been caught between the islands in a fearful storm; while doing something to his sail his thumb was torn off. With great presence of mind he put it, in sea water, in the milk can, but it was another ten hours before he could bring his boat in to shore. The doctor sewed the thumb on, the bone immediately began to mend, father and thumb are both doing well. *'Ce n'est pas l'eau de la Seine qui aurait fait cela,'* said the doctor.

October 11, 1953

*

I have been staying, as I stay every October, with a friend in the Seine et Marne. The sunny plain to the east of Paris, whose flatness is relieved by avenues of poplars rushing to every horizon, is covered at this time of year with the fruits of its enormous fertility. Haystacks, cornstacks, and heaps of dung dot the landscape; the beet-fields, scarlet with poppies, are full of bending harvesters; huge and ancient wagons, drawn by Percherons, lurch along the fawn-coloured roads. The modern world seems far away.

Meanwhile the modern world gets more and more horrible. What a million ages in fact, though only about fifty years in time, have gone by since Mr McGregor chased Peter Rabbit with his rake. The Mr McGregor of today is called Docteur Armand-Delille:

he got tired of chasing Peter, who had done some damage to his young plantations in Eure et Loir. So he caught him, injected him with myxomatosis, and sent him back to the nice sandy floor of his burrow. Poor Peter. His little head swelled, he became blind and deaf, he lurched pathetically round the potting shed and presently he died. Flopsy, Mopsy and Cottontail suffered the same fate, and so apparently did every wild rabbit, and many tame ones, in Northern France.

The disease, *'bondissant par dessus le Massif Central,'* has now reached beyond Charente in the South, and has passed the Belgian frontier. Nothing, it seems, can stop it from affecting the whole of Europe and Asia.

This affair is very unpopular. The farmers, who might have been pleased, since they will benefit from an increase in crops, love *la chasse.* The wild rabbit, or *garenne*, is a staple article of diet here; it is said that the doctor's ill-considered action has sent the cost of living up by a point or two. The breeders of tame rabbits must have them inoculated every six months, at a cost of 30 francs a time, because the disease is carried into their hutches by mosquitoes. The fur trade faces enormous losses and the makers of shot-guns and cartridges are already turning away workmen from the factories.

The Americans have very kindly suggested lending and leasing some of their rabbits, which are immune from myxomatosis. But American rabbits are as large as lions and as fierce as tigers. In fact, to read the French papers on the subject, one would suppose that skyscrapers were invented to take the Americans as far away as possible from their rabbits. These ravaging rodents have been refused with thanks.

I said to a député of my acquaintance 'Just remind me exactly how the président de la République is elected?' 'We all (the Assemblée Nationale and the Sénat) go down to Versailles and elect him there.' 'And who will you vote for?' 'Oh, my dear, one doesn't vote *for*. One votes *against*.'

November 8, 1953

Britain Revisited

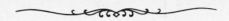

[In July 1950, Nancy Mitford toured Great Britain, with the cast of *The Little Hut*, a play by André Roussin, which she had translated.]

Like Marie Stuart, and complaining twice as loud, I have left Paris for Edinburgh; like her, I am here for professional reasons. I love Scotland but I always hate to leave Paris, particularly during the hot summer months and oh, the weather! France lay in the blue and pink glow of a heat wave; half-way across the Channel a curtain of cloud descended; it was pitch dark in Kent and pouring with rain in London, where everybody was muttering about St Swithin. Next day I came to Edinburgh by train.

Why are the trains so dreadful in England? Is there an explanation? If so it should be written up in every carriage with the Railway Executive's abject apologies.

'I feel ashamed for foreigners to come here,' said a young soldier on leave from Berlin with whom I had tea, 'it's all so dirty and ugly.' And indeed the journey through the Midlands was nine hours of solid drizzling ugliness, made even worse by the fact that the windows of the carriages were thick with grime.

Edinburgh, however, is not ugly. It so happens that I have never been here before; expecting to find a prim little Northern Bloomsbury I was quite unprepared for the dark, romantic, John Martin-like view which extends from my bedroom window. A castle-crowned cliff hangs over a valley full of trains and tomb-stones and classical buildings, all in various shades of black, and all enveloped in a murky fog. It has an extraordinary beauty, though I could never love so cold and so dirty a town.

I was unprepared, too, for the collection of pictures, few, but beautifully chosen and arranged, in the Scottish National Gallery. I had supposed that it would be given over to Raeburn and Allan

Ramsay, but in fact it contains wonderful treasures – a first-class Watteau, the most beautiful portrait by Greuze, of a little boy at his lessons, I have ever seen, several Poussins, a Tintoretto, an El Greco, and a particularly exquisite Rembrandt. There is, of course, a whole roomful of sandy, optimistic Scottish faces by Raeburn, a painter who bores me as a rule, though here I loved his skating clergyman.

I must say I feel very much cut off from Paris. I can't get the *Figaro*, let alone the sporting paper *Equipe* with its news of the *Tour de France*, and, greatly to my chagrin (not being very mechanically minded it came as an entire surprise to me), my little wireless no longer talks French. Instead of the furious arguments alternating with opera arias on cracked records to which I am accustomed, I now hear polite English voices playing paper games. It is very disconcerting.

'I like the cold weather, Jeannie, it braces y'up.' I heard a woman say. It seemed to me that she was getting what she liked. But I have since become conscious of the fact that Edinburgh considers itself in the grip of a torrid heat wave. The lift man says 'awful close' every time I see him, and one local newspaper spoke of our play's having filled the theatre on a hot summer night. By no stretch of imagination, however, is it warm enough for cotton dresses, so the Edinburgh women pay a tribute to the season by wearing white shoes, hats, bags and gloves with their tweed suits.

I said to a nice woman in the train that surely the English put up with too much. 'You ought to revolt,' I said, 'against such horrors as the National butter – if nobody bought it the Government would be obliged to supply something else.' I told her how the French Government had tried to foist frozen meat on the public because it is easier to distribute – fresh meat disappeared from the shops and awful stuff called Frigo took its place. The housewives revolted, nobody bought any meat for a fortnight, and that was the end of Frigo. She pondered over this and then said, with pride, '*We* revolted once you know, over tinned beetroot.'

The first sight of Glasgow is not attractive, especially when it rains, and I think it's the dirtiest town I ever was in. Furthermore, it doesn't like the play. 'This play may be screamingly witty in

French, if so poor Miss Mitford has rather missed the point' say the local critics.

All very discouraging. But I can't be totally miserable in a town which has a good restaurant (Rogano's is first class by any standards at all) and wonderful pictures. The Glasgow Art Gallery has an enormous collection in which nearly all the European schools are represented. I could have spent hours there. But we are busier than ever with the play, I am half the time struggling with new dialogue in my hotel bedroom (no rocky view here, just a belching factory chimney), and the other half in the theatre. I did manage to go over a shipyard, I am glad to say, and was deeply fascinated by the beauty of the scene and the skill of the workmanship.

Having had quite enough of British Railways I went from Glasgow to Newcastle by bus. I see now that, as in Spain, the trains here have become obsolete and that buses are the only possible form of transport. The employees are polite, the seats are comfortable, the windows are clean and the saving in money is great. The first few minutes of this particular journey were a little bit agitating owing to a shower of ginger beer bottles from the rack, but when that was over I settled down to six hours of beautiful border scenery, punctuated by great ruined abbeys, and have seldom enjoyed myself more.

The thing about Newcastle is that the people are so nice. They like the play and they seem to like us, so spirits have risen. Also I have now at last visited Seaton Delaval, the burnt-out ruin of a little Vanbrugh house, which I have always wanted to see and which more than came up to my expectations. The hall, with its statues blackened by smoke, and its ironwork turned, by the heat of the flames, into brown lace, is almost unbearably romantic, and so is the sightless, crumbling garden front.

Life in France has taught me never to overlook a provincial museum – indeed, the magic word *'Musée'* once got me up an Andorran mountain, to be rewarded by the rather surprising sight of a very old moth-eaten stuffed giraffe.

Motoring from Northumberland, we passed the Bowes

78

museum at Barnard Castle, and, of course, in I went. If ever there was a museum of the stuffed giraffe school, this is it. The oddest collection I ever saw. The handbook describes Madame de Maintenon as the second wife of Louis XVI, thus setting the tone of the whole affair.

Leeds, like Glasgow, filled me with gloom at first sight. But the hotel is so comfortable and the Art Gallery so beautifully run that I soon cheered up. The pictures from Dulwich are on loan here, so are Hogarth's 'Garrick as Richard III' and a beautiful portrait, school of Mignard, of the duchesse de Bourgogne. There is also a Picasso exhibition in progress.

With Leeds the tour came to an end. So now I know what it must feel like to be a foreign tourist in Britain. My impression is that the hotels are good, that the art galleries are full of treasures, and furthermore run with great taste, energy and discrimination, and that the food, though not good, is not as bad as people suppose. The railways are truly terrible, however, and so is the climate. During the whole of this summer month of August I have worn nothing but last winter's clothes, and I think there has hardly been one single day without rain.

Sunday Times, August 27, 1950

Chic – English, French and American

Nancy Mitford to Sydney Redesdale October 12, 1951

'I've done an article for an American paper (£100 fee) on English, French and American chic. I've let the English have it – it begins with two English duchesses being turned away from Dior for being too dowdy. However I have said that the two princesses led the world in chic – until they were 8.'

I really prefer the word elegance. 'Chic' has lost value in its native country – '*Chic alors!*' cries the street urchin on finding ten francs in the gutter – and it never had much prestige in England. Roget in his *Thesaurus* lumps it together with 'style, swank, swagger and showing off'; indeed, it represents everything that the English most dislike, a sort of bright up-to-date fashionableness they have never aspired to. For elegance in England is of such different stuff from that in any other country that it is not easy to make foreigners believe in it at all. (As regards the women, that is. English men and small children are universally admitted to be the model of good dressing; our Queen and Princess Margaret set the fashion for the world until they were ten.) It is based upon a contempt of the current mode and a limitless self-assurance.

When the Empress Eugénie paid a state visit to England she went with Queen Victoria to the opera. The Londoners sighed a little as the two ladies stood together in the Royal Box during the playing of the National Anthem; the beauty in her Paris clothes beside chubby little red-faced Victoria. Then the time came for them to take their seats. The Empress, with a graceful movement, looked round at her chair, but Queen Victoria dumped straight down, thus proving unmistakably that she was of Royal birth and upbringing. Had that chair not been in its place the skies would have fallen, and she knew it. The audience was proud of its Queen and never gave the parvenue Empress another thought – indeed, nobody in England was at all surprised when shortly afterwards the Second Empire collapsed.

Nearer our own time two English duchesses were turned away from Christian Dior. The people at the entrance considered them too dowdy to be admitted. In England, if you are a duchess you don't need to be well dressed – it would be thought quite eccentric. I cannot imagine why they ever had the idea of going to Dior, where they would certainly not have ordered anything. Perhaps they were tired after extensive sight-seeing and thought they would like to sit for a while, having a vision of Monsieur Worth's soothing empty salons in the days when their mothers dressed there. (In the days of their grandmothers Monsieur Worth came to the house like any other tradesman.) They had surely not envisaged the scented scramble at the top of the stairs, the enervating atmosphere of a salon where no window may ever be opened, the hideous trellis of crossed nylon legs round the room, and the all-in wrestling match for each and every chair. The duchesses went quietly, and if they did not quite realize what an escape they had had, they were probably rather happy to sit on a bench in the avenue Montaigne and watch the motors go by.

At the beginning of this century the English were rich and pleasure-loving; foreign currency was no problem; society women bought all their clothes in Paris. When the dresses were delivered they were put away for at least two years, since, in those days, nothing was considered so common as to be dressed in the height of fashion. Harlots and actresses could flaunt the current clothes, it was quite all right for them, and indeed a mark of their profession, but 'one of us, dear child', never. Even the men would not think of wearing a new suit until it had spent one or two nights in the garden, making it look at least a year old.

Now this tradition continues in London. The dressmakers there slavishly follow the Paris fashion of two years before, while people in the streets lag another year, so that to anybody arriving from Paris the clothes have an odd and disproportioned look, skirts too long or short, waists too high or too low, and so on. Anyhow, the word elegant cannot truthfully be applied to the English by day. Ladylike is the most that can be said. They really have no idea of what day-clothes should be; and contrary to what is sometimes supposed, their sports and country clothes are

81

deplorable. They are of tweed thick and hard as a board, in various shades of porridge, and made to last for ever. For the town English women have only one solution, a jacket and tight skirt with what the fashion papers call 'a cunning slit up the back', which, when they walk, divides rather horribly over their calves.

Women seen about in London streets give a general appearance of tidy dreariness, but these same women at a ball are a surprise and a delight. In the evening they excel. With their beautiful jewels glittering on their beautiful skins, with their absolute unselfconsciousness, put them in any old satin skirt and deep décolleté and they are unbeatable. There is no more dazzling sight than a ball at Buckingham Palace.

French women, we are often told, are the most elegant. But where are they? Foreigners visiting Paris for the first time are often disappointed because they never see anybody well dressed. The fact is that elegance in Paris is confined to a small group of women who are seldom seen in public and never in the streets. They get into their own motors inside their own courtyards, rarely eat in restaurants or appear at the big dressmakers' (a selection of the clothes is sent for them to see at home), and in short it is an act of faith for the ordinary tourist to believe that they exist at all. They do, however, and are absolutely powerful in the world of elegance, since it is their taste which, in the end, everybody follows.

French dress designers, hairdressers, and cooks are admitted to be unbeatable, but they lose their eye, their hand, their skill after a few years in England or America. Why? Because they are no longer under the disciplinary control of *les femmes du monde* – that is to say, of a very few rich, ruthless, and savagely energetic women who know what they want and never spare anybody's feelings in their determination to get it. Back goes the dress, back goes the dish, back into the washtub goes the head, until the result is perfect – then and then only is heard the grudging *'Pas mal'*. Their vigilance extends to the smallest details. I once bought a suit in an expensive English shop and gave it to my Paris dressmaker for some minor alteration. She told me she had been obliged to take it home and do it herself, since she could not risk letting the girls in her workroom see how badly it was finished off. 'But how could you have accepted it?' she kept saying. I didn't like to tell her that I had not turned it inside out, as any French woman

82

would have done, so had no idea how the seams were sewn.

Anglo-Saxons do not quite understand French elegance and what it is. They have a vague romantic notion that any French woman can take any old bit of stuff, give it a clever twist, and look chic in it. This may be true of Italian peasants, but not of Parisians. Dressing, in Paris, is not a craft; it is an art not to be come by easily or cheaply; Parisians are not peasants, but citizens of the most civilized town in the world. When they cannot afford the time and money to be really well dressed, they abandon the idea of clothes and concentrate instead upon cooking and their children's education. Dresses with a cheaply fashionable air do not appeal to French women.

In writing about Americans I find myself at a disadvantage so great that perhaps I really should not attempt it. For I have never been to America. I study it, of course. I look at *Life* and *Time* and the *New Yorker*; I hang about behind Americans at cocktail parties and listen to what they are saying to each other. I read their books, in many of which they seem to behave oddly, nipping off their own breasts with garden shears and so on, but no more oddly I suppose than the English of *Wuthering Heights*. America is to me some great star observed through a telescope, and I never feel quite sure that it exists, now, or whether its light is not coming to me across centuries of time (future time, of course).

If I may venture then to speak about American elegance, as observed through my telescope during many a long wakeful night, I should say it is the elegance of adolescence. The bobby-soxers, the teen-agers, who seem to what we call 'come out' so very young, are beautifully dressed. Their neat little clothes have more than an echo of Paris; the skirts are the right length, the waists in the right place, and they are, very suitably for children, under-stated. I imagine it would not do to turn them inside out and examine the seams. These young Americans do not care to have one good dress and wear it a whole season; they would rather have a quantity of cheap dresses and throw them away after two or three wearings. As I look through my telescope I see a charming flock of radiant little girls, in pretty dolls' clothes, clean, shining, with regular if rather big, teeth, wonderful figures and china skins. I also see a crowd of gracious ladies in canasta gowns, impeccable, not one blue hair out of place. But what happens to the intermediate ages? At what point do old little girls turn into young old ladies? Where are the grown-up women in the prime of life dressed as adults?

I think that the elegance of these three countries can be summed up by saying that in England the women are elegant until they are ten years old and perfect on grand occasions; in France a few women are entirely elegant always; in America most women are smart and impeccable, but with too much of an accent on immaturity for real elegance. The Latin American woman dressed in Paris is the very height of perfection, however.

Atlantic Monthly, 1951

Rome is Only a Village

Evelyn Waugh to Nancy Mitford January 8, 1952

'I liked your Rome article very much. I expect you are now reading many protests giving the precise dimensions of St Peters & St Giles. I thought it a good joke. Pope & Vicar less funny but it has a sort of relation to the truth.'

Nancy Mitford to Sydney Redesdale January 23, 1952

'The Romans it seems are furious about my article, what they mind is the lesser country house.'

Peacock cries of Ma-ri-a, a clock striking the quarter and then the preceding hour (the only logical way for a clock to strike), a fountain splashing far below in the courtyard – I had woken up in Rome. I should have known where I was without these noises by the smell of damp plaster, coffee, and wood smoke which exists nowhere else and is one of the most delicious of all town smells. (I always wonder whether the Paris smell of Gauloises, garlic and a tiny tang of drains is as intrinsically heavenly as it seems to me or whether I love it so much because of its associations.)

It must be a form of mental laziness that whereas we can hear and smell places for ourselves we always see them through the eyes of painters. Rome appears to me through those of Hubert Robert, Corot, and Victorian great-aunts clever with their brushes. The great-aunts were especially fascinated by Roman washing, and so am I. Surely no other capital city can be quite so uninhibited about its underclothes or allow them to hang like flags across the streets.

But Rome is a capital city only in name; in fact and at heart it is a village, with its single post office, single railway station and life centred round the vicarage. There is only one thing going on at a time in Rome. You are asked to a tea-party; you hesitate. 'But of course you can come – there is no other tea-party tomorrow.' At luncheon you say to some charmer: 'I do wish I could see you again.' Hey presto! At tea your wish is already granted. At the cocktail party there he is, at the dinner party he is across the table and next morning, as you brush away a tear over the heart of Shelley, you observe him brushing one away over the grave of Keats. Thereafter you meet him every time you walk into the Piazza di Spagna, the village green.

And as for the village streets! Arnold Bennett once said that 'pavement' is the most beautiful word in the English language, a sentiment which must be echoed by anybody who has tottered about on Roman cobbles and splashed in and out of Roman puddles, trying to avoid death from the huge buses which squeeze their way between the palaces at ninety miles an hour.

It would really be too trite to enlarge upon the beauties of Renaissance Rome, but I must say that most of the baroque there is too much for me. I cannot but feel as grateful to Louis XIV for sending Bernini home, loaded with money and honours but without a commission (except for the splendid bust at Versailles), as to Madame de Pompadour for directing French taste away from rococo. But most English people like Italian baroque and I quite see why: It makes them feel at home. Indeed St Peter's, seen from the colonnade, is very much like a lesser country house.

The English have always been close to Italy and love the gay, good-natured Italians, a sentiment which is entirely reciprocated. Since the war the Italians have had great hopes that we shall take a lead in Europe; over and over again I was asked to explain our apparent non-co-operation. Whereas the French have always understood that it is impossible for us to join any sort of federation the Italians seem to have expected us to do so and are now both puzzled and disappointed by our attitude.

I was staying next door to the Farnese palace, the French embassy and incidentally the only French public building which is still covered with *fleurs de lis*; they have been left there because they are, in this case, the Farnese and not the Bourbon coat of arms.

86

This is one of the two most perfect embassies in the world, the other being ours in Paris. Our old Roman one by the Porta Pia was not up to much as a house, but it had charm, and civilized memories of the days when Maurice Baring, Lord Berners, Geoffrey Scott, the present Duke of Wellington and Sir D'Arcy Osborne were young men in the chancery there, under various urbane and scholarly ambassadors. After the war we saw fit to install our Ambassador and his enormous staff in the former German embassy with its frightful architecture, inconvenient situation and what are now called unpleasant associations, in other words still-reeking torture chambers. Several old palaces in the heart of Rome could have been bought for a derisory price. Gone are the days when Lord Stuart de Rothesay could acquire the *'Nid de Pauline'* for the nation, complete with all its furnishings.

Sunday Times, January 6, 1952

The Mystery of the Missing
Arsenic

Nancy Mitford to Raymond Mortimer February 7, 1953

'*Picture Post* rang up and offered £100 for an article on Marie Besnard so I've been literally buried in her. It meant one day in newspaper offices mugging her up & one day to write 1200 words & telephone them to London & as a result I am in bed with waves of nausea. How can anybody be a journalist?'

This week the trial of Marie Besnard re-opens at Poitiers after having been adjourned for exactly one year. The French newspapers, with their usual lack of inhibition, have called her the Lafarge or Brinvilliers of our age, after those two famous female poisoners. Her neighbours are convinced that she is a mass murderess and so was the whole of France until, suddenly and dramatically in the middle of her trial, the case for the prosecution seemed to crumble away to nothing. Here is the story of Marie Besnard, but we must take into account the fact that it is told by her deeply prejudiced neighbours. She seems to be without one friend in the world and nobody has a good word for her.

Marie Besnard was born in 1898; her parents were well-to-do peasants, what we should call smallholders. They sent her to school at the local convent, where the other children disliked her so much that, when she made her first communion no little girl could be found to walk up the aisle with her. In 1920, she married Auguste Antigny, a poor creature, said by her to be tubercular. Nine years later he got very thin and died. Now, widows, in provincial France, are expected to mourn. They envelope themselves in a huge black veil, yards and yards of crêpe, and may not go to any place of amusement or even play the piano for at least two years. To the horror of her neighbours, however, the Widow Antigny threw her black veil into a bed of nettles and went gallivanting off to the circus with a new acquaintance, Léon Besnard. Worse still, she was heard to call him 'tu', the equivalent of our 'darling'. She then married him quite respectably and they appear to have been perfectly happy. Her new in-laws, however, hated her from the beginning; in 1930 her sister-in-law wrote of her as 'this horror of a woman'. The Besnards were comfortably off. They owned two farms and a vineyard and bred horses. 'We were not Rothschilds, but we lived well'. Today Marie Besnard owns about £15,000, three hotels at Loudun, two farms and 50 hectares of land. The Besnards came through the war without inconvenience, except for the difficulty of getting help on the farm. In 1947 they engaged a German prisoner, Dietz, a handsome boy of twenty-four, to work for them. He was not, he said, a Nazi. The neighbours thought that Marie Besnard was falling in love with Dietz; she took to rouge, considered a terrible sign of wickedness in the provincial bourgeoisie; she shortened her skirts. (This piece of evidence is not very convincing since it refers to the year of the New Look when most women were frantically adding false hems to all their garments.) She certainly must have needed a little relaxation since for ten years she seems to have spent most of her time at sick-beds, death-beds and the graveyard. Except for her mother and husband, all her relations and her two closest friends had now died. She had looked after them herself; worn out with nursing, she had then been obliged to arrange and pay for their funerals (first-class), because it so happened that she and her husband were heirs, direct or indirect, of each and all of these loved ones. The declared value of the legacies, it is true, was not very much, varying from £3 to £500; however nobody in rural France declares their money and everybody has a stocking more or less filled with gold. The Besnards probably inherited a few thousand pounds in all. While the neighbours were gossiping about Marie and Dietz, Léon Besnard became very thin. He is supposed to have said to a friend: 'If I die, see there is an autopsy'. He did die, soon to be followed to the churchyard by his mother-in-law. Marie Besnard and Dietz were now alone in the house together, but not for long. They were arrested; Dietz was set free again the same day, and Marie was tried for having forged the signature of some deceased relation on a money order. She was found guilty and sent to prison for two years.

Meanwhile, the loved ones were being dug up out of their graves, and their remains were packed off to Marseilles. There they were analysed by Dr Béroud, who found that every single body contained a heavy dose of arsenic. They were:

Aunt Louise, who died in 1938. When Besnard learned at the funeral that she had left her money to his mother and sister and not to him, he flung a little holy water on her grave and went off in a rage.

1939: The great friend, Toussaint Rivet, who spent every Sunday with the Besnards. Marie Besnard was his wife's heiress.

1940: Marie's father. Died after taking a purge administered by her.

1940: Léon's father. He left £227. Marie said, 'I can't imagine how the doctor found arsenic in him; I was not even there'.

1941: Léon's mother.

Two months later, Léon's sister Lucie was found hung up and strangled. Verdict of suicide. She was a fervent Roman Catholic, and had a happy life with her flower garden, her poultry and her rabbits.

1941: Marthe Rivet, widow of the great friend. She had made over her house to the Besnards in return for £2.10s. a year and free lodging, and died almost immediately afterwards.

1945: Pauline and Virginie Lalleron, cousins of Léon, both over 80. Virginie only left £3 but was supposed to wear a little bag of gold round her waist day and night. She told a policeman that Léon was trying to take it away from her, but the policeman does not seem to have pursued the matter. Pauline and Virginie were both rather simple.

When the analyst's report was delivered, Marie Besnard was brought to trial and accused of having murdered all these people. In the dock she presented the classical appearance of a poisoner. She was dressed in shiny black and wore a black lace mantilla: her hideous face was chalk white. Though a sturdy, masterful-looking woman, she spoke in a sinister little voice, thin and high as a reed. 'I pray for my dead every day'. As the prosecution told the story of these deaths and spoke of 36, 48, 50 milligrams of arsenic (over ten is a fatal dose), nobody doubted for a moment that she was guilty. But then came the turn of maître Gautrat, counsel for the defence. Almost at once things began to look quite different. There had clearly been a great deal of carelessness in the Marseilles laboratory and the various exhibits were hopelessly mixed up.

Maître Gautrat's cross-examining the doctor:

'Marie Besnard's mother's remains were put into ten tubes, duly sealed and inventoried. Why, then, did 11 tubes turn up at Marseilles, of which two were different from those that were sent?' ... 'You say that Virginie contained 24 milligrams of arsenic; but did not Virginie's body crumble into dust?'

The doctor soon became flustered and then angry. 'All you Parisians have a down on Marseilles'. This is rather true. The Northern French love the people of Provence, but never take them very seriously. 'But my methods were undisputed and my instruments are pure.'

Maître Gautrat: 'Now here are six tubes which you say contained traces of arsenic. Which of these contains arsenic? Between ourselves, they contain no arsenic at all; three of them contain antimony.' Collapse of the doctor. Commotion in court.

The case was immediately adjourned so that the bodies could be analysed again, this time under the auspices of Professor Fabre, head of the Faculty of Medicine in Paris. He and his three assistants have now finished their work, and we shall know next week what they have found. Meanwhile, Marie Besnard sits in a little cell looking over the gardens, waiting. She is said to be perfectly cheerful and confident.

Picture Post, February 21, 1953

The English Aristocracy

Nancy Mitford to Violet Hammersley March 15, 1955

'I've been asked to write a hugely long article for *Encounter* on the English Aristocracy. Can't quite decide, but if I do it will contain volleys of teases.'

Nancy Mitford to Sydney Redesdale May 2, 1955

'My article is screamingly funny as you will see. And very fair – but full of teases of course – quite good tempered ones.'

Nancy Mitford to Sydney Redesdale Sepetember 14, 1955

'A flood of letters re *Encounter* – mostly fans, though some abuse "I am circulating it in the monastery – the Prior much impressed by it" "My typist is so angry she refuses to type a letter to you" & so on. It was wicked old Spender, eye on sales, who egged me on to do the U stuff. I went to WHS here yesterday – manager dashed at me saying all sold out the first day. Heywood [Hill], who usually sells 20 has sold over 100 last week. I'm pleased, as they gave me 3 times their usual rate, so I feel I've earned it.'

Nancy Mitford to Sydney Redesdale April 30, 1956

'I keep getting perfectly serious letters from people saying things like I am descended from Alfred the Great's sister & would like to congratulate you on your splendid stand for people of our sort.'

Nancy Mitford to Evelyn Waugh May 11, 1956

'Can you get over them going *on* with U? I mean really we've had enough – even I have & you know how one loves ones own jokes.'

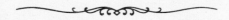

The English aristocracy may seem to be on the verge of decadence, but it is the only real aristocracy left in the world today. It
has real political power through the House of Lords and a real
social position through the Queen. An aristocracy in a republic is
like a chicken whose head has been cut off: it may run about in a
lively way, but in fact it is dead. There is nothing to stop a
Frenchman, German, or Italian from calling himself the Duke of
Carabosse if he wants to, and in fact the Continent abounds with
invented titles. But in England the Queen is the fountain of
honours and when she bestows a peerage upon a subject she
bestows something real and unique.

The great distinction between the English aristocracy and any
other has always been that, whereas abroad every member of a
noble family is noble, in England none are noble except the head
of the family. In spite of the fact that they enjoy courtesy titles, the
sons and daughters of lords are commoners – though not so
common as baronets and their wives who take precedence after
honourables. (So, of course, do all knights, except Knights of
the Garter who come after the eldest sons and the daughters
of barons, but before the younger sons.) The descendants of
younger sons, who, on the Continent would all be counts or
barons, in England have no titles and sit even below knights.
Furthermore, the younger sons and daughters of the very richest
lords receive, by English custom, but little money from their
families, barely enough to live on. The sons are given the same
education as their eldest brother and then turned out, as soon as
they are grown up, to fend for themselves; the daughters are given
no education at all, the general idea being that they must find
some man to keep them – which, in fact, they usually do. The rule
of primogeniture has kept together the huge fortunes of English
lords; it has also formed our class system.

But there is in England no aristocratic class that forms a caste.
We have about 950 peers, not all of whom, incidentally, sit in the
House of Lords. Irish peers have no seats, though some Irish
peers have a subsidiary UK peerage giving a seat; Scottish peers
elect sixteen representatives from among themselves. Peeresses
in their own right are not, as yet, admitted. Most of the peers share
the education, usage, and point of view of a vast upper middle
class, but the upper middle class does not, in its turn, merge
imperceptibly into the middle class. There is a very definite

border line, easily recognizable by hundreds of small but significant landmarks.

When I speak of these matters I am always accused of being a snob, so, to illustrate my point, I propose to quote from Professor Alan Ross of Birmingham University. Professor Ross has written a paper, printed in Helsinki in 1954, for the *Bulletin de la Société Néo-philologique de Helsinki*, on 'Upper Class English Usage.' Nobody is likely to accuse either this learned man or his Finnish readers of undue snobbishness. The Professor, pointing out that it is solely by their language that the upper classes nowadays are distinguished (since they are neither cleaner, richer, nor better-educated than anybody else) has invented a useful formula: U (for upper class) speaker versus non-U-speaker. Such exaggeratedly non-U usage as 'serviette' for 'napkin' he calls non-U indicators. Since 'a piece of mathematics or a novel written by a member of the upper class is not likely to differ in any way from one written by a member of another class . . . in writing it is in fact only modes of address, postal addresses and habits of beginning and ending letters that serve to demarcate the class.' . . . The names of many houses are themselves non-U; the ideal U-address is PQR where P is a place name, Q a describer, and R the name of a county, as 'Shirwell Hall, Salop.' (Here I find myself in disagreement with Professor Ross – in my view abbreviations such as Salop, Herts, or Glos, are decidedly non-U. Any sign of undue haste, in fact, is apt to be non-U, and I go so far as preferring, except for business letters, not to use air mail.) 'But,' adds Professor Ross, 'today few gentlemen can maintain this standard and they often live in houses with non-U names such as Fairmeads or El Nido.' Alas!

He speaks of the U-habit of silence, and perhaps does not make as much of it as he might. Silence is the only possible U-response to many embarrassing modern situations: the ejaculation of 'cheers' before drinking, for example, or 'it was so nice seeing you,' after saying goodbye. In silence, too, one must endure the use of the Christian name by comparative strangers and the horror of being introduced by Christian and surname without any prefix. This unspeakable usage sometimes occurs in letters – Dear XX – which, in silence, are quickly torn up, by me.

After discoursing at some length on pronunciation, the professor goes on to vocabulary and gives various examples of U and non-U usage.

94

Cycle is non-U against U *bike*.

Dinner: U-speakers eat *luncheon* in the middle of the day and *dinner* in the evening.

Non-U-speakers (also U-children and U-dogs) have their *dinner* in the middle of the day.

Greens is non-U for U *vegetables*.

Home: non-U – 'they have a lovely *home*'; U – 'they've a very nice *house*.'

Ill: 'I was *ill* on the boat' is non-U against U *sick*.

Mental: non-U for U *mad*.

Note paper: non-U for U *writing paper*.

Toilet paper: non-U for U *lavatory paper*.

Wealthy: non-U for U *rich*.

To these I would add:

Sweet: non-U for U *pudding*.

Dentures: non-U for U *false teeth*. This, and *glasses* for *spectacles*, almost amount to non-U indicators.

Wire: non-U for U *telegram*.

Phone: a non-U indicator.

(One must add that the issue is sometimes confused by U-speakers using non-U indicators as a joke. Thus Uncle Matthew in *The Pursuit of Love* speaks of his *dentures*.)

Finally Professor Ross poses the question: Can a non-U-speaker become a U-speaker? His conclusion is that an adult can never achieve complete success 'because one word or phrase will suffice to brand an apparent U-speaker as originally non-U (for U-speakers themselves never make mistakes).' I am not quite sure about this. Usage changes very quickly and I even know undisputed U-speakers who pronounce girl 'gurl,' which twenty years ago would have been unthinkable. All the same, it is true that one U-speaker recognizes another U-speaker almost as soon as he opens his mouth, though U-speaker A may deplore certain lapses in the conversation of U-speaker B.

From these U-speakers spring the sensible men of ample means who generally seem to rule our land. When the means of these sensible men become sufficiently ample they can very easily be ennobled, should they wish it, and join the House of Lords. It might therefore be supposed that there is no aristocracy at all in England, merely an upper middle class, some of whom are lords; but, oddly enough, this is not so. A lord does not have to be born to his position and, indeed, can acquire it through political activities, or the sale of such unaristocratic merchandise as beer, but though he may not be a U-speaker he becomes an aristocrat as soon as he receives his title. The Queen turns him from socialist leader, or middle-class businessman, into a nobleman, and his outlook from now on will be the outlook of an aristocrat.

Ancestry has never counted much in England. The English lord knows himself to be such a very genuine article that, when looking for a wife, he can rise above such baubles as seize quartiers. Kind hearts, in his view, are more than coronets, and large tracts of town property more than Norman blood. He marries for love, and is rather inclined to love where money is; he rarely marries in order to improve his coat of arms. (Heiresses have caused the extinction as well as the enrichment of many an English family, since the heiress, who must be an only child if she is to be really rich, often comes of barren or enfeebled stock.) This unconcern for pedigree leads people to suppose that the English lords are a jumped-up lot, and that their families are very seldom 'genuine' and 'old'. One often hears it said, 'No Englishman alive today would be eligible to drive in the carriage of a King of France.' 'Nobody really has Norman blood.' 'The true aristocracy of England was wiped out in the Wars of the Roses.' And so on.

There is some truth in all these statements, but it is not the whole truth. Many of our oldest families have never been ennobled. Some no longer hold peerages. The ancient Scrope family has, in its time, held the baronies of Scrope of Marsham and Scrope of Bolton, the earldoms of Wiltshire and of Sunderland, the sovereignty of the Isle of Man, but the head of the family is now Mr Scrope. If he should be offered a peerage he would no doubt proudly refuse. The only existing families known to descend from knights who came over with William the Conqueror in time to fight at Hastings, the Malets, the Giffards, and the Gresleys, are another case in point. Of the Norman knights who came during William's reign or later, some were never anything but country gentlemen, but some are the direct ancestors of modern peers: St John, Talbot, West, Curzon, Clinton, Grey, Seymour, St Aubyn, Sinclair, Haig, and Hay, for instance. There are 100 peers of England from before the Union (including Prince Charles, as Duke of Cornwall). All of them are descended in the female line from King Edward III, except possibly Lord Byron, though a little research would probably find him an Edward III descent. All peers, except barons, are officially styled 'Cousin' by the Queen; as regards most dukes and earls this is not so much fiction as a distant truth. Only 26 earls have been created in this century and they have all been great men like Lloyd George and Haig. (The Haigs have borne arms and lived at Bemersyde since the twelfth century but had never previously been ennobled.)

The dukes are rather new creations. When James I came to the throne there were no dukes at all, the high traitors Norfolk and Somerset having had their dukedoms attainted. They were both restored in 1660. Between 1660 and 1760, 18 dukedoms were created. On the whole, Englishmen are made dukes as a reward for being rich or royal (4 descend from bastards of Charles II), though dukedoms have sometimes been bestowed for merit. The oldest title is that of Earl. Several medieval earldoms still exist. 65 barons hold titles from before 1711. 327 of the present-day peerages were created before 1800, 382 belong to families which have borne arms in the direct male line since before 1485 and which are therefore eligible, as far as birth is concerned, to be Knights of Malta.

But whether their families are 'old' or 'new' is of small account – the lords all have one thing in common: they share an aristocratic attitude to life. What is this attitude? The purpose of the aristocrat is to lead, therefore his functions are military and political. There can be no doubt of the military excellence of our noblemen. 214 peers alive today have been decorated in battle or mentioned in despatches. The families of the premier duke and the premier earl of England hold the George Cross. In politics, including the unglamorous and often boring local politics, they have worked hard for no reward and done their best according to their lights.

The purpose of the aristocrat is most emphatically not to work for money. His ancestors may have worked in order to amass the fortune which he enjoys, though on the whole the vast riches of the English lords come from sources unconnected with honest toil; but he will seldom do the same. His mind is not occupied with money, it turns upon other matters. When money is there he spends it on maintaining himself in his station. When it is no longer there he ceases to spend, he draws in his horns. Even the younger sons of lords seem, in all ages, to have been infected with this point of view: there is nothing so rare as for the scion of a noble house to make a fortune by his own efforts. In the old days they went into professions – the Army, the Navy, diplomacy, and the Church – in which it is impossible to earn more than a living. Those who went to the colonies were administrators, they rarely feathered their nests – the great nabobs were essentially middle class. Nowadays younger sons go into the City, but I have yet to hear of one making a large fortune; more often they lose in unwise speculations what little capital they happen to own.

All this should not be taken as a sign that our lords are lazy or unenterprising. The point is that, in their view, effort is unrelated to money. Now this view has, to a large extent, communicated itself to the English race and nation with the result that our outlook is totally different from that of our American cousins, who have never had an aristocracy. Americans relate all effort, all work, and all of life itself to the dollar. Their talk is of nothing but dollars. The English seldom sit happily chatting for hours on end about pounds. In England, public business is its own reward, nobody would go into Parliament in order to become rich, neither do riches bring public appointments. Our ambassadors to foreign states are experienced diplomatists, not socially ambitious millionairesses.

This idiosyncratic view of money has its good side and its bad. Let us glance at the case history of Lord Fortinbras. Fortinbras is ruined – we are now in the 1930's. (All English noblemen, according to themselves, are ruined, a fantasy I shall deal with later, but Fortinbras really is.) He is not ruined because of death duties, since his father died when he was a child, before they became so heavy, but because he and his forbears have always regarded their estates with the eyes of sportsmen rather than of cultivators. It is useless for him to plead that the policy of cheap corn has been his downfall; an intelligent landowner has always been able to make money with prize cattle, racehorses, market gardens, timber, and so on. But Fortinbras's woods have been looked after by gamekeepers and not by woodmen, his farms have been let to tenants chosen for their tenderness towards foxes and partridges rather than for their agricultural efficiency. His land is undercapitalized, his cottagers live in conditions no better than those of their Saxon forbears, water and electric light are laid on in his stables but not in the dwellings of his tenantry. He has made various unwise speculations and lost a 'packet' on the Turf. In short, he deserves to be ruined and he is ruined.

Now what does he do? He is young, healthy, and not stupid; his wife, the daughter of another peer, is handsome, bossy, and energetic. She is the kind of woman who, in America, would be running something with enormous efficiency and earning thousands. They have two babies, Dominick and Caroline, and a Nanny. Does it occur to either Lord or Lady Fortinbras to get a job and retrieve the family fortunes? It does not. First of all they sell everything that is not entailed, thus staving off actual want. They shut up most of the rooms in their house, send away the servants (except, of course, Nanny) and get the Dowager Lady Fortinbras and her sister to come and cook, clean, dust, and take trays upstairs to the nursery. Old Lady Fortinbras is quite useful, and Lady Enid is a treasure. The Fortinbrases realise that they are very lucky, and if at heart they wish there were a mother's hall for the two ladies to sit in of an evening, they never say so, even to each other. Fortinbras chops the wood, stokes the boiler, brings in the coal, washes the Morris Cowley, and drives off in it to attend the County Council and sit on the Bench. Lady Fortinbras helps in the house, digs in the border, exercises the Border terriers, and also does a great deal of committee work. They are both on the go from morning to night, but it is a go that does not bring in one penny. Their friends and neighbours all say, 'Aren't the Fortinbrases wonderful?'

Comes the war. They clear the decks by sending Nanny and the children to an American couple, the Karamazovs, whom they once met at St Moritz and who have sent them Christmas cards ever since. Fortinbras goes off with his territorials and Lady Fortinbras joins the ATS. Their war records are brilliant in the extreme, their energy, courage, and instinct for leadership have at last found an outlet, and in no time at all they both become generals. After the war they are not surprised to find themselves more ruined than ever. The Karamazovs, whose lives for several years have been made purgatory by Dominick, Caroline, and Nanny, especially Nanny, send in a modest bill for the schooling of the young people which Fortinbras has no intention of settling. It would seem unreasonable to pay for one's children to be taught to murder the English language and taught, apparently, nothing else whatever. Dominick, failing to get into Eton, has had to be sent to some dreadful school in Scotland. Besides, what did the Karamazovs do in the war? Nothing, according to Nanny, but flop in and out of a swimming pool. The Karamazovs come to England expecting to be thanked, fêted, and paid, only to find that their friends have left for the Northern Capitals.

Now the Fortinbrases are getting on, over fifty. Dominick having come of age, they have broken the entail and sold everything, very badly, as the house is full of dry rot and the farms are let to tenants who cannot be dislodged. However, a little money does result from the sale. They arrange a mews flat behind Harrods where, generals once again, they will continue to cook and wash up for the rest of their days. They both still sit on endless committees, Fortinbras goes to the House of Lords, they kill themselves with overwork, and have never, except for their Army pay, earned one single penny. 'Aren't the Fortinbrases wonderful?' Well yes, in a way they are.

Now, while the Fortinbrases have the typical aristocratic outlook on money, the state of their finances is by no means typical. Most people, nowadays, take it for granted that the aristocracy is utterly impoverished, a view carefully fostered by the lords themselves. It takes a shooting affray, letting police and reporters into a country house, to remind the ordinary citizen that establishments exist where several menservants wait on one young woman at dinner. There are still many enormous fortunes in the English aristocracy, into which income tax and death duties have made no appreciable inroads. Arundel, Petworth, Hatfield, Woburn, Hardwicke, Blenheim, Haddon, Drumlanrig, Alnwick, Stratfield Saye, Harewood, Knole, Knowsley, Wilton, Holkham, Glamis, Cullen, Cliveden, Highclere, Althorp, Mentmore – all vast houses – are still inhabited by lords who have inherited them, and this little list is a mere fraction of the whole. The treasures such houses contain are stupendous. When the Duke of Buccleuch came to visit the Louvre, the curator, who had been to England and seen the Duke's collection of French furniture, greeted him with the words: 'I apologize for the furniture of the Louvre, M. le Duc.'

Another English duke owns a collection of incunables second only to that formerly in the possession of the Kings of Spain, and more Grolier bindings than the Bibliothèque Nationale. A jeweller told me that out of the one hundred finest diamonds in the world, sixty are in English families. One could go on citing such instances indefinitely.

The English, so censorious of those foreigners (the French peasantry for instance) who do not pay their taxes as they should, have themselves brought tax evasion within legal limits to a fine art. Death duties can be avoided altogether if the owner of an estate gives it to his heir and then lives another five years. One agreeable result of this rule is that old lords are cherished as never before. Their heirs, so far from longing to step into their shoes, will do anything to keep them alive. Doctors and blood donors hover near them, they are not allowed to make the smallest effort, or to be worried or upset, and are encouraged to live in soft climates and salubrious spots.

The crippling effects of supertax also can be overcome in various ways by those who own large capital sums. The aristocrat can augment his fortune in many a curious manner, since he is impervious to a sense of shame (all aristocrats are: shame is a bourgeois notion). The lowest peasant of the Danube would stick at letting strangers into his home for 2s. 6d., but our dukes, marquesses, earls, viscounts, and barons not only do this almost incredible thing, they glory in it, they throw themselves into the sad commerce with rapture, and compete as to who among them can draw the greatest crowds. It is the first topic of conversation in noble circles today, the tourists being referred to in terms of sport rather than of cash – a sweepstake on the day's run, or the bag counted after the shoot.

'I get twice as many as Reggie, but Bert does better than me.'

The baiting of the trap is lovingly considered.

'Mummy dresses up in her Coronation robes, they can't resist it.'

'I say, old boy, look out – you don't want to pay entertainment tax.'

'No, no – I've taken counsel's opinion.'

'We've started a pets' cemetery – a quid for a grave, three quid for a stone, and a fiver if Daphne writes a poem for it.'

Of course the fellow countrymen of people who will descend to such methods of raising cash imagine that they must be driven to it by direst need. The fact is they thoroughly enjoy it. Also it has become a matter of policy to appear very poor. The Lords are retrenching visibly, and are especially careful to avoid any form of ostentation: for instance, only five of them saw fit to attend the last coronation in their family coaches. Coronets on luggage, motor cars, and so on are much less used than formerly. Aristocrats no longer keep up any state in London, where family houses hardly exist now. Here many of them have shown a sad lack of civic responsibility, as we can see by looking at poor London today. At the beginning of this century practically all the residential part of the West End belonged to noblemen and the Crown. A more charming, elegant capital city would have been far to seek. To the Crown – more specifically, I believe to King George V in person – and to two Dukes, Westminster and Bedford, we owe the fact that London is not yet exactly like Moscow, a conglomeration of dwellings. Other owners cheerfully sold their houses and 'developed' their property without a thought for the visible result. Park Lane, most of Mayfair, the Adelphi, and so on bear witness to a barbarity which I, for one, cannot forgive.

The lords have never cared very much for London, and are, in this respect, the exact opposite of their French counterparts who loathe the country. But even where his country house is concerned, the English nobleman, whose forbears were such lovers of beauty, seems to have lost all aesthetic sense, and it is sad to see the havoc he often brings to his abode, both inside and out. His ancestors spent months abroad, buying pictures and statues, which he cheerfully sells in order to spend months abroad. Should one of his guests perceive that a blackened square of canvas in a spare bedroom is a genuine Caravaggio, that picture will appear at Christies before you can say Jack Robinson, though there is no necessity whatever for such a sale. The Caravaggio buyer planted his estate with avenues and coppices and clumps of cedar trees. The Caravaggio seller fiddles about with herbaceous borders, one of the most hideous conceptions known to man. He never seems to plant anything larger than a flowering prunus, never builds ornamental bridges, or digs lakes, or adds wings to his house. The last nobleman to build a folly on his estate must have been Lord Berners and he was regarded as foolish indeed to do such a thing. The noble eccentric, alas, seems to be dying out. Lord Berners was one, another was the late Duke of Bedford, pacifist, zoologist, and a good man. One of the chapters of his

102

autobiography, I seem to remember, was headed 'Spiders I have Known,' and he tells of one spider he knew whose favourite food was roast beef and Yorkshire pudding. The great days of patronage, too, are over, though there are country houses which still shelter some mild literary figure as librarian. The modern nobleman cannot, however, be blamed for no longer patronizing art, music, and letters. Artists, musicians, and writers are today among the very richest members of the community and even an English aristocrat could hardly afford to maintain Mr Somerset Maugham, M. Stravinsky, or M. Picasso as part of his establishment.

Voltaire very truly said that those who own are those who wish to own: this wish seems to have left the English lords. Divest, divest, is the order of the day. The nobleman used to study a map of his estate to see how it could be enlarged, filling out a corner here, extending a horizon there. Nowadays he has no such ambitions; he would much rather sell than buy. The family is not considered as it used to be; the ancestors are no longer revered, indeed they are wilfully forgotten, partly perhaps from a feeling of guilt when all that they so carefully amassed is being so carelessly scattered. The dead are hardly mourned. 'Far the best for him,' the children say, cheerfully (so long, of course, as he has lived the requisite five years). Nobody wears black any more. The younger generation is no longer planned for, and there is a general feeling of *après nous le déluge.'*

The instinct of the lords to divest themselves of age-long influence and rights extends to their influence and rights in the Church. Most of them are members of the Church of England; though there are forty-seven Roman Catholics with seats in the House of Lords. On the whole, the lords, in common with most of their fellow countrymen, have always regarded religious observance as a sort of patriotic duty. The Church is the Church of England and must be supported to show that we are not as foreigners are. A friend of mine voiced this attitude during the war: 'Well, you know, I don't do fire-watching or Home Guard and I feel one must do something to help the war, so I always go to Church on Sunday.' I am sure he did not imagine that his prayers would drive back the German hordes; he went as a gesture of social solidarity. Hitherto, the livings of our Church have been the gift of landowners, who have generally chosen downright, muscular Christians of low Church leanings. 'Don't want lace and smells in my Church.' Zeal has always been frowned upon. As it is impossible to remove a parson once he is installed in his living, some of the most ringing rows of all time have been between the Manor and the Vicarage. Now, however, faithful to the spirit of divest, divest, the temporal lords are busily putting their livings at the disposal of their spiritual colleagues, the Bishops. Many people think that this will lead to more lace, more smells, and more un-English zeal in the Church, and indeed greatly alter its character. Incidentally, the marriage customs of the peerage have lately become very lax. One peer in eight has divested himself of his wife, and foreigners notice that there are rather more duchesses than dukes in London society today.

As for the House of Lords which gives the English aristocrat his unique position, Lord Hailsham, himself an unwilling member, says that the majority of peers are voting for its abolition 'with their feet,' by simply neglecting their hereditary duties. It must be said that the number of regular attendants has never been very large, and the august chamber has always been characterized by an atmosphere of the dormitory if not of the morgue. This is distressing to an active young fellow like Lord Hailsham but it is nothing new. One of the merits of the Upper House has been to consist of a hard core of politicians reinforced now and then by experts, and only flooded out in times of crisis by all its members. These have hitherto proved not unrepresentative of public opinion. Now, however, it seems that it is hardly possible to get through the work, so small is the attendance.

Does this apparent abdication of the lords in so many different directions mean that the English aristocracy is in full decadence and will soon exist only like the appendix in the human body, a useless and sometimes harmful relic of the past? It would not be safe to assume so. The English lord has been nurtured on the land and is conversant with the cunning ways of the animal kingdom. He has often seen the grouse settle into the heather to rise and be shot at no more. He has noticed that enormous riches are not well looked on in the modern world and that in most countries his genus is extinct. It may be that he who, for a thousand years has weathered so many a storm, religious, dynastic, and political, is taking cover in order to weather yet one more. It may be that he will succeed. He must, of course, be careful not to overdo the protective colouring. An aristocracy cannot exist as a secret society. Nor must he overdo an appearance of destitution. There is the sad precedent of George Neville who was deprived of his dukedom (Bedford) by act of Parliament because 'as is openly known he hath not, nor by inheritance may have, any livelihood to support the name, estate and dignity . . .'

But the English lord is a wily old bird who seldom overdoes anything. It is his enormous strength.

Encounter, September 1955

Wicked Thoughts in Greece

Nancy Mitford to Mark Ogilvie-Grant June 2, 1955

'I thought I was flying away from noise & smell & cocktail parties to small pink islands and Byzantine churches, but these seem so difficult to attain. Nobody will – or can – tell me what to do . . . You know I had quite a wrong idea of Athens. I thought of it as very small rather like Naples or Toulon, I'd no idea it was a sort of New York.'

Nancy Mitford to Sydney Redesdale June 4, 1955

'I'm alive & in perfect happiness. Boiling heat . . . telephone calls from old friends and many strangers inviting me to this and that the moment I arrived.'

Nancy Mitford to Mark Ogilvie-Grant June 9, 1955

'I plan to come here every time I can afford it – I'm so hot and happy. I even like the food.'

Nancy Mitford to Mark Ogilvie-Grant July 3, 1955

'Busy cooking up a *S. Times* article for 17 July.'

The visitor to Greece must not be put off by first impressions of Athens. It is probably the ugliest capital in Europe, worse, even, than Madrid, tying for horror with Moscow, which it resembles in that both are formless conglomerations of modern buildings overlooked by an immortal monument. Furthermore, it has a dreadful air of prosperous vulgarity which one does not expect to see this side of the Atlantic. The traffic is noisier, wilder, more evidently intent on homicide than that of Paris, and consists entirely of enormous pastel-coloured American motor-cars. Streets of new houses are going up everywhere, and one very inconvenient result of this is that nobody can tell you the way –

106

neither taxi-drivers nor passers-by nor even the policemen know one street from another, everything is so new and uniform. And this hideous newness extends, in every direction, as far as the eye can see – Athens from the air is a desert of khaki-coloured cement.

I had the idea of walking up to the Parthenon instead of taking a cab; fortunately, because within a stone's throw of the hotel there is another world. A little old town, called the Plaka, covers the lower slopes of the Acropolis. It is very much like hundreds of Mediterranean hill-towns – Hyères, for instance – with narrow streets ending in flights of steps, houses washed in clear pale colours and roofed with Roman tiles, courtyards crammed with geraniums, pinks, orange and fig-trees; vines over everything, drains in the street – my first whiff of the south – the old ladies sitting beside them chatting their lives away.

The unique quality of the Plaka comes from the fact that round every corner there is some classical monument or fragment or Byzantine church, while overhead hangs the tremendous Parthenon. All is as Lord Byron must have seen it, though his hosts, the French monks, and their monastery have disappeared and fields of corn no longer wave between it and the Piraeus. Houses, churches, and monuments are on the right scale and at the right distance from each other, a rare and precious balance of which modern architects seldom take account. Alas! After ten minutes of happy wandering the dream is shattered and the dreadful wasteland of the Agora appears.

Here the American School of Classical Studies seems to have torn down whole streets in order to search for a few pots. Here the Americans are building, in a ghastly graveyard marble, the Stoa, said to be 'of Attalos', but really of Mr Homer A. Thompson. And here a gracious garden will be planted, complete, no doubt, with floral clock. This is only a beginning. The Greeks have been made to feel that the Plaka is insanitary and (dread word) picturesque, an unworthy slum in a brave new capital city, and that it ought to go.

I went to see a learned English friend and found him sitting, like a Turkish lady, on his balcony. (Turkish ladies have their drawing-rooms built out at right-angles to the street so that they can see what goes on there.) His conversation was interspersed with remarks like: 'There's the yoghourt boy – late as usual. See that man with one leg? He's my plumber. I hope he's coming here. Oh well, another day no doubt.'

He said, 'Are you going to write about Greece?' 'I don't know,' I replied. 'Everybody is so kind to me and I'm having such a lovely time, and yet when I take up my pen my thoughts are wicked.' 'You must get out of Athens, or your thoughts will get wickeder and wickeder.' He was perfectly right, of course.

I visited one or two islands, and a learned American friend took me to Knossos, a fraudulent reconstruction like the Stoa, English this time, alas, and built in an *art nouveau* style reminiscent of Paris metro stations. It is evident that Anglo-Saxons should be kept away from Mediterranean sites; French and German archaeologists never make these dreadful errors of taste. Knossos, however, matters less than the Stoa, because it is out in the country and does not spoil anything else. The Stoa in all its vileness hits the eye from the Acropolis and the Temple of Hephaestus. It is as though the French had allowed Frank Lloyd Wright to build his idea of a Petit Trianon at the bottom of the *tapis vert* at Versailles. Apart from Knossos, I greatly enjoyed three days in Crete and had the agreeable experience of meeting one of Paddy Leigh Fermor's partisans in a bus. He was treating Paddy's book, with a photograph of himself, rather like a passport, bringing it out on every occasion. Finally I hired a motor-car and went with my learned American for a tour of the Peloponnese, returning by Delphi. Only then did I understand the real point and greatness of Greece.

We know that Greece is beautiful, just as we know that Heaven is, but knowing is not the same as seeing. Photographs are not much help. The works of man are thin on the ground compared with any other civilized country – indeed, my learned English friend in Athens greeted me with the words, 'There is nothing to see here, you know' – but man himself is splendidly in harmony with a splendid land.

The Peloponnese has many different sorts of scenery: it can resemble Provence, Tuscany, and even Scotland, each at its very best, and it is inhabited by a race of beauties. It breathes the prosperity, real, solid and eternal, which comes from hard work on fertile soil, very different from the meretricious prosperity of Athens, based on the whimsical dollar. I liked to see the people living on such good terms with their beasts. The roads, where motors hardly ever appear, are covered with mules and goats and cows; my little chauffeur drove with great consideration and never once made a baby donkey jump or an old lady run for dear life.

We went first to Eleusis: still under the dead hand of Athens, it sits in a cement factory; no magic here. Then to Nauplia for a swim, and then Mycenae. 'Great God, this is an awful place.' And haunted. If Miss Jourdain and Miss Moberley had come here instead of that other palace at Versailles they might have had An Adventure indeed. The golden treasure, by the way, is no longer shown to the public, but lies buried in the Bank of Greece. Was it for this that Frau Schliemann, surrounded by armed troops, worked with her penknife day and night for three weeks, robbing the ancient dead? Here, at Olympia and at Delphi the excavations have all been carried out in perfect taste; the ruins lie in their own wonderful background and tell their own wonderful story. The museums are a model; the hotels, even, are not horrible to look at.

Perhaps best of everything I liked Hosios Loukas, the Byzantine church in its almond grove on a mountainside, still tended, as it has been for nearly a thousand years, by the monks of its own monastery. Unspoilt both inside and out, with its incomparable mosaics and brickwork, Hosios Loukas gives the happy, holy feeling of a great work of art. Mercifully, it is very far from Athens. We must hope that Mr Homer A. Thompson will never get there.

Back in Athens for a last dinner-party with a learned Greek friend whom I am obliged to call the Desecrator, because he goes round the country removing *bondieuseries* from churches. He does it with the purest intentions and in the interests of good taste. But I believe Byzantine churches are meant to be filled with holy clutter: if you take away the eikons and put them in museums or the Desecrator's dining-room and throw away the little images beloved of the peasants, the Bon Dieu himself flies out of the windows. However, I can forgive the Desecrator a great deal on account of his dinners. Abler pens than mine have described the horrors of Greek food (in the country places one is obliged to exist on bread and water, both excellent). But Greece is not a country of happy mediums: everything there seems to be either wonderful or horrible, and my friend's food is wonderful. It is worth the voyage from Paris to dine with him; his cook must be one of the best in Europe.

Sunday Times, July 24, 1955

A Queen of France

Evelyn Waugh to Nancy Mitford July 23, 1955

'Of course I was as shocked as any frog by your attack on Marie-Antoinette . . . Some of my informants in Paris say you may be readmitted to the fringes of Society. Others that you will have to change your name & go to Dakar.'

Nancy Mitford to Evelyn Waugh July 25, 1955

'Gaston [Palewski] says Anglo–French relations haven't been so bad since Fashoda (I don't really know what all the fuss is about as I am on *their side* for cutting off the head of an Austrian spy). Why do we dance on 14th July then?'

Nancy Mitford to Evelyn Waugh November 19, 1955

'M. de Mun, whose name speaks for itself, told me that the *culte* for MA is something quite new, I think I am forgiven, but I shall have to watch my step.'

To me Marie-Antoinette is one of the most irritating characters in history. She was frivolous without being funny, extravagant without being elegant, her stupidity was monumental: she was one of those people who cannot put a foot right.

She disliked elderly folk, said she wondered that anybody over thirty dared show themselves at Court, and referred to them as *les siècles*; but she always took the side of old reactionaries in politics. She amused herself with silly and immoral courtiers and constantly set at naught the etiquette with which the French liked to surround their sovereign, yet made an uncomfortable situation for years by refusing to be civil to Mme Dubarry. In the end, putting class before country, she sent military secrets to the enemy, through her lover Fersen. She certainly deserved a traitor's death.

Her mother, the Empress, who tried for years to keep her in

order, writing letter after letter of loving and sensible advice – *'nous ne sommes pas dans ce monde pour nous divertir'* – realized that the case was incurable. Indeed, the naughty, pert, spoilt little girl from Vienna certainly did more than anybody to force the French Revolution into the form it took. And yet, when all hope was gone, she became an exemplary figure. In prison, at her trial and on the scaffold she showed that she had an imposing and noble side to her nature, of which she gave no indication during her better days.

Many people, however, love Marie-Antoinette, and I have often been dreadfully scolded, sometimes almost assaulted, for saying these things. In any case, whether one loves or hates her, there can be no two opinions on the exhibition of her belongings which has just opened at Versailles. The French have a particular talent for such exhibitions, as faithful visitors to the Bibliothèque Nationale are well aware, but this one surpasses all I have ever seen.

We owe it to the initiative, energy and learning of two young amateurs, Baroness Elie de Rothschild and the duc de Mouchy, and one young professional, the new curator of Versailles, M. van der Kemp. They were helped by the devoted band of experts on the curator's permanent staff. The catalogue, a monument of scholarship, which will be an indispensable addition to the libraries of all who like eighteenth-century art, was compiled by Mlle Jallut, a lifelong student of Marie-Antoinette and one of the curators of the château.

Last Monday morning the exhibition was opened by the Minister of Education, after which the moving spirits received a few friends and showed them their handiwork. The duc de Brissac, Président des Amis de Versailles, dispensed champagne in an atmosphere of happy, smiling congratulation.

The exhibition is on the ground floor of the château and begins, suitably enough, in the rooms where Marie-Antoinette lived when she was Dauphine. The fifth Dauphine at Versailles, she was the only one to become Queen – the two Queens who reigned there before her were never Dauphines. These rooms were always considered the most desirable in the whole palace – facing south and west, flooded with sunshine, their French windows opening on to the parterre, they were decorated more like a country house than a palace. Most of this decoration has disappeared, but the rooms retain a great deal of charm.

The exhibition also occupies the former apartment of Mme de Pompadour; it has been entirely remodelled since her day, so that nothing remains of what she saw there but the view from the windows, facing due north. Though there are nearly a thousand objects on view there is so much space, and they are so beautifully arranged, that everything can be seen even when there is a crowd.

The walls are hung with the portraits of all the familiar figures in Marie-Antoinette's story. Here are the three friends of her heart, princesse de Lamballe, Madame de Polignac and Count Fersen, who redeemed the wicked silliness of their youth by perfect faithfulness at the end. (Madame de Polignac was forced to leave the Queen and go into exile, but when she heard how her friend had perished she put her hand to her heart and fell dead.)

There are Rose Bertin, surely the worst modiste of all time, who made a pearly queen of poor Marie-Antoinette with a mass of mad feathers, and Mique, the third-rate architect so beloved of the Queen, who allowed him to scatter his dreary little summer houses and temples among the masterpieces of Gabriel; there are the two statesmen Choiseul and Kaunitz, who between them arranged her marriage; there are dear, good Louis XV, good, sad Louis XVI, foxy Louis XVIII, the cardboard Don Juan Charles X (who, typically, was Marie-Antoinette's favourite) and, of course, all the members of the French and Austrian royal and imperial families. There is an excellent likeness of the Emperor Francis, in crayon, drawn by Marie-Antoinette at the age of ten. A pen-and-ink drawing of the execution of Louis XVI has written on it *'Infâme Pitt, c'était ton ouvrage, et le Roi Louis XVI le scavait.'* The Intelligence Service up to its tricks as usual!

Among the objects shown, perhaps the most splendid and original is the bronze clock *La Négresse*, in the form of a negress's head, lent by Her Majesty the Queen. When one of the earrings is pulled, hours and minutes appear in its eyes, when the other is pulled the clock plays sixty different tunes. The mechanism was broken when the Prince Regent bought this marvellous object in 1807 – it was restored by Vulliamy of London.

Of great interest is the *nécessaire*, without which Marie-Antoinette refused to embark on the journey that ended at Varennes and the making of which caused a fatal delay. It is the equivalent of our picnic basket, silver articles for eating and dressing in a plain mahogany case. No doubt a crowd will always

113

be found in front of the famous necklace, the *collier de la Reine*, which was fraudulently ordered on her behalf and of which she knew absolutely nothing. A contemporary paste reproduction of the original necklace has been lent by a descendant of the jeweller who made it: twenty-two enormous matching diamonds from the necklace itself are lent by the Duchess of Sutherland.

The Comte de Paris has lent a parure of sapphires and diamonds made for the Queen and subsequently presented by Napoleon to Joséphine. The duc d'Orleans bought it from Joséphine's heirs and it has remained in his family ever since. The huge and wonderful diamond earrings which Marie-Antoinette had in her pocket on the flight to Varennes are also here; they were in the Youssoupoff family until the Russian revolution.

Of the furniture, which comes from collections all over the world, my prize goes to the Jacob armchairs with eagles' heads, but many people will like the mother-of-pearl writing table by Riesener. There is a great deal of beautiful silk and lace; I could have wished to see more china, morocco bindings and silver.

Sunday Times, May 22, 1955

Channel-Crossing

Letters from Madame de Sévigné

Translated by Violet Hammersley. Secker & Warburg

Nancy Mitford to the Duchess of Devonshire January 7, 1956

'The Wid [Violet hammersley] very nervous about my review in NS and writes most civilly all of a sudden. I've toned it down a bit – one must remember she won't be here for ever. Even so, she may not like it, she only likes *total* praise.'

The problem of translation must always exercise those who write in English on French matters. Are the publishers quite correct in assuming that the common reader has no French? It is a new idea. In the past there have been many English editions of French classics – Mrs Paget Toynbee's *Madame du Deffand* for instance, where the letters are in their original French. Until the war nobody thought twice about quoting French in an English text. Nowadays it seems that every word has to be translated. The bookshops are loaded with English versions of the French classics, while quotations in French are very much frowned upon. (A notable exception is made by Messrs Longmans, who bravely allowed Mr John Lough to quote extensively from French writers in his *Introduction to Seventeenth-Century France*.) Some of these translations jar the reader unmercifully. It is a shock to hear that a Princess of France 'has guts,' or that one of Saint-Simon's characters is 'positively airborne.' Others may be not too accurate. In *Dearest Bess*, Napoleon is quoted as having said, on the eve of his Russian campaign, 'This old Europe bores me.' What did he really say? *'Cette vieille Europe m'ennuie'*? If so, the meaning is very

115

different. The reader who knows French is puzzled and tantal-ized; he who does not may be deceived.

Perhaps the public must be spoon-fed, to ensure that books shall have a great circulation and publishers a great super-tax; if so, then the spoon should contain real food, not a tinned and frozen substitute covered with sauce *à l'Américaine*. Of all forms of writing, a letter is the most difficult to translate, since it echoes the very voice of its author and inevitably, in a foreign language, that echo is lost. Mrs Hammersley has overcome this difficulty by writing in her own voice. She has not so much translated the letters as rewritten them in English, and the result is a very odd, amusing book. Nobody is so well qualified as she for such a venture, since she is herself a modern Mme de Sévigné. Born in the English Embassy at Paris, in the same room (though not at the same time) as Mr Somerset Maugham, they bowled their hoops together in the Tuileries Gardens. Her girlhood was spent between the banks of the Thames and the banks of the Marne, and when she married she made a centre for all that was intellectual, odd and *frondeur* in London society – the exact equivalent of Mme de Sévigné's circle in the Paris of 200 years before. This charmer then, to the joy of her readers, has been transported by the wave of a magic wand (like the Yankee at the Court of King Arthur) to live at the Hôtel Carnavalet and Les Rochers. As we read the well-known letters in this new voice it is Mrs Hammersley, with her vivid El Greco looks, rather than the slightly bovine Mme de Sévigné whom we picture, arriving at some country house by torchlight, 'strolling, parasoled and veiled' under the orange trees, seated at her writing table: 'M. le Chevalier, is that you I hear? And pray how have you borne the fatigues of the journey?' It is certainly Mrs Hammersley who seizes upon Dangeau as her partner at the card table, so that she will be sure to win.

The charm of Mme de Sévigné's letters lies above all in the picture they give of *vie de château*. This has changed less in France than anywhere; it has always been very different from English country-house life. House parties as such, of specially chosen guests staying between two dates, hardly exist. Instead there is a constant trickle of friends who come and go when it suits them. The accent is on food and religion, rather than on sport and politics, as with us. The local Bishop wanders in, and there are

116

few meals without some curé or abbé to say the grace. Nature is loved, but in a different, larger way and where an Englishwoman would go out and plant a Michaelmas daisy, Mme de Sévigné planted forest trees with her own hands.

Unlike M. de Saint-Simon, Mme de Sévigné has always been a favourite in England. It is to be hoped that this new translation, which is a work of art on its own account, will lead an ever increasing public to her letters in their original tongue.

New Statesman, January 14, 1956

A Heart of Stone

Strawberry Fair: Biography of Frances,
Countess Waldegrave: 1821–1879
by Osbert Wyndham Hewett. Murray

The Victorian hostess, 'last of the great ladies,' Frances Lady Waldegrave, could hardly have had a more unpromising start in life. She was born in 1821, daughter of a Jewish opera singer but, to look at, a golden-haired, blue-eyed English rose. While still in her teens she married a Mr Waldegrave, hardly out of his, the elder, illegitimate, brother of Lord Waldegrave. The two brothers, who were inseparable, were almost idiotic; their sole occupations were gambling, shooting, drinking and beating up old women. Mr, Mrs and Lord Waldegrave lived cheerfully together at Strawberry Hill for a year or so, until Mr Waldegrave had a fit, or delirium tremens, and died. His widow then married her brother-in-law. Soon after the wedding the bridegroom was sent to prison for assaulting a policeman after knocking up a woman who kept a mangle. 'When Lord Waldegrave arrived in the Queen's Bench he proceeded to the coffee room of the prison. He has the apartments over the lobby . . .' Lady Waldegrave joined him. 'We are as comfortable as can be – have our own servants . . .' – and soon they were giving delightful parties.

When Lord Waldegrave had served his sentence he sold Horace Walpole's collections and left Strawberry Hill an empty shell. This was to avenge himself on the Borough of Twickenham, whose bench had sent him to the assizes. On the sixth anniversary of his wedding he died of cirrhosis of the liver. Both the Waldegrave brothers left everything to Frances, who now owned several large country houses, huge estates and some £20,000 a year. Having had enough of jolly young hooligans, she took in 1847 as her third husband a sixty-year-old Mr Harcourt of

Nuneham Park. He was to teach her the ways of the world and was soon a good deal too successful for his own peace of mind.

Frances became a political hostess. The parties were in splinters, nobody could form a durable government, nobody could work with anybody else. 'So much selfishness and intrigue that no reliance can be placed on what is to come.' In these troubled waters Lady Waldegrave fished for admirers and soon landed an outsize bag, which included the whole Liberal party, not a few Tories, all the Ambassadors and most of the Royal Family. We like her better when she was being Wendy to the Waldegraves. Poor old Mr Harcourt never had her to himself, never had another moment of peace. When they went abroad half the House of Commons would pop up in their path, even when they were stranded in an Alpine snowstorm a young Secretary of State happened to be sheltering in the same mountain hut. He was a Mr Fortescue, perhaps more madly in love with her than anybody. He gave up his mistress and devoted his life to the 'darling lady.' Unfortunately Lady Waldegrave was strictly virtuous; poor Mr Fortescue broke out in spots and stammers, became a shadow of his former self and jeopardized his political career with attacks of nerves.

However, Mr Harcourt mercifully died. Richer than ever, she was free to reward Mr Fortescue for eleven years of chaste devotion. Though now forty-two, she went to the altar in a white lace crinoline. The whole thing was too much for some spiteful person, who wrote over the signature of 'Bluemantle' to the *Daily Telegraph* and queried her right to go on calling herself Lady Waldegrave. A thousand swords flew from their scabbards in her defence and 'Bluemantle' must have been thankful that he had not revealed his identity. Lady Waldegrave she remained, even after Mr Fortescue was raised to the peerage.

Everything pleases in this amusing book except its heroine. She was too much of a good thing, and under all the charm, vitality, beauty and sex appeal we sense a heart of stone. Perhaps great hostesses are never really human.

The New Statesman & Nation, February 11, 1956

In Defence of Louis XV

Life of Louis XV by G. P. Gooch. Longmans

Nancy Mitford to Evelyn Waugh February 24, 1953

> 'I suppose we belong to the last generation which will be able to understand the mentality of a man like Louis XV. He was not so different from – say – my father or Eddy Devonshire in outlook & prejudices, but the type will soon have died out I imagine.'

Nancy Mitford to Raymond Mortimer December 18, 1955

> 'You do hate Louis XV as much as Macaulay hated Charles II. I think it must be the strong strain of puritanism inherent in even the most broad-minded of English writers. During the life of Pomp [Madame de Pompadour] there were no great painters, don't count horrid old Chardin (Frag: still studying in Rome) but consider: Panthéon, Ecole Militaire, p. de la Concorde were all ordered *& paid for* by dear good [Louis]. Van Loo was the court painter – Boucher & la Tour greatly patronized by dear good as were all the great ébénistes & sculptors of the time. Think of our Queen & Annigoni.'

Dr Gooch is one of our most revered historians, but he is not interested in human beings. Occupied with historical trends and political events, he sees the characters concerned in them as the stereotyped heroes and villains of a fairy story: the Great King, the Bad King, the Good Prince (who always, alas, dies young), and Princess Charming. In his *Life of Louis XV* he describes that complicated freak Louis XIII as colourless. He sees the Duchesse de Bourgogne as a sort of female Lord Fauntleroy, the darling of the Great King's heart; no mention of her ugliness, her orgies of eating and drinking, her lovers, the fact that, like Marie-Antoinette, she constantly sent State secrets to her own relations when they were fighting the French, and her disconcerting habit of having an enema in front of the drawing-room fire before dinner. All who knew her adored her in spite of her faults and oddities, and therein lies her interest; to Dr Gooch she is simply the Rose of Savoy. Her husband was a Good Prince and they both died young, greatly regretted by Dr Gooch. But this Good Prince had the faults of his virtues. He was very bigoted. His son Louis XV is blamed for persecuting the *philosophes* – would Bourgogne have persecuted them less? Another Good Prince who died young, also regretted by Dr Gooch, was the 'Polish Dauphin', the son of Louis XV, who thought that Voltaire should be tortured to death. Had he come to the throne there might have been some very odd goings-on.

Dr Gooch's theme and subtitle is Monarchy in Decline. Now, we all like to give the French Revolution a single author. *'Voltaire a fait tout ce que nous voyons,'* said Condorcet in 1793. *'Infâme Pitt, c'était ton ouvrage,'* cried Soulavie. Nobody knows better than Dr Gooch the responsibilities of Marie-Antoinette in this matter. But she is a Princess Charming and must not be scolded, so he points his accusing finger at the Bad King, Louis XV. Please, Sir, may I speak? Surely if any one person was to blame it was the Great King, Louis XIV. He died leaving France more ruined than ever in her history, the country one enormous hospital. He eliminated the admirable Huguenots. He separated the King of France from his subjects and the nobles from their domains, and knitted up a political tangle which could never be unravelled and which finally had to be cut by the guillotine.

However, Dr Gooch very much prefers him to Louis XV, who would not 'mend his ways'. What were his ways? He was merciful, 'too weak to punish', and wished for peace, 'too easy-going'. He lacked self-confidence and left important decisions to his Ministers. (He would have been a good constitutional monarch had the Great King seen fit to leave any sort of constitution.) He is reproached for laziness; this is simply unfair. He got up at five o'clock every morning, lighting his own fire in the winter, in order to get through the work on hand. He had a series of incompetent ministers – this may or may not have been his fault. The politicians, like the generals of his reign, were a poor lot. Cut off as he was, by the Great King's dispositions, from the life of his capital, it is difficult to know how he should have set about making

121

the clean sweep which alone would have been of any use. Dr Gooch hardly mentions the work he was doing with Maupeou which was interrupted by the King's death and the Chancellor's dismissal, yet some historians think that had it been achieved the course of events would have been very different.

What Dr Gooch cannot forgive is his love of pleasure. Surely a King who loves pleasure is less dangerous than one who loves glory? It should be remembered, too, that in the eighteenth century pleasure was not regarded with the cold disapproval of our dismal age. Helvétius thought it was the ultimate good; even Frederick the Great said it was the truest reality of our existence. It would have been very strange had Louis XV felt like the Prince Consort about pleasure. Dr Gooch also furiously takes him to task for loving women. Oddly enough, some men do.

Most of the facts marshalled against Louis XV in this book come from the memoirs of disgruntled Ministers. But memoirs are not always reliable evidence, as everybody knows who has reached an age when contemporaries are writing them. Dr Gooch is inclined to quote only from those which prove his case. (Mme de Pompadour's letter on the Calas affair: *le bon coeur du roi a bien souffert au récit de cette étrange aventure et toute la France crie vengeance* is, of course, ignored.) He takes the death-bed scene from Liancourt, who says that the King's cowardice was beyond description, rather than from Cröy, who says the exact opposite. But the Bad King must come to a Bad End, to serve him right for having had a Good Time.

Sunday Times, 1956

Portrait of a French Country House

Nancy Mitford to Evelyn Waugh September 30, 1950

'I've been staying with my dear old Mme Costa de Beauregard in a house in which nothing has changed for 100 years. In the drawing room sit 4 old ladies, who have stayed there all of every summer since they were born & M. le Curé aged 87, who has been M. le Curé there since he was 27. Last All Saint's Day he asked Mme Costa, as he always does, for her list (people to pray for) & she gave him by mistake her private list, so he read out Louis XIV, Thérèse (old cook), Landru, le duc d'Aumale, Marie-Ange (old gardener) etc. etc. We asked her why Landru & she said she heard he had no family to pray for him so she does every day. The house is like that in *Les Malheurs de Sophie*, extremely elegant in front & backing onto a *basse-cour* with vast manure heaps covered with hens. The farmer, a handsome young man, has 18 children & to Mme Costa's sorrow none of them intend to take orders. But the youngest is only 4. The eldest daughter brought her fiancé to see Mme Costa while I was there, a ravishing young man who has been in the Congo & SEEN PIGMIES. It is all like another world, the world you love but which would bore me, though I like to see it in progress.'

Nancy Mitford to Diana Mosley October 7, 1948

'Did I ever tell you about Wid's [Violet Hammersley] sister Mme Costa who confesses nearly everyday so at last somebody said to the priest what *can* an old lady of 80 have to confess? "Oh it's always the same, *j'ai été odieuse avec les invités*."' [I've been horrid to the guests.]

I always spend the autumn in a French country house which I will call the Château de Sainte Foy. I look forward to this visit all the year; the weeks pass much too quickly; it is a happy time.

Sainte Foy is a long, low white house, like that in *Les Malheurs de Sophie*. It occupies one side of a square on the other side of which are farm buildings; the whole surrounds the *basse-cour*, where lively, noisy peasants in blue overalls, horses and big wooden farm carts, a herd of cows, tractors and the farmer's own little motor go endlessly to and fro under a tower which dates from the time of Henri IV. In front of the house there is a wooded park intersected by canals, containing two ancient chapels, a dovecote, a kitchen garden and a charmille or hornbeam avenue without which no French park is complete.

An important convent which stood here until the Revolution was razed to the ground; the house remained; it was built in the eighteenth century to put up the friends and relations of the nuns. Perhaps this is why it is such a perfect place for guests. Its owner, Mme de Florange, fills it with people whenever she is there; so did her parents before her; for a century Sainte Foy (unchanged, except that now every bedroom has its bathroom) has sheltered a cheerful company.

Many of my fellow guests have been coming here ever since they were born, as their parents came before them. They keep the same rooms and leave various belongings from one visit to another. Impossible to convey the prettiness of these rooms, with their old-fashioned furniture, amateur water-colours and double taffeta curtains, pink and white. They are all on the east front, away from the farmyard, the only manifestation of which is an occasional rich whiff of manure. At night one hears the owls, the noise, like rain, of wind in the poplars and the thud of walnuts falling from the tree.

I arrive at Sainte Foy on September 1. It is one o'clock and the party is gathered among the orange tubs in front of the house. There are cries of joy, hugs; cares and bothers fall away – for many weeks now we shall be free of them. The atmosphere at Sainte Foy is very much like that in a Russian play – endless chat, endless leisure, a little plotting, secrets in the charmille; the difference is that ennui does not exist. (In all the years I have lived in France I have never come across it, although in the eighteenth century people here were eaten by it.)

The house party, as in Russian plays, is composed of disparate elements, young and old, egg-heads and bone-heads, saints and sinners, grasshoppers and ants. We are seldom fewer than eight or more than twelve. A grave element is provided by one or two Abbés, a learned lady who knows all about medieval architecture, and the tutor of Mme de Florange's grandchildren. They regard Mrs H, M. d'Albano, aged ninety-five, M. de la Tour and myself as agreeable but weightless.

M. d'Albano composes definitions: *'Yes. Ne veut vraiment dire oui . . . qu'à toutes choses anglaises.' 'Héros. Beaucoup ne tiennent pas à l'être mais combien voudraient l'avoir été.'*

M. de La Tour restores pictures and has turned a blackened canvas on the staircase into a (perhaps) Bassano – I sometimes wish he hadn't, the head of St John the Baptist is so very unpleasant. He is a Chekov character, young, romantic, elusive, elegant and rather mysterious; he desperately loves the beauty of this world and feels the approach of an engulfing tide of ugliness which he doubts being able to survive. This makes him melancholy.

Cares and bothers fall away at Sainte Foy, but not for Mrs H, since caring and bothering are her hobbies; she exudes a sort of frivolous pessimism which nobody takes very seriously. She is the most French English person I know. Her father was on the staff of Lord Lyons and she was born at the Paris embassy, in the same room, though not at the same time, as Mr Somerset Maugham. They bowled their hoops together in the Tuileries gardens. She first came to Sainte Foy when she was six weeks old; her girlhood was spent between the banks of the Thames and the banks of the Marne; when she married she made a centre for the intellectual element in London society. She has a tragic greenish face with huge black eyes, and dresses in the colours of mourning. She said to me once 'Child' (I am *Child* to her and *La Petite* to Mme de Florange, it is so agreeable) 'Child, you should never put any make-up on your face – artists do not admire it'. 'All very well for you' I said 'since you look like El Greco's mistress. If I put no make-up on I look like an old English governess.' While the others are greeting me with every appearance of satisfaction, Mrs · H, whom I have not seen for months, only says 'Have you brought a paper, Child? No paper? Of course, you care nothing for the break-up of civilization.'

125

For some reason civilization always seems nearer its break-up in September than at any other time of year, an added reason for spending that fidgety month at Sainte Foy, where the sound of drums is muffled. No daily paper is seen there, except the English ones which Mrs H and I receive by post, two days late. 'As you have the *Daily Telegraph*, Child, I will arrange to have *The Times*'. There is an antique wireless in the drawing-room, but it gives a powerful electric shock to anybody rash enough to turn it on.

None of us minds not knowing the latest news except Mrs H who, gloomily fascinated by the break-up of civilization, simply longs for a peep into the present. At the time of Suez I used to take pity on her and manipulate the wireless with an india-rubber. 'This is the end!' Like all English people she and I took sides over Suez and furious were our arguments. The French rather agreed about its being the end, but they did not fly at each other's throats – they shrugged their shoulders and blamed the Americans.

Mme de Florange is a tall, beautiful, elegant woman, born the same year as Sir Winston Churchill, Dr Adenauer and the late Pope. Like them she is extremely authoritarian; the world has always been at her feet and she gets her own way. She happens to be a saint. Saints are seldom easy of commerce; Mme de Florange resembles the eagle rather than the dove. She is a rebel and something of a phenomenon; in her world, Catholic, royalist, *bien pensant*, Action Française, it is most unusual to be, as she is, a firm Gaullist. The cry generally goes up: 'I vote for the General with both my hands so as to avoid shaking his.' They vote for him because 'who else is there?' But they hate.

Mme de Florange, and this too is unlike many of her compatriots, is full of fantasy. Impossible to guess how she will take things. She is not shocked by Voltaire or Anatole France (though the children are not allowed to read them) or even by Mendès-France; she positively enjoys *L'Express* for its vile cleverness. She has always been interested in contemporary art, was painted by Cubists and made great friends with Bonnard, who gave her a picture. Somebody once found the list of people she prays for every day – in among the family names there were Louis XIV and Landru. 'Poor man,' she said when asked why Landru, 'it seems he has no relations to pray for him.' Exceedingly religious, she spends more time in church than in the drawing-room. She is not

126

with the others when I arrive; her maid is on her way to the Chapel to tell her that luncheon is ready.

Meanwhile Mrs H, who came from England an hour ago, is recounting her news, all bad. 'My doctor I was so fond of has gone into broilers.' *'Brolairs? Qu'est ce que c'est que ça?'* 'A kind of chicken you keep in the dark and feed with injections. He says they can't ring him up in the night – oh, it is too hard.'

'But these broilairs must be very nasty?' They are more concerned with the sufferings of the consumer than those of the hen.

'Oh, very. But nobody cares. Veal in England now tastes of blotting-paper – why? Because the calves live in Turkish baths,' she adds, conjuring up a picture of Hammams all over England's green and pleasant land.

The day begins at Sainte Foy, as in all French houses, by the noise, like pistol shots, of wooden shutters being thrown back. Not mine. I sleep with everything open, so I love the French window which marries a house to the firmament instead of dividing them like the stuffy sash.

Soon Mme Congis appears with coffee and croissants. She lives, with lucky, lucky M. Congis, in a village some miles away; comes pedalling over on her bicycle before breakfast and leaves again after tea, laden with black-edged letters for the post. She is passionately interested in the goings-on at Sainte Foy; having dumped the tray on one's knee, she folds her arms, says *'Voilà!'* and then makes an announcement.

'Voilà! M. l'Abbé Fesch got on to one of the children's donkeys after Mass, for a joke, and has been carried away over the hill. Mme la Comtesse is most worried.'

'Voilà! Meeses H has got raging toothache and she is going now to the dentist at Meaux.' All heads out of all windows as the motor is heard; Mrs H, wrapped in shawls, emerges from the house, looks up like a Gothic saint, cries, 'Pray for me' and is driven off to her martyrdom.

Once a year Mme Congis announces: *'Voilà!* Madame knows that tomorrow is Bishop's Day?' Everybody enjoys this. Monseigneur, who is a great dear, comes, with his chaplain, and says Mass at nine o'clock. After a vast breakfast for all the tenants he retires to a room put at his disposal and does his morning's work. Luncheon is a gargantuan feast attended by many priests (some of

127

whom come from Paris) and neighbours. The women all curtsy to the Bishop and kiss his ring. Madame de Florange's beautiful English daughter-in-law once met him unexpectedly in the charmille. He held out his ringed hand – she took it – absent-mindedly and said 'Oh, what a pretty stone!' At the luncheon table where, like a king, he acts as host, the foreigners, Mrs H and I sit on each side of him and she pumps him for all she is worth about civilization's break-up. But he is a jolly, optimistic character to whom the next world is more real than this one; Nasser and the Bomb leave him singularly unmoved. After luncheon he and the other priests sit drinking coffee, smoking, chatting and laughing. They look like a picture of the Cardinal School.

André the butler comes into his own on the Bishop's Day, which is largely organized by him. He is an adorable man. A walking encyclopaedia, he suffers, at meals, from loose statements of uncertain facts. Sometimes his lips move frantically as he tries, without actually speaking, to prompt some hesitating speaker.

'Who came after Sadi Carnot?' M. de La Tour said, vaguely. That evening he found a neat list of the Presidents of the Republic, and their dates, on his dressing-table. At dinner a fellow guest, shouting at a deaf lady, said: 'La rue de Tilsit – Tilsit comme la bataille.' I couldn't resist saying in a know-all voice: 'There was no battle at Tilsit.' 'Will you bet?' Fortified by a nod from André, I betted and won 100 francs. Coming down early for dinner one often finds him looking up something in Larousse. If I sit down absentmindedly before some visiting Abbé has said grace, André gives me a sharp thump on the back. Somebody once asked what he would like for a Christmas present and he replied, 'A love poem by Alfred de Vigny, framed.'

His predecessor was a Moor called Mahmoud who had been condemned to death by his compatriots and therefore never wanted a day off. However, he fell, with lustful intent, upon Bernadette the between-maid and had to be sacked. Soon afterwards poor Mahmoud was found with his throat cut.

On Friday various men who work in Paris come down *en weekend*. Mrs H awaits them as if they were the Messiah, hoping to glean much information on current affairs. Indeed, they are full of it and soon she knows exactly what is being said at the Jockey Club. It seldom tallies with what she sees in her *New Statesman and Nation*, so she tries to arrive at some truth half-way between the two.

They bring heaps of newspapers, sweets and flowers for Mme de Florange (in France flowers are taken to, not from the country) and any new books which the authors happen to have given them. Most of the books lying about on the drawing-room table are written by dukes and duchesses. This does not mean that we are down to society memoirs; there are some highbrow French dukes; three of them are in the French Academy, where they may soon be joined by the duchesse de La Rochefoucauld as the first woman member.

When people ask me what I do all day at Sainte Foy I am at a loss to reply. I only know that the time seems to be crammed with delightful ploys and that I never can count on doing any work there. We pose for Mme de Florange, who paints enormous, masterly altar-pieces. We have all figured in these as angels or devils or victims of the plague.

We play a good deal of bridge. The visit always begins with me imploring our hostess to allow us to play for two sous instead of one. 'Certainly not. We have always played here for one sou and we always shall.' She is a wild overbidder and hates winning. Mrs H is a wild underbidder and hates losing. 'Child, you always win except when you are playing with me, it is so hard.' We have furious struggles and acid arguments, sometimes ending in a telephone call to a friend of Albarron in Paris to settle the matter.

Incidentally the farmers in this part of Seine et Marne are terrible gamblers. The Mayor of Pouy, who has one of the biggest farms in the district, often comes to play with us (for one sou). He tells of really mad poker games; one of his colleagues recently lost a team of horses to another – they were sent over the next morning, their carter in floods of tears. This charming Mayor takes me and M. de La Tour every year to the forest of Ermenonville to hear the stags roaring under a full moon. The forest is full of creatures crashing about, the stags sound like lions, it all seems as primitive as the Congo and yet is less than an hour's drive from Paris.

Sainte Foy is plumb in the battlefield of the Marne; the two wars are still the chief topic of conversation between the peasants and a foreigner like myself. They had a bad time here with the Germans and show no enthusiasm at all for United Europe.

129

There is a touching little book, printed locally after the first war, telling exactly what happened to the inhabitants of five neighbouring villages in the autumn of 1914.

The Mayor of Pouy has fascinating stories of the Battle of the Marne, in which he fought as a very young man. He will never forget how one morning, after several nights of no sleep for anybody, he saw an Indian officer calmly sitting by the road while an orderly wound his turban. He says the mules of the Indian regiment always looked as if they had just that minute been polished. In this district the English are regarded as faithful brothers in arms; Mers el Kebir and our (real or imagined) behaviour, hostile to France, in Arab lands have made no impact here. In 1943 M. Gouasc, Mme de Florange's farmer, hid an English captain for many months and received a constant flow of *parachutages*. Gouasc was finally caught, taken to Germany and died as a result of his treatment there. The Captain got away; he was finally killed in Burma. *'Le pauvre Capitaine – il était bien gentil.'* When the peasants tell you these things they extol each other's behaviour but never speak of their own.

One of my fellow guests who was a girl in 1914 was doing her embroidery in a little summer house, which we still use, perched up on the park wall like a bird's nest, when suddenly she saw Uhlans galloping over the hill. In those early days with the armies on the move, there was often no means of knowing that the enemy was near. The family then went to Paris, leaving Sainte Foy in the charge of their groom. A few days later a German officer rode up the drive, made straight for the harness room and helped himself to a bridle. He asked the groom 'where are M. de Florange and M. d'Albano?' 'With their regiments.' He spoke about one or two other friends of the house and then went off down a path across the fields which no stranger could have found. Who was this mysterious person? None of them knew any German officer. So it is thought that the children's Fraulein must have been a man all along – she always looked like one they say and had a distinct moustache.

There are lovely walks at Sainte Foy. You can go over the uplands, past the corn ricks and the old windmill to Pouy, which consists of a dozen white-washed houses, with red and blue roofs, clustering round a Romanesque church; down a dusty white lane, bordered by nuts and blackberries, to Mareilly, where the village

130

shop can sometimes provide a copy of *L'Aurore*, or through a poplar wood to the watercress beds.

When M. de La Tour was restoring a naïve fresco in Pouy church I used to go up there, after tea, and walk home with him. Like many French people, he pretends to regard his compatriots as worse than idiotic, 'The boobies – *(crétins)* – what do they care about their beautiful church?' So it was a pleasant surprise when he received a round robin from all the parishioners thanking him for his trouble.

When I first knew this country, just after the war, the aspect of the villages was decidedly grubby, but lately there has been an improvement, due, I think, to a few Parisian weekenders who have bought cottages. The town mouse has taught the country mouse to paint his woodwork, hang pretty curtains, cook on Butagaz, and plant flowers in his garden. Perhaps everybody is richer now, but I believe lack of imagination, rather than of cash, was often responsible for the old sad look. This year I noticed one or two washing-machines but I have yet to see a television set.

The farms in this part of France are large enough to be prosperous. The chief crops are wheat, maize, and beet. Modern appliances are used more and more; at Sainte Foy the forty Friesian cows are milked and fenced in by electricity; there is a big Ferguson tractor and other motorized equipment; but Champagne, a dear white horse, who loves his carter so much that he watches him all the time, like a dog, and Jean-Mermoz, a nappy old chestnut, still do a lot of work. The French consider that horses are useful when the soil is wet, they produce manure and can eventually be eaten, none of which can be said for the tractor.

A horrible manifestation of the modern world, hitherto so remote, came to Sainte Foy last year. Some clever young Civil Servants arrived in a caravan to prospect for oil. They dug an enormous crater in a wheat field just outside the park wall and set up a pump which made a deafening noise night and day; powerful searchlights glared behind the trees; the whole effect was hellish. We were warned that if oil was found, a shanty town would spring up on the pastures; the atmosphere would be laden with petrol; the pump and the searchlights become a permanence. Furthermore, Mme de Florange and young M. Gouasc, her farmer, would receive a tiny sum in compensation, but not a penny of profit, because, since long before the Revolution, everything under the earth in France has belonged to the State. Mercifully the prospectors drew a blank. They gave the farmer £100 for temporarily ruining his field, filled in the crater, and moved off to find a substantial layer of oil some twelve miles away.

Sainte Foy was saved, but for how long? Near as it is to Paris, will it not soon become part of the *agglomération parisienne*? Will all the clever, handsome peasants be crammed into factories to make unnecessary objects for the use of other peasants in other factories? Will the poplar trees be cut down to be replaced by *Unités*, i.e. blocks of flats with their own shops and swimming baths, rising out of concrete car parks?

Perhaps not, after all. I really cannot imagine Mme Congis or the Mayor of Pouy living in a *Unité*.

PS. I showed this account of Sainte Foy to a French friend who said, 'My dear, if the English think we all live like this, they will never join the Common Market.' I said, 'Don't worry at all, the English don't believe a word I tell them; they regard me as their chief purveyor of fairy tales.'

Sunday Times, August 6, 1961

Reading for Pleasure

As far as I am concerned, all reading is for pleasure. My eyesight is erratic and when I am bored by a book physical agony soon compels me to put it down. On the other hand, if I am interested and amused I can go on for quite a long time. Of course, this has not always been so. I cannot remember not being able to read and as a child I lived in books; my most vivid early recollections come from them. Public events such as the outbreak of war or the murder of the Romanovs made more impression on me than family ones, because they were part of that fascinating serial called History. I read quickly and guiltily. Reading was tolerated but not at all encouraged by my father, who thought it a waste of time. 'If you've got nothing to do', he would say, finding one with a book, 'run down to the village and tell Hooper . . .'

There were certain very strict rules, continually broken. Reading in bed and in the bath were forbidden; novels not allowed before luncheon; library books to be read in the library only. By good luck all my forebears except my father were literate and our house was full of books – classics in the library and the usual (excellent) children's books of the day in the schoolroom, left there by my aunts, the youngest of whom was only eight years older than me. Though my father never read himself, he had learnt from his father to respect a volume as an object, and if I had lost or mutilated one I would never have been allowed in the library again. It never occurred to him that beautiful calf or morocco might contain inflammatory material.

I mention these early years and our library because no doubt my taste in reading was formed by its contents – French and English biography, history and belles lettres, with some German philosophy, out of my reach. (My grandfather had translated Kant and Houston Stewart Chamberlain.) There were no novels, no books of travel and very little poetry. I still read more biography, memoirs and letters than anything else; I like to get into some lively set, and observe its behaviour. The Encyclopaedists or Byron and his friends are supreme entertainers, but any small society will provide an interesting study in human relationships if one or two of its members can write.

They need not be professional writers – men of action not infrequently have literary gifts. We know all about Captain Scott and his companions from his own journal and Cherry Garrard's *The Worst Journey in the World*, two books I love. Here is the Englishman as he was when I was a child, of whom it has been said that his favourite words in his favourite poem were 'someone had blundered'. Scott struggled to the Pole by the most difficult route; he took insufficient rations and he went on foot because he thought it would be cruel and unfair to use dogs. The realistic foreigner who got there first raced along comfortably, his sledge drawn by dogs which he ate on the way. Would the modern Englishman hesitate between the two methods? Something seems to have happened in the past fifty years to make him more practical, less idealistic, much less respectful of animals, which are now ruthlessly sacrificed in the interests of science or expediency.

My greatest pleasure is reading to gather up material for a biography. The driest, longest book becomes a treasure chest if one is rummaging about in it for appropriate facts. The *Mémoires* of the Duc de Luynes would be unreadable to the ordinary person; they are in about sixteen volumes, pedestrian in style and written without a scrap of the sparkling malice which drives Saint-Simon's pen. But their day-to-day exactitude makes them perfectly fascinating to anybody who wants to describe Versailles in the reign of Louis XV and I raced through them at top speed when writing *Pompadour*.

Most people like reading about what they already know – there is even a public for yesterday's weather. I know about the personalities of seventeenth- and eighteenth-century Europe and I read nearly everything which appears on the subject. Much of it irritates me profoundly and I think the best books on the eighteenth century are still those written before 1914. Modern writers have dug up a few new facts, but they are too much inclined to make a long book about some hangers-on of whom Sainte-Beuve has told the essentials in a few thousand words. Their predecessors were more talented. Carlyle's *Life of Frederick the Great*, though dishonest to a comic degree about Frederick's morals, is a work of art; the secondary characters are brilliantly portrayed;

134

Voltaire is summed up once and for all. His *French Revolution* has the grandeur of a thunderstorm. These are books I can read over and over again, and so are Macaulay's Essays, 'freighted with the spoils of the ages', and his *History of England*, Michelet's *History of France*, Sainte-Beuve's *Lundis*, and Lord Acton's Essays and Lectures. I also like the works of the Goncourts, Funck-Brentano, Pierre de Nolhac, George Saintsbury, Charles Whibley, Lenotre and others of that school, now out of fashion; nearer my own age, in the same tradition of civilized writing, I admire Lytton Strachey, Harold Nicolson, Virginia Woolf's *Common Reader* and E. M. Forster's *Abinger Harvest*.

In the matter of novels, with few exceptions and those the greatest, I demand jokes. In my time I have enjoyed most of the French, English and Russian masterpieces, but now I hardly ever read novels. Exceptions are those of Evelyn Waugh, P. G. Wodehouse, Rose Macaulay, and E. F. Benson's Lucia books. (Will somebody not reprint these soon?) I liked *Lucky Jim* for its funniness, but it made me sad, as do all evidences of declining civilization.

I never read travel books, partly, no doubt, because I seldom travel. I cannot read criticism – I would be incapable of reading Sartre on Genet, for instance – nor can I manage literary weeklies, English or French. The English yellow Press, so much enjoyed by so many, is no good to me; when I go home I am like Rip Van Winkle, ignorant of many a household word and looming row. French popular papers have a certain charm because, long as I have lived here, I am still enchanted by such headlines as '*Excédé par le soupirant de sa gouvernante, l'octogénaire décharge son revolver sur lui.*' But nothing is so bad for the eyes as newsprint.

To sum up – I like fact better than fiction and I like almost anything that makes me laugh. But my favourite book falls into neither of these categories: it is *La Princesse de Clèves*.

The Times, November 20, 1961

Blor

Nancy Mitford to Evelyn Waugh April 10, 1962

'A piece on Blor will appear in *Sunday Times* soon. Fancy, they offered me £100 – I replied well, but I got £500 for Fontaines [Portrait of a French Country House], they replied "did you, how ghastly, must have been a mistake. All right will give you £250 for Blor". Really don't you think it rather peculiar? They don't seem to know the value of money.'

Sydney Redesdale to Nancy Mitford August 18, 1962

'The first chapter gives a charming account of the dearest Blor, though somehow she remains a shadowy figure. I wish only one thing, that you would exclude me from your books, I don't mind what you write about me when I am dead, but do dislike to see my mad portrait while I am still alive.'

Nancy Mitford to Evelyn Waugh August 22, 1962

'My mother is displeased with what I shall say about her in the ST . . . It comes from seeing ones own life & all ones relations as a tremendous joke which one expects them to share. Bother.'

Unlike my sister Diana, who declares (and she is rather a truthful person) that she remembers having a bottle, I can remember almost nothing about my early childhood. It is shrouded in a thick mist which seldom lifts except on the occasion of some public event. For instance, I see our dining-room at 1 Graham Street (now Graham Terrace), the house where I was born; my father and mother, at breakfast, are reading newspapers with black edges to them and they are both crying. The tears startle me – so does the news; the King is dead. The King was Edward VII. Now, the funny thing about this mental tableau is that, whereas in fact my parents were beautiful and young at the time, aged thirty and thirty-one, they appear in it as two old people, contemporaries of the King whom they mourn. The room, the wallpaper (white with a green wreath round the cornice), the street outside and the black-edged *Times* are a real image; the two living creatures are seen subjectively and I very much doubt if those tears really flowed at all. So much for my memory.

Soon after this we moved to Victoria Road. Another tableau: walking towards the Park I am saying to Blor, who is pushing one or two of my sisters in a pram: 'How big is the *Titanic*?' 'As big as from here to Kensy High Street.' To this day I see the *Titanic* as Victoria Road, houses, trees and all, steaming through the icebergs. Its sinking gave me ideas, of a rather dreadful kind, I am sorry to say. My father and mother used to go every other year to Canada in order to prospect for gold. Poor but optimistic, they were quite sure that sooner or later their ship would come home. But I became very hopeful that on one of these journeys their ship would go down; then, no doubt, like Katy in *What Katy Did*, I would gather up the reins of the household in small but capable hands and boss 'the others'. (It never occurred to me that, in fact, some uncle or aunt would no doubt take us over and boss us all.) I remember scanning Blor's *Daily News* for an account of the shipwreck: 'Mr and Mrs Mitford are among the regretted victims.' I knew this delightful day dream would never come true; no doubt if it had I would have been as sad as one can be at seven years old, because in fact I loved my parents, while later in life all my faults and disabilities would have been put down to this early tragedy.

By far the most vivid of my fitful recollections is the outbreak of war in 1914. When it appeared to be imminent Blor told me to pray for peace. But I thought, if we had war, England might be invaded; then, like Robin Hood, one would take to the greenwood tree and somehow or another manage to kill a German. It was more than I could do to pray for peace. I prayed, as hard as I could, for war. I knew quite well how wicked this was; when my favourite uncle was killed I had terrible feelings of guilt.

My prayer having been granted as prayers so often are, I was soon sitting like a *tricoteuse*, on the balcony of Grandfather Redesdale's house in Kensy High Street, crocheting an endless purple scarf while the troops marched by on their way to France. (There was no khaki wool to be had so early in the war – you took

137

what you could get.) I and the others, Pam, Tom and Diana, Blor and Ada, the nursery maid, were staying with my grandfather because my mother was, as usual, increasing the number of the others, an occupation which I thought extremely unnecessary. On 8th August a girl was born; she was christened Unity, after an actress my mother admired called Unity Moore, and Valkyrie after the war maidens. This was Grandfather Redesdale's idea; he said these maidens were not German but Scandinavian. He was a great friend of Wagner's and must have known. Then we all went back to Victoria Road. The war turned out to be less exciting than I had hoped, though we did see the Zeppelin come down in flames at Potters Bar. I fell in love with Captain Platt in my father's regiment, an important General of the next war, and crocheted endless pairs of khaki mittens for him – I am not sure that they were inflicted on him. In any case, all this crocheting was the nearest I ever got to killing an enemy, a fact which I am still regretting.

I don't remember much more of my early childhood; what I am now going to recount mostly comes from family hearsay. Our first Nanny was Lily Kersey; 'Ninny Kudgey', daughter of the captain of Grandfather Bowles's yacht. My mother adored the sea, which she saw in terms of Tissot rather than Conrad; she christened me Nancy in the hopes that a sailor's wife a sailor's star I'd be; she gave me in charge of Ninny so that a love of ocean waves should be implanted in my young psychology. It all turned out rather differently, however. Ninny was quite untrained and knew nothing about babies; she laid the foundations of the low stamina which has always been such a handicap to me in life. I think she was also partly responsible for my great nastiness to the others. My next sister Pam was born three days before my third birthday; Ninny Kudgey instantly transferred her affections. My mother used to hear me saying, 'Oh Ninny how I wish you could still love me!' In the end, she says, I became too sad and Ninny was sent away. But she was succeeded by the Unkind Nanny. The Unkind Nanny is a legendary figure in the family. Had we been slightly older she might well have found herself the biter bit, but it must be borne in mind that at this time I was between three and six and the others between nothing and three. I am not quite sure what form the unkindness took. I, of course, cannot remember; the others were really too little (Diana, the great rememberer, was only four

138

months old when she left) and my mother seems to have a certain feeling of guilt which prevents her from discussing the subject. Did the Nanny beat us or starve us or merely refuse to laugh at our jokes? I shall never know. Another thing, like the False Dimitris there may have been more than one Unkind Nanny, though this is not certain. In short, the three years after the departure of Ninny Kudgey were a kind of Mitford dark ages, full of mystery, wickedness and horror. No reliable records exist of this period and we turn our minds from it with relief. During it, Tom was born and then Diana.

My mother has always lived in a dream world of her own and no doubt was even dreamier during her many pregnancies. Later in life she has taken to reading, preferring, like Mr Raymond Mortimer, books about Victorian clergymen to any others, so that my biographies are not much good to her. But when she was young she never opened a book and it is difficult to imagine what her tastes and occupations may have been. My father and she disliked society, or thought they did – there again, later on they rather took to it – and literally never went out. She had no cooking or housework to do. In those days you might be considered very poor by comparison with other people of the same sort and yet have five servants in a tiny house. How different are the lives of such young couples now! Last time I was in London I met a friend pushing her granddaughter round Eaton Square in a pram. We chatted for a while; the wind was bitter; I said: 'Why don't we go and put our toes in the nursery fender and let Nanny give us some tea?' 'There is no nursery, there is no fender, there is no Nanny.' We took the baby home and handed it over to an Italian girl who was ironing in the drawing-room; no fire; indeed no fireplace. It had been turned into a cupboard for hunting-boots.

So what did my mother do all day? She says now, when cross-examined, that she lived for us. Perhaps she did, but nobody could say that she lived with us. It was not the custom then. I think that nothing in my life has changed more than the relationship between mothers and young children. In those days a distance was always kept. Even so she was perhaps abnormally detached. On one occasion Unity rushed into the drawing-room, where she was at her writing-table, saying: 'Muv, Muv, Decca is standing on the roof – she says she's going to commit suicide!'

'Oh, poor duck,' said my mother, 'I hope she won't do anything so terrible' and went on writing.

We were looked after by a nurse and nursery maid; we 'came down' to see our parents finishing their breakfast and again, dressed up in party clothes, after tea. Occasionally, of course, there were treats; we went to Gorringes or the Zoo, or an aunt or uncle took us to a pantomime, after which, all having fallen desperately in love with some character on the stage, we would be insupportable for weeks. But we spent the major part of our lives in the nursery. My mother says she has forgotten how she found out about the Unkind Nanny's (or Nannies') unkindness. Little children, of course, never tell tales about those in authority. Perhaps the neighbours sent for the police, but I don't think so. Even I would have noticed the irruption of a bobby in the nursery, I suppose. The house was minute; probably my parents, having heard unmistakable sounds of torture going on upstairs for a few months, decided that the time had come for another change. I do vaguely remember the sacking of the Nanny. My mother retired to bed, as she often did when things became dramatic, leaving my father to perform the execution. There was a confrontation in the nursery as of two mastodons; oddly enough, throughout the terrifying battle which ensued, I felt entirely on the side of the Nanny.

It took my mother some time to find a successor. She had no wish to fall upon another False Dimitri; she longed to finish bringing up her children with no more changes. She interviewed about a dozen nurses, including one with the almost irresistible name of Lily Duck. When she saw Blor, who was 39, she thought her too old and frail to look after a large and growing family. Blor herself wondered whether she could manage to push a pram, with two children and a sort of *strapontin* for a third, all the way from Graham Street to the Park. However, when she saw the baby, Diana, all these doubts vanished. 'I can see her face now,' says my mother, 'as she said, "Oh! what a lovely baby!"' So she moved into our family and never moved out again. Of course, I can remember nothing of all this; it happened just before my sixth birthday. I was reading *Ivanhoe*, so Blor has often told me, and my furious little round face was concealed behind the book as she took off hat and cape for the first time, in our nursery. I remember every word of *Ivanhoe*, which I have never read since, but have no recollection of the advent of Blor. No doubt it seemed at once as though she had been with us for ever.

Her name was Laura Dicks and she came from Egham. Charming to look at, she had a kind, white face, with curly reddish-brown hair. Out of doors she wore a bonnet, of shiny black straw trimmed with a velvet bow and strings. The French painter Helleu used to say he could live in London if only because of the bonnets of the Nannies in the Park. When Blor changed her flat bow for a velvet ruche, Diana, who was about two, says she noticed it and cried. Mr Dicks, the father of Blor, looked like God the Father with a long white beard; he was a smith – he made wrought-iron gates and grew black pansies. Her many brothers and sisters looked like her. They were all clever and had success-ful careers. The family was advanced in its views, liberal and non-conformist, very different from the one in which she was to spend the rest of her life. My parents were ultra-conservative and Church of England, with the emphasis on England. They went to church regularly, in order to support the State; I doubt if either of them ever had a conventionally religious thought. Indeed, my mother used to say: But what happens when people pray? How can they think of enough things to ask for? Somebody once told her about the resurrection of the body and she became quite hysterical at the idea; in spite of the fact that she proclaimed her belief in it, out loud, every Sunday, she had not considered its strange implications. Blor stuck to her guns and never changed her way of thinking. She was very religious and I believed she suffered from not being able to go to her own church during the months, sometimes years, on end that we lived in the country. She attended the village church and she asked Mr Ward, our vicar, if she could take Communion there, but he was obliged to say no. When the Liberal Party declined, Blor took to voting Labour, to the horror of my sisters. 'How did you vote, Blor?'

'Well, darling, to vote for the Liberal candidate would only put in the Conservative, you know.'

'Blor! Never tell me you voted for the Socialists?'

'Yes, darling, that's just what I did.'

'Oh! You are naughty! What will the Führer say?'

Even I, who voted Labour myself, felt rather shocked. Such frivolities seemed unsuitable for Blor.

141

However, she is one of the few people with whom none of us ever had a political quarrel – or indeed a quarrel of any sort. The strong passions that raged in our house were kept on the other side of the nursery door; even my father, armed with hunting crop or croquet mallet, in pursuit of a screaming but delighted quarry, would go so far and no further. Somehow the egg-shell skull of the current baby was protected from its rampaging relations by Blor's personality. She had a wonderful capacity for taking things as they came and a very English talent for compromise. In two respects she was unlike the usual Nanny. We were never irritated by tales of paragons she had been with before us; and she always got on quite well with our governesses, upholding their authority as she did that of our parents. When we grew up she never interfered in our lives. If she disapproved of something one said or did, she would shrug her shoulders and make a little sound between a sniff and clearing her throat. She hardly ever spoke out – perhaps never – and on the whole our vagaries were accepted with no more stringent comment than 'Hm' – sniff – 'very *silly*, darling.' A strong Puritan streak made her despise pleasure. Her father disapproved of the theatre and she had never seen the inside of one until I badgered and wheedled my mother to let me go to the opera. I was fifteen and under the influence of Tolstoy's novels at the time. The word opera to me signified the World in all its wickedness and glamour; nothing to do with the performance, of course – I was after the House, with its boxes, its foyer and its *coulisses*, gallant men in opera hats and lovely women in opera cloaks, gazing at each other through opera glasses. Blor and I went off together to a matinée of *Faust*, at Oxford. I need say no more.

When we left the schoolroom and began to live for pleasure its occupational complaints got no sympathy from Blor. One tottered, lean and pale, into the nursery, having danced until dawn: 'Oh, Blor I'm so tired!' The reply was: 'I don't pity you!' My first ball dress was viewed without enthusiasm. 'You'll be cold.' On Diana's wedding day, when she was trying to arrange her veil to its best effect, Blor remarked: 'Don't worry, darling – nobody's going to look at *you*.'

She once said to Unity: 'I do wish you wouldn't keep going to Germany, darling.'

'Why, Blor?'

Sniff. 'All those men!'

What could be more descriptive of Hitler's Germany?

When Diana's boys began using four-letter words Blor said: 'I'm afraid nobody will like them when they are grown up if that's how they talk!'

My mother, whose views on health were rudimentary, who had never heard of hygiene and did not really believe in illness, had one medical superstition which nothing could shake. Pig, she thought, was unclean and, like the Jews and the Arabs, we were strictly forbidden to eat it. The perfect health of Arabs is a very current English belief. How many times have I been told not to expose myself to the sun because they wear blankets in heatwaves! (Most of those I see are noticeable for their poor physique, but let that pass.) Of course, we don't go so far as to copy their ablutions; true cleanliness is considered rather immoral by my compatriots, who lie for hours in hot baths, but are maddened at the sight of a bidet.

The ruling that deprived us children of pig also forbade horse and oysters; that was not a real hardship, because no other member of the family ate horse, and oysters are seldom seen in the Cotswolds. But pig! Whiffs of fried bacon from my father's breakfast and the sight of him tucking into sausage rolls or sausage mash, cold gammon and cranberry sauce, pork chops with apple sauce, pigs' thinkers and trotters and Bath chaps were daily tortures; the occasional sucking-pig which crackled into the dining-room hardly bears contemplating, even now. Our craving for the stuff amounted to an obsession. Others have told how my young sisters were to be seen concealing sausages up their knickers and running off to eat them in some secluded spot; the first letter my brother Tom wrote from his private school simply stated 'We have sossages every day.' Blor must have thought this 'no pig' rule eccentric, if not rather mad; she never commented on it and always upheld it, except on one occasion. She and convalescent Debo were sent to a seaside hotel for a breezy fortnight. Ordering luncheon on the first day Debo said to the waiter, in what she thought was a grown-up voice: 'I'll have a very little bit of ham.' Then she looked at Blor to see what the reaction would be. Blor gave her disapproving sniff, but she only said: 'Well, it must be a very, very little bit of ham.'

My parents, as is only human, had favourites among their

daughters. Tom was their adored only son who could do no wrong in their eyes – and then he had the advantage of being away at school. Luckily, perhaps, their favourites were not always the same. For my father there would be one child who was allowed every licence and one who was getting what we used to call rat week – the rest of us floated in a sort of limbo between these two extremes. The change would come with dramatic suddenness and for no apparent reason. Of course, one kept a weather eye open for it, but even after years of experience nobody could prophesy when it would occur or what direction it would take. My mother, who was not violent like my father, never seemed, as he often did, actively to loathe any of us. She was entirely influenced by physical beauty; those who were passing through an awkward or ugly age was less in favour than their prettier sisters.

Blor, however, must have been superhuman; she seemed to have no favourites at all. If she felt on the side of the little ones, especially her own baby, Diana, against the bully that I was, she never showed it. Her fairness always amazed me, even as a child. My vile behaviour to the others was partly, I suppose, the result of jealousy and partly of a longing to be grown up and live with grown-up people. The others bored me, and I made them feel it. They banded together against me; my mother still has a badge carefully embroidered with 'Leag against Nancy, hed Tom'. I expect I would have been much worse but for Blor. My mother's scoldings and my father's whippings had little effect, but Blor at least made me feel ashamed of myself. Of course, I ought to have gone to school – it was the dream of my life – but there was never any question of that.

Diana thinks that the one Blor really preferred was Decca. 'Hurry up, Jessica – stop dawdling.' She was a dawdler if ever there was one. 'Put those shoes on, Jessica. Whatever are you doing?' 'I love yer, m'Hinket' (her own name for Blor). Personally, I thought it was Debo. But I believe there was very little in it; she loved us all.

Long after we were grown up she went back to Egham to live with her brother and sister. She died at a great age, nearly ninety.

Useless to pretend that the Nanny in *The Blessing* is not based on Blor. She has all her mannerisms and many of her prejudices, but she is a caricature. When I sent Blor the book I said: 'This is a story about a Nanny very much unlike you, darling.' She wrote back; '. . . I felt quite sorry for the poor Nanny – all that packing!' I have written this about her to try and present her as she really was.

Sunday Times, 1962

The Other Island

Nancy Mitford to Evelyn Waugh April 12, 1952

'Have you ever been to Ireland? It's very pretty. But nothing one didn't know before so not very easy for an article. I can't think of one original thing to say. How can people live in the country?'

Irish reader to Nancy Mitford

'Hell would be a more suitable place for you than Ireland.'

Ireland has changed its name to Eire and its charming people, whose qualities of heart and mind were so cruelly misused for so many centuries, are busily making a nation, but it is still the Emerald Isle of nineteenth-century literature, exaggeratedly itself. I go there every spring to stay with various friends; my spirits rise with my body as the little Aer Lingus plane flaps away from Le Bourget like an owl. It is well named Friend Ship; whereas other airlines are beginning to follow the horrid maxim of BEA 'do not spoil the passengers', the Friend Ship is organized to please. There is a delicious luncheon of hot soup, fresh salmon and hot coffee, after which the passengers settle down to enjoy the soothing headlines of *The Irish Times* and *The Cork Examiner*: 'Dublin Nun Found Dead in Drain', 'Priest Hurt in Collision with Cart', 'Departing Nuncio's Tribute to Ireland'. The new, restless Europe is already far away. The Friend Ship's wings are above the cabin so that one can see out as from a helicopter. England is a jewel wrapped in cotton wool, but over the Irish Channel a blue horizon glimmers and in it lies the dark green velvet land. A cold sun shines on the fields; they are dotted with small houses like the ancestral home of President Kennedy, that white-washed box with two tiny windows which has figured on many a Christmas card. The Irish are naturally proud of this local boy who has made so very good.

146

There is an hour or two to spend in Dublin before catching a train to the south. It is a prim little eighteenth-century town, sometimes compared to Bath, though this is doing it too much honour; and unspoilt. So, come to think of it, are most capital cities in Western Europe – hard to name another that has suffered like our poor London. (How can a rich and civilized race, devoted to its own history, have come to allow such destruction? Once a charming city, London is now a heap of rubbishy jerry buildings. No wonder the young citizens march about and sit down pro-claiming that they do not want it to be defended and have no intention of dying for it.)

A little wait at Dublin station, time enough to write one's name in tin for a penny and weigh oneself for another. The May wind is bitter. Some American women are shivering on a bench, huddled in their plastic cloaks. One of them goes to the refreshment-room in search of hot coffee – comes back and says: 'Don't go in there, it's just dismal.' The train is an omnibus. Four nuns make a quick dash to install themselves by the four front windows, which they open. The wind rushes in; it beats on the plastic garments of the Americans and disturbs their hair-nets; they suffer for a while and then one of them goes forward: 'Pourdon me, could you close the windows?' But the nuns, in their veiling and men's boots are feeling the heat; they observe custody of the eyes and pretend not to have heard. If the temperature totters into the forties the Irish, as it were, reach for their solar topees. There are many farmers in the train who have been to an agricultural show; they, too, are feeling the heat, there are sighs and groans and mopping of brows. They scrape manure off their trousers with knives and talk like an Abbey Theatre play. 'I've had another anonymous letter from Dooley O'Sullivan.' Delicious dinner of bacon and eggs and then we arrive at Limerick Junction. The cold sun is still shining, though it is now half past nine.

The plain of Tipperary is the richest farm land in Western Europe, so fertile that farming there requires little skill; beasts are simply left in the fields until they are fat enough to be sold. It is beautiful beyond words and empty. People leave Eire as they have always left Ireland, at an enormous rate. Every village, however small and poor, has a luggage shop. The plan on which the villages are built, one long, immensely wide street which can be used as a market, bordered by tiny houses, accentuates their

147

emptiness. The admirable roads are bare of traffic – for miles and miles there is nothing except, occasionally, an enormous man spanking along in a donkey cart or a Rolls-Royce with American tourists buried in white satin luggage. The cottagers' dogs are so unused to motor traffic that they crouch and spring dangerously at passing cars. The green deserted fields lying beneath blue deserted mountains; the windowless mills dripping with creepers; the towers for captive princesses inhabited by owl and raven; the endless walls surrounding ghostly demesnes, the lodge gates, rusted up and leading into hay; the roofless churches, with elegant neo-Gothic spires rising out of nettle-beds make a melancholy but enchanted impression. Everywhere are nettles and those black birds, rooks, crows, ravens, jackdaws, which, in France, are indiscriminately known as *corbeaux*.

Historians of England record with surprise that Anglo-Saxons were never known to dwell in Roman villas left vacant by the fall of the Empire and the departure of their owners. The villas were solidly built of stone with such conveniences as central heating and baths, but the natives preferred to live out their short and brutish lives in horrid little wooden or wattle huts. This situation is strangely repeated today in Eire. What was good enough for President Kennedy's ancestors is good enough for the Irish. Within a stone's throw of their cabins there may be a great beautiful house deserted by its owners during the Troubled Times, positively inviting tenants. Why does not the whole village move in – plenty of room for everybody? But it remains empty. Eventually such houses are pronounced unsafe and blown up with gunpowder; sometimes the stones 'go on the roads', but often they lie in great heaps on the beautiful sites (walled or terraced gardens, lakes, avenues, carefully planted arboreta), monuments to the oddity of mankind. The Irish Government is not interested in 'ascendancy architecture' and would exchange any amount of Wyatt houses against one Celtic cross.

Those of the Anglo–Irish who have held on to their places are now happy in them again. An occasional reminder of the civil war, such as machine-gun marks in the nursery passage, framed, with the date, is only the relic of an historical past. If the Irish still hate us they show no signs of it, beyond an understandable gloating when President Kennedy turns the screw. Country house life resembles the French *vie de château* more than the quick weekend dash of the English. As in France, small unfortified country houses are called Castle. Guests move in for a good long stay, with their dogs, children, embroidery and fishing-rods. There is generally an invalid to be tenderly inquired for. 'She was wandering this afternoon and then went into such a very sound sleep that I sent for the doctor. He hopes that next time the chemist won't muddle up the labels.' A couple is invited from another part of Ireland; they reply by telegram: 'Bother arrive by car Tuesday.' 'If it's such a bother –' says the hostess crossly until she realizes that the word should be both.

The houses are beautiful in their provincial way and have such romantic names as Ann's Grove, Dereen, Newtown Anner. They are full of treasures (with the oddest attributions, like *Madame du Barry by Largilliere*) in a hotch potch of rubbish. The china cabinet will contain Rose Pompadour Sèvres cheek by jowl with A Present from Bexhill; old *Tatlers* in a bookshelf are muddled up with Oudry's *Fables de La Fontaine*. All this is a happy hunting-ground for dishonest dealers. The famous Irish plaster work is often coarse and rather ugly, too much like the plaster in which somebody's leg has recovered from a Swiss accident stuck on the wall. French gardening amateurs, who arrived in a bus, annoyed one of my hostesses by exclaiming: *'Comme c'est charmant, tout ce désordre britannique!'*

There is still a feudal flavour about domestic life, for servants abound, and delightful they are. The kitchen teems with scullions and the servants' hall nourishes many more people than actually work in the house. The atmosphere below stairs is jolly; quarrels are rare. Food is of paramount importance and the houses vie with each other to delight the guests. It is rather too rich for me, based on cream. A typical Irish dinner would be: cream flavoured with lobster, cream with bits of veal in it, green peas and cream, cream cheese, cream flavoured with strawberries. I crave skim milk from an English coalmine, but then I have not been on the river all day to sharpen my appetite. Sometimes we lunch, on cold cream, in the fishing-hut. There is a sheaf of telegraph forms hanging up in case somebody feels like having a bet, when a boy on a pony is sent off to the nearest post office.

The village is a splendid shopping centre. It has not yet got a boutique (pronounced bowtike), like Clonmel, but the draper, whose white china horse in the window proclaims him to be a

Protestant, has a range of lovely cotton dresses for 12s. 6d., and I stock up with his nylons for the whole year. Medical Hall keeps French cosmetics and scent. Next door to where it says 'Yoke your Team to a Pierce Machine' there is an exciting new notice: Modern Hairstyling. I ask about it in Medical Hall. Oh yes, there are two young ladies trained in New York and they wash your hair backwards. The young ladies have already lost some of the transatlantic hustle, I note. It is half past eleven when I ring their bell; the receptionist is still in her dressing-gown. However, my hair is beautifully washed and the bill is 6s.

The Troubled Times are wonderfully over, but can never be forgotten. Their history is that of all resistance movements, ruthless and terrible, with internal factions and betrayals that engendered the blackest hatreds.

'Twas the twenty-eighth day of November
Outside of the town of Macroon
The Tans in their big Crossley tender
Were hurtling along to their doom.
The lads in the column were waiting
Their hand grenades primed, on the spot,
And the Irish Republican Army
Made balls of the whole fucking lot.

It seems strange that the kindly, gentle, rather lazy Irish should have been the first to prove that in our modern communities violence always pays. The nation which now comes into being after such revolutionary birth throes has some unexpected features. It is prim like Dublin architecture; it submits to Rome; it is old-fashioned. When *The Irish Times* publishes the titles of current successful novels, including at least one book which has been warmly praised by Catholic writers in other lands, it is not 'for holiday reading'; it is a list of the books banned in Eire on moral grounds. In the same issue a letter from Mr John Moore complains that a novel of his, which *The Irish Times* itself has described as 'unremittingly pleasant' and which has been read out on the English wireless as A Book at Bedtime, is on the list.

The piety of the Irish has often been turned to patriotic ends and still has a nationalistic flavour. To this day there is not much fraternization with Protestants. I asked my hostess what would happen if she asked the priest to dinner. 'If he came,' she said, 'he would very soon be moved to another parish.' A pagan element, too, remains and it is sometimes difficult to know whether saints are being honoured or the Little People. Rags tied to thorn bushes are said to be for the latter, but they look like the ribbons which French peasants tie on the Virgin and the thorn tree surely has a Christian association. I would like to hear more of the Little People, but nobody talks about them very much and they seem to have gone underground. The barrows and prehistoric earthworks still may not be excavated for fear of disturbing them. I asked an old keeper, but he had only seen their pipes – when I looked disappointed he said: 'I saw a sow where never a sow there was,' and that was the nearest I have ever got to them. There is said to be a fairy's shoe in the Dublin museum. It was found in a bog and the fact that it is worn out proves it is not a doll's shoe.

The rulers of Eire want the people to speak Irish. It is taught in the schools as a second language; all official notices and forms are written in it, with an English crib. It is really rather easy, the sort of language one could invent oneself. *Corneal* = corner, *telefon* = telephone, *aerphort* = airport, etc. But parents do not approve of their children being made to waste time learning Irish at *scoil* and there is a good deal of resistance to it. Some Common Market language would certainly be more useful. In fact, Eire does not live with the times. Before the English ascendancy Ireland ignored 'the new restless Europe with its Crusades and Hilde-brandine movements, its stone castles, cathedrals, its feudalism, its charters, its trade routes and all the stir of modernity',[1] and now that the ascendancy is over she turns her back on the atomic age.

It might be easier to foresee the future of Ireland if one knew the inwardness of her past. She has had no Michelet, no Trevelyan, of her own. Perhaps historiography is not an Irish talent; an Englishman might well find the close scrutiny of his own ancestors at their very worst rather depressing. For reasons of space, historians of England can only present this strange people, in its fairy-like island, as John Bull's worrying neighbour; this is not good enough. Some young genius ought now to begin his life's work, a great History of Ireland.

The Water Beetle, 1962

[1]G. M. Trevelyan.

A Bad Time

Nancy Mitford to Evelyn Waugh April 10, 1962

'I have written a long description of Captain Scott's last minutes. (It made me cry twice). I do wonder *why* I have!'

Apsley Cherry Garrard has said that 'polar exploration is at once the cleanest and most isolated way of having a bad time that has yet been devised'.[1] Nobody could deny that he and the twenty-four other members of Captain Scott's expedition to the South Pole had a bad time; in fact, all other bad times, embarked on by men of their own free will, pale before it. Theirs is the last of the great classic explorations; their equipment, though they lived in our century, curiously little different from that used by Captain Cook. Vitamin pills would probably have saved the lives of the Polar party, so would a wireless transmitter; an electric torch have mitigated the misery of the Winter Journey. How many things which we take completely as a matter of course had not yet been invented, such a little time ago! Scott's *Terra Nova* had the advantage over Cook's *Resolution* of steam as well as sail. Even this was a mixed blessing, as it involved much hateful shovelling, while the coal occupied space which could have been put to better account in the little wooden barque (764 tons). Three motor-sledges lashed to the deck seemed marvellously up-to-date and were the pride and joy of Captain Scott.

The *Terra Nova* sailed from London 15th June 1910 and from New Zealand 26th November. She was fearfully overloaded; on deck, as well as the motor-sledges in their huge crates, there were 30 tons of coal in sacks, 2½ tons of petrol in drums, 33 dogs, and 19 ponies. She rode out a bad storm by a miracle. 'Bowers and Campbell were standing upon the bridge and the ship rolled sluggishly over until the lee combings of the main hatch were under the sea . . . as a rule, if a ship goes that far over she goes

[1]Unless otherwise stated, the quotations in this essay are from *The Worst Journey in the World*, by Cherry Garrard.

down.' It took her thirty-eight days to get to McMurdo Sound, by which time the men were in poor shape. They had slept in their clothes, lucky if they got five hours a night, and had had no proper meals. As soon as they dropped anchor they began to unload the ship. This entailed dragging its cargo over ice floes which were in constant danger of being tipped up by killer whales, a very tricky business, specially when it came to moving ponies, motor sledges and a pianola. Then they built the Hut which was henceforward to be their home. Scott, tireless himself, always drove his men hard and these things were accomplished in a fortnight. The *Terra Nova* sailed away; she was to return the following summer, when it was hoped that the Polar party would be back in time to be taken off before the freezing up of the sea forced her to leave again. If not, they would be obliged to spend a second winter on McMurdo Sound. Winter, of course, in those latitudes, happens during our summer months and is perpetual night, as the summer is perpetual day. The stunning beauty of the scenery affected the men deeply. When the sun shone the snow was never white, but brilliant shades of pink, blue and lilac; in winter the aurora borealis flamed across the sky and the summit of Mount Erebus glowed.

The Hut, unlike so much of Scott's equipment, was a total success. It was built on the shore, too near the sea, perhaps, for absolute security in the cruel winter storms, under the active volcano Mount Erebus, called after the ship in which Ross discovered these regions in 1839. It was 50 feet by 25, 9 feet high. The walls had double boarding inside and outside the frames, with layers of quilted seaweed between the boards. The roof had six layers of alternate wood, rubber and seaweed. Though 109 degrees of frost was quite usual, the men never suffered from cold indoors; in fact, with twenty-five of them living there, the cooking range at full blast and a stove at the other end, they sometimes complained of stuffiness.

Life during the first winter was very pleasant. Before turning in for good they had done several gruelling marches, laying stores in depots along the route of the Polar journey; they felt they needed and had earned a rest. Their only complaint was that there were too many lectures; Scott insisted on at least three a week and they seem to have bored the others considerably – except for Ponting's magic lantern slides of Japan. A gramophone and a pianola provided background music and there was a constant flow of witticisms which one assumes to have been unprintable until one learns that Dr Wilson would leave the company if a coarse word were spoken. In the Hut they chiefly lived on flesh of seals, which they killed without difficulty, since these creatures are friendly and trustful by nature. 'A sizzling on the fire and a smell of porridge and seal liver heralded breakfast which was at 8 a.m. in theory and a good deal later in practice.' Supper was at 7. Most were in their bunks by 10 p.m., sometimes with a candle and a book; the acetylene was turned off at 10.30 to economize the fuel. Cherry Garrard tells us that the talk at meals was never dull. Most of these men were from the Royal Navy, and sailors are often droll, entertaining fellows possessing much out-of-the-way information. (Nobody who heard them can have forgotten the performances of Commander Campbell on the BBC – he was one of the greatest stars they ever had, in my view.) Heated arguments would break out on a diversity of subjects, to be settled by recourse to an encyclopedia or an atlas or sometimes a Latin dictionary. They wished they had also brought a *Who's Who*. One of their discussions, which often recurred, concerned 'Why are we here? What is the force that drives us to undergo severe, sometimes ghastly hardships of our own free will?' The reply was The Interests of Science – it is important that man should know the features of the world he lives in, but this was not a complete answer. Once there was a discussion as to whether they would continue to like Polar travel if, by the aid of modern inventions, it became quite easy and comfortable. They said no, with one accord. It seems as if they really wanted to prove to themselves how much they could endure. Their rewards were a deep spiritual satisfaction and relationships between men who had become more than brothers.

Their loyalty to each other was fantastic – there was no jealousy, bickering, bullying or unkindness. Reading between the lines of their diaries and records it is impossible to guess whether anybody disliked anybody else. As for The Owner, as they called Scott, they all worshipped and blindly followed him. Cherry Garrard, the only one who could be called an intellectual and who took a fairly objective view of the others, gives an interesting account of Scott's character: subtle, he says, full of light and shade. No sense of humour – peevish by nature, highly strung, irritable, melancholy and moody. However, such was his strength of mind that he overcame these faults, though he could not entirely conceal long periods of sadness. He was humane, so fond of animals that he refused to take dogs on long journeys, hauling the sledge himself rather than see them suffer. His idealism and intense patriotism shone through all he wrote. Of course, he had the extraordinary charm without which no man can be a leader. In his diaries he appears as an affectionate person, but shyness or the necessary isolation of a sea-captain prevented him from showing this side to the others. He was poor; he worried about provision for his family when it became obvious that he would never return to them. Indeed, he was always hampered by lack of money and never had enough to finance his voyages properly. Lady Kennet, his widow, once told me that Scott only took on Cherry Garrard because he subscribed £2,000 to the expedition. He thought him too young (23), too delicate and too short-sighted, besides being quite inexperienced; he was the only amateur in the party. It is strange and disgraceful that Scott, who was already a world-famous explorer, should have had so little support from the Government for this prestigious voyage.

These men had an enemy, not with them in the Hut but ever present in their minds. His shadow fell across their path before they left New Zealand, when Captain Scott received a telegram dated from Madeira, with the laconic message *Am going South Amundsen*. Now, Amundsen was known to be preparing Nansen's old ship, the *Fram*, for a journey, having announced that he intended to do some further exploring in the Arctic. Only when he was actually at sea did he tell his crew that he was on his way to try and reach the South Pole. There seemed something underhand and unfair about this. Scott's men were furious; they talked of finding the Amundsen party and having it out with them, but Scott put a good face on it and pretended not to mind at all. The two leaders could hardly have been more different. Amundsen was cleverer than Scott, 'an explorer of a markedly intellectual type rather Jewish than Scandinavian'. There was not much humanity or idealism about him, he was a tough, brave professional. He had a sense of humour and his description of flying over the North Pole in a dirigible with General Nobile is very funny indeed. Nobile was for ever in tears and Amundsen on the verge of striking him, the climax coming when, over the Pole,

155

Nobile threw out armfuls of huge Italian flags which caught in the propeller and endangered their lives. All the same, Amundsen died going to the rescue of Nobile in 1928.

No doubt the knowledge that 'the Norskies' were also on their way to the Pole was a nagging worry to Scott all those long, dark, winter months, though he was very careful to hide his feelings and often remarked that Amundsen had a perfect right to go anywhere at any time. 'The Pole is not a race,' he would say. He (Scott) was going in the interests of science and not in order to 'get there first'. But he knew that everybody else would look on it as a race; he was only human, he longed to win it.

The chief of Scott's scientific staff and his greatest friend was Dr Wilson. He was to Scott what Sir Joseph Hooker had been to Ross. (Incredible as it seems, Hooker only died that very year, 1911. Scott knew him well.) Wilson was a doctor of St George's Hospital and a zoologist specializing in vertebrates. He had published a book on whales, penguins and seals and had prepared a report for the Royal Commission on grouse disease. While he was doing this Cherry Garrard met him, at a shooting lodge in Scotland, and became fired with a longing to go south. Wilson was an accomplished water-colourist. Above all, he was an adorable person: 'The finest character I ever met,' said Scott. Now Dr Wilson wanted to bring home the egg of an Emperor Penguin. He had studied these huge creatures when he was with Scott on his first journey to the Antarctic and thought that their embryos would be of paramount biological interest, possibly proving to be the missing link between bird and fish. The Emperors, who weigh 6½ stone, look like sad little men and were often taken by early explorers for human natives of the South Polar regions, are in a low state of evolution (and of spirits). They lay their eggs in the terrible mid-winter, because only thus can their chicks, which develop with a slowness abnormal in birds, be ready to survive the next winter. They never step on shore, even to breed; they live in rookeries on sea-ice. To incubate their eggs, they balance them on their enormous feet and press them against a patch of bare skin on the abdomen protected from the cold by a lappet of skin and feathers. Paternity is the only joy known to these wretched birds and a monstrous instinct for it is implanted in their breasts; male and female hatch out the eggs and nurse the chicks, also on their feet, indiscriminately. When a penguin has to go in the sea to catch his dinner he leaves egg or chick on the ice; there is then a mad scuffle as twenty childless birds rush to adopt it, quite often breaking or killing it in the process. They will nurse a dead chick until it falls to pieces and sit for months on an addled egg or even a stone. All this happens in darkness and about a hundred degrees of frost. I often think the RSPCA ought to do something for the Emperor Penguins.

Dr Wilson had reason to suppose that there was a rookery of Emperors at Cape Crozier, about sixty miles along the coast. When the ghastly winter weather had properly set in he asked for two volunteers to go with him and collect some eggs. It was one of the rules in the Hut that everybody volunteered for everything, so Wilson really chose his own companions: 'Birdie' Bowers, considered by Scott to be the hardest traveller in the world, and Cherry Garrard. The three of them left the light and warmth and good cheer of the Hut to embark upon the most appalling nightmare possible to imagine. The darkness was profound and invariable. (They steered by Jupiter.) The temperature was generally in the region of 90 degrees of frost, unless there was a blizzard, when it would rise as high as 40 degrees of frost, producing other forms of discomfort and the impossibility of moving. The human body exudes a quantity of sweat and moisture, even in the lowest temperatures, so the men's clothes were soon frozen as stiff as boards and they were condemned to remain in the bending position in which they pulled their sleigh. It was as though they were dressed in lead. The surface of the snow was so bad that they had to divide their load and bring it along by relays. They could never take off their huge gloves for fear of losing their hands by frostbite; as it was, their fingers were covered with blisters in which the liquid was always frozen, so that their hands were like bunches of marbles. The difficulty of performing the simplest action with them may be imagined; it sometimes took over an hour to light a match and as much as nine hours to pitch their tent and do the work of the camp. Everything was slow, slow. When they had a discussion it lasted a week. If Cherry Garrard had written his book in a more uninhibited age he would no doubt have told us how they managed about what the Americans call going to the bathroom.[1] As it is, this interesting point remains mysterious. Dr

[1] They [the savages] go to the bathroom in the street.' (Report from a member of the Peace Corps in the Congo.)

Wilson insisted on them spending seven hours out of the twenty-four (day and night in that total blackness were quite arbitrary) in their sleeping-bags. These were always frozen up, so that it took at least an hour to worm their way in and then they suffered the worst of all the tortures. Normally on such journeys the great comfort was sleep. Once in their warm dry sleeping-bags the men went off as if they were drugged and nothing, neither pain nor worry, could keep them awake. But now the cold was too intense for Wilson and Cherry Garrard to close an eye. They lay shivering until they thought their backs would break, enviously listening to the regular snores of Birdie. They had got a spirit lamp – the only bearable moments they knew were when they had just swallowed a hot drink; for a little while it was like a hot-water bottle on their hearts; but the effect soon wore off. Their teeth froze and split to pieces. Their toe-nails came away. Cherry Garrard began to long for death. It never occurred to any of them to go back. The penguin's egg assumed such importance in their minds, as they groped and plodded their four or five miles a day, that the whole future of the human race might have depended on their finding one.

At last, in the bleakest and most dreadful place imaginable, they heard the Emperors calling. To get to the rookery entailed a long, dangerous feat of mountaineering, since it was at the foot of an immense cliff. Dim twilight now glowed for an hour or two at midday, so they were able to see the birds, about a hundred of them, mournfully huddled together, trying to shuffle away from the intruders without losing the eggs from their feet and trumpeting with curious metallic voices. The men took some eggs, got lost on the cliff, were nearly killed several times by falling into crevasses and broke all the eggs but two. That night there was a hurricane and their tent blew away, carried out to sea, no doubt. Now that they faced certain death, life suddenly seemed more attractive. They lay in their sleeping-bags for two days waiting for the wind to abate and pretending to each other that they would manage somehow to get home without a tent, although they knew very well that they must perish. When it was possible to move again Bowers, by a miracle, found the tent. 'We were so thankful we said nothing.' They could hardly remember the journey home – it passed like a dreadful dream, and indeed they often slept while pulling their sleigh. When they arrived, moribund, at the

158

Hut, exactly one month after setting forth, The Owner said: 'Look here, you know, this is the hardest journey that has ever been done.'

I once recounted this story to a hypochondriac friend, who said, horrified, 'But it must have been so *bad* for them.' The extraordinary thing is that it did them no harm. They were quite recovered three months later, in time for the Polar journey, from which, of course, Wilson and Bowers did not return, but which they endured longer than any except Scott himself. Cherry Garrard did most of the Polar journey; he went through the 1914 war, in the trenches much of the time, and lived until 1959.

As for the penguins' eggs, when Cherry Garrard got back to London the first thing he did was to take them to the Natural History Museum. Alas, nobody was very much interested in them. The Chief Custodian, when he received Cherry Garrard after a good long delay, simply put them down on an ink stand and went on talking to a friend. Cherry Garrard asked if he could have a receipt for the egg? 'It's not necessary. It's all right. You needn't wait,' he was told.

The Winter Journey was so appalling that the journey to the Pole, which took place in daylight and in much higher temperatures seemed almost banal by comparison; but it was terribly long (over seven hundred miles each way) and often very hard. Scott left the Hut at 11 p.m. on 1st November. He soon went back, for a book; was undecided what to take, but finally chose a volume of Browning. He was accompanied by a party of about twenty men with two motor-sledges (the third had fallen into the sea while being landed), ponies and dogs. Only four men were to go to the Pole, but they were to be accompanied until the dreaded Beardmore glacier had been climbed. The men in charge of the motors turned back first, the motors having proved a failure. They delayed the party with continual breakdowns and only covered fifty miles. The dogs and their drivers went next. The ponies were shot at the foot of the glacier. The men minded this; they had become attached to the beasts, who had done their best, often in dreadful conditions. So far the journey had taken longer than it should have. The weather was bad for travelling, too warm, the snow too soft; there were constant blizzards. Now they were twelve men, without ponies or dogs, manhauling the sledges. As they laboured up the Beardmore, Scott was choosing the men

159

who would go to the Pole with him. Of course, the disappointment of those who were sent home at this stage was acute; they had done most of the gruelling journey and were not to share in the glory. On 20th December Cherry Garrard wrote: 'This evening has been rather a shock. As I was getting my finesko on to the top of my ski Scott came up to me and said he had rather a blow for me. Of course, I knew what he was going to say, but could hardly grasp that I was going back – tomorrow night . . . Wilson told me it was a toss-up whether Titus [Oates] or I should go on; that being so I think Titus will help him more than I can. I said all I could think of – he seemed so cut up about it, saying "I think somehow it is specially hard on you." I said I hoped I had not disappointed him and he caught hold of me and said "No, no – no", so if that is the case all is well.'

There was still one more party left to be sent back after Cherry Garrard's. Scott said in his diary: 'I dreaded this necessity of choosing, nothing could be more heartrending.' He added: 'We are struggling on, considering all things against odds. The weather is a constant anxiety.' The weather was against them; the winter which succeeded this disappointing summer set in early and was the worst which hardened Arctic travellers had ever experienced.

Scott had always intended to take a party of four to the Pole. He now made the fatal decision to take five. Oates was the last-minute choice; it is thought that Scott felt the Army ought to be represented. So they were: Scott aged 43, Wilson 39, Seaman Evans 37, Bowers 28, and Oates 32. The extra man was *de trop* in every way. There were only four pairs of skis; the tent was too small for five, so that one man was too near the outside and always cold; worst of all, there were now five people to eat rations meant for four. It was an amazing mistake, but it showed that Scott thought he was on a good wicket. The returning parties certainly thought so; it never occurred to them that he would have much difficulty, let alone that his life might be in danger. But they were all more exhausted than they knew and the last two parties only got home by the skin of their teeth, after hair-raising experiences on the Beardmore. Scott still had 150 miles to go.

On 16th January, only a few miles from the Pole, Bowers spied something in the snow – an abandoned sledge. Then they came upon dog tracks. Man Friday's footsteps on the sand were less dramatic. They knew that the enemy had won. 'The Norwegians have forestalled us,' wrote Scott, 'and are first at the Pole . . . All the day dreams must go; it will be a wearisome return'. And he wrote at the Pole itself: 'Great God! This is an awful place!'

Amundsen had left his base on 20th October with three other men, all on skis, and sixty underfed dogs to pull his sleighs. He went over the Axel Herberg glacier, an easier climb than the Beardmore, and reached the Pole on 16th December with no more discomfort than on an ordinary Antarctic journey. His return only took thirty-eight days, by which time he had eaten most of the dogs, beginning with his own favourite. When the whole story was known there was a good deal of feeling in England over these animals. At the Royal Geographical Society's dinner to Amundsen the President, Lord Curzon, infuriated his guest by ending his speech with the words, 'I think we ought to give three cheers for the dogs.'

And now for the long pull home. Evans was dying, of frostbite and concussion from a fall. He never complained, just staggered along, sometimes wandering in his mind. The relief when he died was tremendous, as Scott had been tormented by feeling that perhaps he ought to abandon him, for the sake of the others. When planning the Winter Journey, Wilson had told Cherry Garrard that he was against taking seamen on the toughest ventures – he said they simply would not look after themselves. Indeed, Evans had concealed a wound on his hand which was the beginning of his troubles. A month later, the party was again delayed, by Oates's illness; he was in terrible pain from frostbitten feet. He bravely committed suicide, but too late to save the others. Scott wrote: 'Oates' last thoughts were of his mother, but immediately before he took pride in thinking that his regiment would be pleased at the bold way in which he met his death . . . He was a brave soul. He slept through the night, hoping not to wake; but he woke in the morning, yesterday. It was blowing a blizzard. He said "I am just going outside and may be some time."'

All, now, were ill. Their food was short and the petrol for their spirit lamp, left for them in the depots, had mostly evaporated. The horrible pemmican, with its low vitamin content, which was their staple diet was only bearable when made into a hot stew. Now they were eating it cold, keeping the little fuel they had to make hot cocoa. (This business of the petrol was very hard on the survivors. When on their way home, the returning parties had made use of it, carefully taking much less than they were told was their share. They always felt that Scott, who never realized that it had evaporated, must have blamed them in his heart for the shortage.) Now the weather changed. 'They were in evil case but they would have been all right if the cold had not come down upon them; unexpected, unforetold and fatal. The cold in itself was not so tremendous until you realize that they had been out four months, that they had fought their way up the biggest glacier in the world, in feet of soft snow, that they had spent seven weeks under plateau conditions of rarified air, big winds and low temperatures.' They struggled on and might just have succeeded in getting home if they had had ordinary good luck. But, eleven miles from the depot which would have saved them, a blizzard blew up so that they could not move. It blew for a week, at the end of which there was no more hope. On 29th March Scott wrote: 'My dear Mrs Wilson. If this reaches you, Bill and I will have gone out together. We are very near it now and I should like you to know how splendid he was at the end – everlastingly cheerful and ready to sacrifice himself for others, never a word of blame to me for leading him into this mess. He is suffering, luckily, only minor discomforts.

'His eyes have a comfortable blue look of hope and his mind is peaceful with the satisfaction of his faith, in regarding himself as part of the great scheme of the Almighty. I can do no more to comfort you than to tell you that he died, as he lived, a brave, true man – the best of comrades and staunchest of friends. My whole heart goes out to you in pity.

Yours R. Scott.'

And to Sir James Barrie:
'We are pegging out in a very comfortless spot . . . I am not at all afraid of the end but sad to miss many a humble pleasure which I had planned for the future on our long marches . . . We have had four days of storm in our tent and nowhere's food or fuel. We did intend to finish ourselves when things proved like this but we have decided to die naturally in the track.'

On 19th March Cherry Garrard and the others in the Hut, none of them fit, began to be worried. The *Terra Nova* had duly come back, with longed-for mails and news of the outer world. They had to let her go again, taking those who were really ill. On

27th March Atkinson, the officer in charge, and a seaman went a little way to try and meet the Polar party, but it was a hopeless quest, and they were 100 miles from where Scott was already dead when they turned back. They now prepared for another winter in the Hut, the sadness of which can be imagined. Long, long after they knew all hope was gone they used to think they heard their friends coming in, or saw shadowy forms that seemed to be theirs. They mourned them and missed their company. Scott, Wilson and Bowers had been the most dynamic of them all, while 'Titus' or 'Farmer Hayseed' (Oates) was a dear, good-natured fellow whom everybody loved to tease. The weather was unimaginably awful. It seemed impossible that the Hut could stand up to the tempests which raged outside for weeks on end and the men quite expected that it might collapse at any time. When at last the sun reappeared they set forth to see if they could discover traces of their friends. They hardly expected any results, as they were firmly convinced that the men must have fallen down a crevasse on the Beardmore, a fate they had all escaped by inches at one time or another. Terribly soon, however, they came upon what looked like a cairn; it was, in fact, Scott's tent covered with snow.

'We have found them. To say it has been a ghastly day cannot express it. Bowers and Wilson were sleeping in their bags. Scott had thrown the flaps of his bag open at the end. His left hand was stretched over Wilson, his lifelong friend.' Everything was tidy, their papers and records in perfect order. Atkinson and Cherry Garrard read enough to find out what had happened and packed up the rest of the papers unopened. They built a cairn over the tent, which was left as they found it. Near the place where Oates disappeared they put up a cross with the inscription: 'Hereabouts died a very gallant gentlemen, Captain E. G. Oates of the Inniskilling Dragoons. In March 1912, returning from the Pole, he walked willingly to his death in a blizzard to try and save his comrades, beset by hardship.'

In due course Cherry Garrard and the others were taken off by the *Terra Nova*. When they arrived in New Zealand Atkinson went ashore to send cables to the dead men's wives. 'The Harbour Master came out in the tug with him. "Come down here a minute," said Atkinson to me and "It's made a tremendous impression. I had no idea it would make so much," he said.'

Indeed it had. The present writer well remembers this impression, though only seven at the time.

Amundsen had won the race, but Scott had captured his fellow countrymen's imagination. It is one of our endearing qualities, perhaps unique, that we think no less of a man because he has failed – we even like him better for it. In any case, Amundsen complained that a year later a Norwegian boy at school in England was being taught that Captain Scott discovered the South Pole.

I don't quite know why I have felt the need to write down this well-known story, making myself cry twice, at the inscription on Oates's cross and when Atkinson said, 'It has made a tremendous impression.' Perhaps the bold, bald men who get, smiling, into cupboards, as if they were playing sardines, go a little way (about as far as from London to Manchester) into the air and come out of their cupboards again, a few hours later, smiling more than ever, have put me in mind of other adventurers. It is fifty years to the day, as I write this, that Scott died. Most of the wonderful books which tell of his expedition are out of print now, but they can easily be got at second hand. I would like to feel that I may have induced somebody to read them again.

Books relating to the Polar journey: *Scott's Last Expedition*; Cherry-Garrard: *The Worst Journey in the World*; Priestly: *Antarctic Adventure*; E. R. Evans: *South with Scott*; Amundsen: *My Life as an Explorer*.

The Water Beetle, 1962

The Last to Be Broken on
the Wheel

Voltaire and the Calas Case by Edna Nixon. New
York: The Vanguard Press

In 1761 a French Protestant merchant called on Voltaire at his house near Geneva and told him a story, which may be briefly summarized as follows. A highly respected Protestant citizen of Toulouse, Jean Calas, had been accused of murdering his eldest son, the alleged motive being that the son was about to become a Roman Catholic. In fact young Calas had gone mad and hanged himself. Jean Calas defended himself steadfastly at the trial and displayed great fortitude under torture. Though the truth was apparent to all but the most bigoted, the Toulouse magistrates could not overcome their anti-Protestant prejudices; they condemned Jean Calas to further torture, to be broken on the wheel and then strangled. His fortune was confiscated, his wife and children left destitute.

This sentence was carried out while Voltaire's visitor was in Toulouse. He felt certain there had been a miscarriage of justice.

When Voltaire heard this story in all its dreadful and interesting details he suffered physically from shock. He was unable to sleep, ran a temperature and was ill for several days. He sent for the youngest Calas son and went most carefully into the sequence of events. Then, convinced that Calas had been innocent, he decided to get his sentence reversed and to rehabilitate the unfortunate family.

The conduct of this affair was Voltaire's masterpiece. He possessed excellent cards for the game: he was in correspondence with several members of the French government – the First

Minister, Choiseul, was an old friend of his; he had a legal training, his father had been a lawyer; he was a man of the world and knew how to arouse and maintain the interest of busy people at court. The Toulouse magistrates very naturally used all the tricks of their trade to obstruct Voltaire's efforts and draw out the affair endlessly, hoping that it would finally be forgotten.

Voltaire, however, never let it rest and he kept his friends up to the mark with a constant stream of brilliant letters. They have the enormous merit of being short and in a beautiful handwriting as easy to read as print. At the beginning, the case in all its horror was stated and the recipient of the letter left to form his own judgment. As the affair dragged on, Voltaire kept it constantly before his correspondents, but was careful never to nag, never to bore them. He generally included a joke or brilliant aphorism which he knew would be widely quoted. For example:

'Honour in your noble profession' he said to Mariette, one of the defence lawyers, 'leads sooner or later to fortune.'

'We must make intolerance intolerable but we must respect prejudice.'

'. . . one of those serious people who are amused by little things.'

The jolly, selfish, cynical Parisian, the courtiers at Versailles and King Louis XV were all horrified by the tale and anxious to do what they could to make amends. Mme de Pompadour wrote: 'The King, in the warmth of his heart has suffered from this strange affair and all France cries out for vengeance.'

Mme Calas and her daughters went to Versailles and were made much of by the lords and ladies there; the Queen herself received them. (Voltaire typically suggested that the prettier of the two daughters should be presented to the King.) However, it is a delicate matter for the ruler of a country to interfere with judges. Toulouse had its own powerful *parlement* whose decrees could only be reversed by the *Maîtres des Requêtes* in Paris, a body of forty magistrates whose duty it was to advise the King on legal matters. At last, three years to the day after his death, the verdict on Calas was quashed.

As far as it went this rehabilitation was a triumph for Voltaire. Public opinion had been aroused and the necessity for legal reform acknowledged. Calas was the last Frenchman ever to be broken on the wheel. But the antiquated legal system remained.

The judges were not sued; their *parlement* disobeyed the order to erase the affair from their registers and to inscribe the final judgment. Mme Calas's confiscated fortune was never restored; Louis XV gave her a pension out of his own money. It was another forty years before Napoleon's genius and dictatorial powers gave France a legal code which every citizen could understand. How Voltaire would have loved and hated that great man!

I admire the clear way in which Edna Nixon has expounded this complicated story, but for fantasy and ornament, for psychological interest, for tears and even for laughter it should be read in Voltaire's own inimitable letters.

The New York Times Book Review, April 14, 1963

The Sun King

Louis XIV by Vincent Cronin. Collins.

Nancy Mitford to Jessica Treuhaft Easter Day 1970

'A man is coming to interview me for BBC. One of the questions: Some historians say your history books are really a description of the Mitford family? Answer: Very true. History is always subjective & the books we yawn over are often the descriptions of the home life of some dreary old professors.'

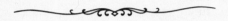

It seems almost impossible to write a satisfactory life of Louis XIV. By far the best account of him is not a biography but the portrait of an age: Voltaire's *Siècle de Louis XIV*. The task is enormous. M. Philippe Erlanger, who is at present engaged on it, tells me that he has written one hundred pages and only arrived at the King's third year. The reign lasted seventy-two years; it was crammed with incident and ornamented by many of the greatest names of our European civilization – an extraordinary galaxy of genius. The King's immediate circle of family and friends were nearly all interesting people about whom a great deal of information is available; not only did many of them write memoirs and letters, but the most talented memorialist of all time lived in their midst.

France was at war during most of the reign, first on the offensive and then on the defensive, and the battles, though conducted according to the rules of chivalry, were bloody. Their outcome was important to the development of modern Europe and the King's foreign policy. The religious problems of an age when people were morbidly interested in theology were inextricably mingled with the political; they have filled many a vast tome; they shook the contemporaries and have retained their fascination to this day. The industrialisation of France was put in train.

The minor arts were brought to perfection. The greatest palace ever seen was built and decorated. From all this material, that which is vital to the author's purpose must be retained and that which seems beside the point must be digested and then cast away.

What is the purpose of the book? Mr Cronin says it is to show the King, surrounded, not by half-forgotten politicians and generals (are Colbert, Louvois, Condé and Turenne forgotten?), but by the men of genius through whom he assured his immortality. Now a biography reveals two characters, that of the hero and that of the author; it can only be a total success when the author has something in his own nature which enables him to understand, to get beneath the skin of the hero. On the evidence of this book, Mr Cronin is good and unworldly – perhaps it takes a more worldly, more cynical mind to get under the skin of Louis XIV and his contemporaries.

I admire his first chapters. His description of the night when Louis XIII was put to bed with his wife after twenty-two years of sterile marriage is a dramatic opening; the attention is captured and held. (He omits the charming story, possibly apocryphal, that as soon as the King and Queen were known to be in bed together the Paris convents were alerted and the nuns prayed all night for a Dauphin.) He gives a masterly account of the Fronde; of Mazarin's last years, death and testament; of the unmasking and arrest of Fouquet.

Then we come to Mlle de La Vallière, blushing to find herself a mistress, a mother, a duchess. Mr Cronin does not approve of adultery, but he sees that, given the Bourbon heredity and the moral standards of the day and with a wife like Marie-Thérèse, it would have been difficult for Louis to avoid committing it. If he must have a mistress, Mr Cronin is all in favour of Louise de La Vallière, whom he finds enchanting. Her large, blue, stupid eyes brimming with tears melt his heart; he would wish the King to keep her for ever. He is against Mme de Montespan. But the King liked clever, amusing people: *'j'aime le gens d'esprit,'* he used to say; he also needed a woman who could help him to entertain the court. It was his misfortune that neither the Queen nor, later on, their German daughter-in-law was the slightest use in the important rôle of hostess. That his own mother had been perfect made him aware of their shortcomings. La Vallière was an excellent

169

rider, but she was provincial and a bore; how could she help the King in his design to make Versailles the hub of the universe?

Mme de Montespan belonged to one of the great French families (much more ancient, she often told the King, than the Bourbons); her two sisters were as beautiful and brilliant as she. The King often slipped into bed with the eldest, Mme de Thianges, and was very fond of the youngest, who, though without any vocation, made an excellent Abbesse of the important Fontevrault. All their relations were good-looking, clever and fashionable; Mme de Thianges used to group them together at parties to show what winners they were. As for Mme de Montespan herself, listen to Mme de Sévigné's description of her after a slimming cure at Bourbon: 'Her looks are amazing, she is half the size she was, but her skin, her eyes and her mouth have not suffered. Her hair, in a thousand curls, was done up with black ribbons; she wore the Maréchale de l'Hôpital's pearl necklace with a clasp and pendants of enormous diamonds – in short a triumphant beauty to dazzle the ambassadors.' The King always liked the ambassadors to be dazzled! Louise de La Vallière could not compete.

Mr Cronin has lost his heroine; he minds. He struggles on and so do we, but the liveliness of the first chapters has gone. Louis conquers Holland, Versailles is finished and decorated, parties are given, quantites of food are eaten, writers write, painters paint, but it all seems rather dull. The men of genius, we note, get less space than the generals and politicians – Pascal about six times less than Condé, Racine half as much as Colbert. Meanwhile, the King, so human and real in the first part of the book, turns into a fatherly barber's block, living for his people. Louis XIV always had a touching side to his character, but surely he became more, not less, tyrannical as the years went on? Mr Cronin is susceptible to his charm and his good manners and turns a blind eye to the sinister undertones – the galleys, the Man in the Iron Mask and Lauzun's dreadful years at Pignerol are not mentioned. He does not say how terrified people were of the King and with what good reason – he could be most kind; he could also be most cruel.

With Mme de Maintenon, Mr Cronin has another heroine to his taste; he can approve of her, the more so that she was wife, not mistress. He greatly over-simplifies her character. It is untrue to

170

say that she did not care about money. She wore no jewels after her marriage to the King (except a cross made of some of the largest diamonds in France), but in her letters to her brother, when he was looking for a wife, she made it quite plain that nothing mattered but the size of the dowry. Nobody can say whether her 'long struggle for the King's soul' was or was not an intrigue to put herself on the steps of the throne, though we can all have our own opinions, but it is certain that she was wordly to the last degree.

She started life by marrying the paralytic Scarron in order to avoid a convent and thereafter lived for society, pleasure and comfort. Considering this, her treatment of the Dames of St Cyr was both cruel and hypocritical. Mr Cronin does not tell how she dragged the charming Mlle de La Maisonfort, half-dead, to the altar and forced her to become a nun. The best thing about Mme de Maintenon was her love of children and even this was turned to her own advantage, since she took the King's fancy through his affection for his children. All the same, it was quite genuine; she probably never loved any man, but with children she was perfect. When they grew up, however, she lost interest in them unless they seemed likely to be useful to her. A light was thrown on her relationship with the King when, on his deathbed, he said he was sorry never to have made her happy – an observation which would reflect badly on any woman.

The subsidiary characters in this book are treated rather too sketchily. Mme des Ursins, for example, at the time when she got the *pour* at Marly, was one of the most important women in the world, a grandee of Spain in her own right, a great friend of the King's. Mr Cronin simply says that she was the wife of an Italian nobleman. It might have been better not to mention the princesse de Conti at all than merely to say she had a cruel, mocking nature. Poor Marie-Anne was an angelic girl, the greatest beauty at the court and as virtuous as such a beauty, widowed at nineteen, was likely to be. Spanheim, the Prussian ambassador, says the reason the atmosphere at Versailles was so decent was because of the Queen's piety, the Dauphine's virtue, Madame's indifference to men and the good behaviour of the lovely princesse de Conti. She was devoted to her mother, Louise de La Vallière, visited her regularly and nursed her on her deathbed. But when she was very young a letter from her to her brother-in-law at the front was intercepted, in a bag with many others, and read by the King. She said she hardly saw anybody but Mme de Maintenon: 'judge what fun that is for me.' Other letters in this bag were even worse and led to many exilings; one courtier said, 'Thank goodness my boy only blasphemed in his – *God forgives*.' Mme de Maintenon never forgave Marie-Anne de Conti.

Mr Cronin comes into his own again when the King is old and sad, implacably, it seems, pursued by the God for whom he thought he had done so much. He writes beautifully about the death. Something went wrong with his book in the middle years, but, as I said earlier, the task is probably insuperable.

Spectator, July 24, 1964

Paris Diary

Michelet thought that the French are divided into Franks and Gauls and nobody who lives here would deny the truth of this theory. The Franks – serious, dour and rather puritanical – build. The Gauls – funny, cynical, clever and frivolous – destroy – they are the revolutionaries and Michelet was on their side. Half one's pleasure in life comes from them, though it is more comfortable to be governed by Franks. At the last Presidential election M. Mitterrand, after voting in the Nièvre, pointed to a nearby hill and said: 'See, that is where Vercingetorix rallied the Gauls!' If ever there was a Gaul it is Mitterrand. Few of my friends seem to have read Michelet's *Histoire de France*, though they can usually recite those famous passages which are used as *dictées* in the schools. Frenchmen often have such serious gaps in their reading because there is no equivalent here of the London Library and books which are out of print are hard to come by. However, the *Histoire de France* is being reprinted at last, in 13 volumes. Meanwhile Barthès' *Michelet par lui-même* (Editions du Seuil) is an excellent appetiser.

Henri de Montherlant, who is seventy, has just brought out a new volume of his notebooks: *Va jouer avec cette poussière*. He says that when he is writing he often pauses for ten minutes searching for *le mot fort*, though he realizes that, out of all the millions of Frenchmen, perhaps 30 will notice that he has got the telling word and in the rest of the world not a single person, since translation kills everything. I disagree about the Frenchmen. If the critics seldom notice whether a book is well or badly written the public does; well written books are those that live. As for translations, they so totally betray the original (even the best of them, even Scott Moncrieff's translation of Proust) that it might really be better to stop publishing them. Then people would learn more languages and publishers would have more room for unknown native writers.

My old servant, Marie, fascinates me with tales of her youth in the Beauce, that fertile plain which surrounds Chartres. She still owns the house there where she was born and which belonged to one of Napoleon's *grognards*, her ancestor. His bronze medal is in the kitchen dresser. Proust's Françoise came from that region and, like her, Marie is characterized by ruthless common sense. I once said 'I'm going to be on television this evening – why don't you go to your niece [who has got a set] and see me?' 'But since I see Madame every day . . .?' I have often thought of writing the memorials of her quiet life, but they would have to be taken down in her own salty language. Now this very thing has been done for a neighbour and exact contemporary of hers, Ephraïm Grenadou. *Paysan Français* (Editions du Seuil) is his life's story as he told it to a young journalist who has gone to live near him: it is a best-seller. Grenadou, the son of a carter and a dressmaker, was born in 1897 at St Loup, the next village to Proust's Illiers. He has never lived anywhere else and is now a prosperous farmer, owning 420 acres. He tells of conditions in the country when he was a boy (vouched for by Marie who was enthralled by the book), of how he survived two wars and the 1931 slump, rising to his present position by his energy, cleverness, interest in modern agricultural methods and constant good luck. He seems to have had a cloudless life. Summing up, he says that a farmer seldom makes much money in cash but he lives like a fighting cock, is his own master and produces happy, healthy children. The opinion polls here say that more than half the French would like to live in the country: this book may well send up the numbers. But Grenadou warns the would-be farmer that only the son and grandson of countrymen can succeed.

M. le Maire is more powerful than an English mayor (for that very reason there is no Mayor of Paris). Once elected, he often keeps the post for life – politics have very little to do with his election. I know a Gaullist who always votes for a communist mayor because he is the only person to understand the vagaries of the village stream. There is an amusing wireless programme every morning on Europe I, *Bonjour M. le Maire*. M. le Maire talks about his town or village, describing its architecture and scenery, enlarging on its historical and literary associations and often ending with the recipe for some local dish. The mayors are eloquent, not to say poetical; the few who have no gift of the gab put up their wives to do the talking, and each manages to present his municipality as the most desirable place on earth – *un petit village plein de félicité*. Their very difficulties evoke bliss. 'Buried as we are in a huge chestnut forest we may soon be cut off from the world as the SNCF threatens to close our line.' 'In our 1,000-year-old village the Beaux-Arts won't allow new buildings.' 'Our streets are too steep and narrow for motor cars and and we have nowhere to put a car park.' 'How to guard our church treasure now that people come from the towns and steal such things?' All this presents *un problème pour M. le Maire*. M. le Curé is apt to be less congenial. He is generally a good man, much poorer than most of his parishioners, but does not put up enough resistance to the dreadful new tendency in the French church towards uglification. Music at weddings, flowers at funerals are discouraged, and so is the use of church ornament. M le Curé himself has shed his *soutane* and dresses *en clergyman*. A church is not a museum, is the cry; people must not be distracted from prayer by looking at works of art or listening to music; the puritanical streak always latent in France has now got the upper hand. Indeed a curious situation has arisen in which M. le Maire is more and more interested in tradition and the arts while M. le Curé is intent upon keeping up with the times.

Bossuet said, too truly, of Versailles: 'This city of the rich will need no enemy to overthrow it – it carries the seeds of its own destruction.' Now a new city of the rich, called Parly 2, is being built within 100 yards of Marie-Antoinette's toy village – vast blocks of luxury flats organized, as Versailles itself was, for communal life (one wonders who will play the part of the king). There are to be swimming-baths, a bridge club, stables for 80 horses, a pool of motor-cars, a *'shopping géant'*, where anything from a large diamond to a tin of sardines can be bought, and a chapel. The specimen drawing-room is furnished in what the Americans call Louis-Louis, complete with chimney-piece. The flats cost between £6,000 and £20,000 each. These machines for modern living are springing up all round Paris and isolate groups of people more and more according to their incomes. I am sure this is a very bad idea. Personally I would rather live in any dear old slum than boxed up with the bourgeoisie in Parly 2.

At the other end of the scale a curious situation has arisen at Meaux. This old town, full of seventeenth-century religious architecture (one can still see the room where Mme Guyon lived while explaining her doctrine to Bossuet), has recently acquired some skyscrapers on its boundaries to be dormitories for Parisian workers. Express trains from the Gare de l'Est take half an hour and have become a cheerful meeting-place for the commuters – they dash in at the last minute, shake hands all round and settle down for a nice chat. Now the planners have had the idea of building factories at Meaux to save people this daily journey. But the workers enjoy the train, *ils y font salon* – it is their drawing-room – they even enjoy the scramble of catching it; they think it would be too dull to walk across the road to their jobs. They go on working in Paris. So the factories at Meaux are staffed by Parisians, who also enjoy the party-like atmosphere of the train.

An English friend who is building some cottages and thinks that the rules about lavatories are too strict asked me to find out what they are here. I went to see my plumber – he couldn't understand what I was getting at for a few minutes, then said brightly: 'Yes, there is a rule – you are not supposed to put a w.c. in a kitchen – but all the houses in the rue de Sèvres have them there!'

New Statesman, July 15, 1966

My Friend Evelyn Waugh

Nancy Mitford to Jessica Treuhaft May 4, 1966

'I'm in despair . . . he was such a close friend & I suppose knew more about me than anybody. I think he was v. miserable in the modern world. It killed Théophile Gautier in 1871 (& may well end by killing me).'

I met Evelyn Waugh in 1928. He had just married my best friend, Evelyn Gardner, (a niece of Lord Carnarvon, who discovered Tutenkhamen's treasures). Evelyn was small and charming to look at, with curly hair and blue eyes that missed nothing. His wife, even smaller than him, looked like a ravishing boy, a page. They seemed a particularly happy couple. Since my parents were in Canada and our house in London closed, I needed a base from which to participate in the frivolities of that year, perhaps the wildest of the interwar years. The Evelyns asked me to move into their small flat in Canonbury Square. Waugh had already published *Decline and Fall*; he was writing *Vile Bodies*. The characters in these books, drawn from life, were if anything less mindless than their real-life counterparts.

The young English upper classes lived a life of total frivolity. The young today seem to me sobriety itself compared to what we were like then. We hardly ever saw the light of day, except at dawn; there was a costume ball every night: the White Party, the Circus Party, the Boat Party, etc. Old-timers still talk about them. Soon the door of my tiny room would no longer shut because of the huge pile of costumes that I had not the courage to pick up. In this mad whirl the two Evelyns' marriage broke up. Caught up in my own affairs, I noticed nothing; I think Waugh, preoccupied with his book, was as surprised as I was.

It was a terrific blow to him. He seemed to change character, he grew serious; became a convert. A few years later he married another young and pretty relation of Carnarvon, Laura Herbert; it was a perfect marriage which produced six children. He continued to observe and chronicle the goings on of his contempories, but more critically and, as it were, from the outside; he was no longer one of those who lived only for fun. As for me, I never saw the other Evelyn again but Evelyn Waugh remained a true and faithful friend. He is one of the people I most loved in the world.

He settled in the country without ever becoming a recluse; he went to London every week where he was a member of White's. He was very fond of a handful of friends and became less and less fond of people he did not know well. Even his close friends were not spared; he criticized everyone fiercely and was a terrible tease, but he set about it in such an amusing way that his teasing was easily forgiven. His genius as a novelist enabled him to see right through people, which could be disconcerting. He was one of the few people today who enjoyed writing and receiving letters.

When his letters are published they will reveal a talent as great as Voltaire's. Indeed, although he detested Voltaire, he was very like him. He had the same goodness hidden beneath the same irascibility. Like Voltaire, Evelyn was an indefatigable worker who enjoyed correcting and rewriting his books that were already in print. His War Trilogy has just been published in one volume. If Waugh does not receive the praise he deserves in France, it is probably because his work is untranslatable.

In the war, as one might expect, he was a hero. He was fearless and asked nothing better than to kill as many foreigners as possible. I think he put all foreigners in the same boat.

Evelyn was not an easy guest. Once when he was in Paris I remember asking him to lunch with Father Couturier. This delightful priest, supposedly too left-wing, did not find favour. Evelyn asked him why Parisian churches had the words *liberté*, *égalité*, *fraternité* written on them. The priest pointed out that they are rather Christian sentiments; Evelyn did not like this answer any more than he liked the priest's comments on the Spanish war. Evelyn pretended to be deaf; when I asked him if he would like to sit nearer the priest so as to hear him better, he replied crossly that he could already hear him only too well.

I think Evelyn's conservative side came from seeing the world from a poetic and romantic point-of-view. The ugliness and mechanization of modern times filled him with terrible sadness. Fiercely patriotic, he believed he was witnessing the decline of his 'unhappy country'. Everyone knows that London, at least from an architectural point-of-view, has become a branch of New York but what is even more depressing is that our country towns have nearly all been gutted and rebuilt in the American manner. All this enraged him, as did modern literature, written in such poor style. But what wounded him most deeply was Vatican II. It was agony for him to listen to the liturgy in dull, flat English. One has the impression that he took refuge against the ugliness of the world in the Catholic church and then, suddenly, was delivered up to his worst enemies. He had slid into a deep depression during these last months; personally, I think he died of a broken heart.

Arts et Loisirs, April, 1966

Garden of Delights

Lucia's Progress and *Mapp and Lucia* by E. F.
Benson, foreword by Michael Mac Liammoir.
Heinemann

At long last, here she is again, the splendid creature, the great, the
wonderful, Lucia. What rejoicing there will be among the
Luciaphils! Those of us who lost her chronicles during the war
and have never, by Clique, by barrow or by theft, been able to
replace them, now find ourselves armed against misfortune once
again; when life becomes too much for us we shall be able to take
refuge in the *giardino segretto*. Messrs Heinemann, in reprinting
Mapp and Lucia and *Lucia's Progress* (and by degrees, one hopes,
the whole saga) have deserved well of all who like to laugh.

Lucia (Mrs Emmeline Lucas) is a forceful lady who lives in the
South of England in two small country towns – that is, when we
meet her first, in the late 'twenties, she is the Queen of Riseholme, but half way through her story (which ends just before the
war) she transfers, presumably so that her creator can pit her
against the formidable Miss Mapp, to Tilling. Tilling, I believe, is
Rye, where E. F. Benson himself lived in the house formerly
occupied by Henry James; this is the very house which Lucia
finally worms out of Miss Mapp.

Lucia's neighbours in both towns are almost all, like herself,
middle-aged people of comfortable means. Their occupations
are housekeeping, at which most of them are skilled (there is a
good deal about food in the books, and lobster à la Riseholme
plays an important part), gardening, golf, bridge and bickering.
None of them could be described as estimable, and they are
certainly not very interesting, yet they are fascinated by each other
and we are fascinated by them.

All this fascination is generated by Lucia; it is what happens with regard to her that counts; she is the centre and the driving force of her little world. As she is a profoundly irritating person, bossy, horribly energetic and pushing, the others groan beneath her yoke and occasionally try to shake it off; but in their heart of hearts they know that it is she who keeps them going and that life without her would be drab indeed.

Mapp and Lucia opens some months after the death of Mr Lucas; Lucia, who has been truly very sad and who has not failed to dramatise her situation, is now longing to emerge from her hermetic widowhood. A suitable occasion for doing so is provided by a forthcoming Elizabethan pageant which was planned by Lucia just before her husband's death. This pageant has fallen into the hands of her most rebellious subject and would-be usurper, Daisy Quantock, who has cast herself in the role of Queen Elizabeth. But everything is going wrong and Daisy is obliged to turn to Lucia for the help and advice – which she is longing to bestow, but of course only if *she* can be Queen Elizabeth.

It soon becomes evident that Daisy hopes that Lucia will run the fête from behind her widow's veil, leaving the limelight to Daisy. She says: 'I was going to suggest that you might take the part of Drake's wife. She comes forward just for a minute and makes her curtsey to me . . .' On hearing these rash words Lucia casts her mourning away; in no time at all Daisy is being Drake's wife and making her curtsey to Lucia. For Lucia always wins and it is a measure of E. F. Benson's talent that we are delighted when she does.

The art of these books lies in their simplicity. The jokes seem quite obvious and are often repeated; we can never have enough of them. In *Lucia in London*, Daisy gets a ouidja board and makes mystical contact with an Egyptian called Abfou. Now Abfou hardly ever says anything but 'Lucia is a Snob,' yet we hang on his lips and are thrilled every time Georgie says, 'I am going to Daisy's, to weedj.' Georgie is the local bachelor who passes for Lucia's lover. Then there is the Italian with which Lucia and Georgie pepper their conversation: '*Tacete un momento, Georgie. Le domestiche.*' It never, never palls. On at least two occasions an Italian turns up and then we learn that Lucia and Georgino mio don't really know the language at all; the second time is as funny as the first.

I must say I reopened these magic books after some thirty years with misgivings; I feared that they would have worn badly and seem dated. Not at all; they are as fresh as paint. The characters are real and therefore timeless; the surprisingly few differences between that pre-war world and its equivalent today only add to the interest. Money of course is one of them – the characters speak of £2,000 as we would of £20,000. At least two people have Rolls-Royces; everybody has *domestiche*. When listening-in begins, Lucia refuses to have a wireless until Olga, a prima donna whom she reveres, owns to having one and listens-in to Cortot on it. None of them ever thinks of going abroad. When Lucia and Georgie want to get away from Riseholme for a little change they take houses at Tilling for the summer; that is what leads to them settling there.

But the chief difference is that, in Lucia's words, 'that horrid thing which Freud calls sex' is utterly ignored. No writer nowadays could allow Georgie to do his embroidery and dye his hair and wear his little cape and sit for hours chatting with Lucia or playing celestial Mozartino, without hinting at Boys in the background. Quaint Irene, in her fisherman's jersey and knickerbockers, would certainly share her house with another lesbian and this word would be used. There are no children in the books – 'Children are so sticky,' says Georgie, 'specially after tea.' After the death of Mr Lucas both Georgie and Lucia are afraid that the other may wish for marriage; the idea gives them both the creeps. However, the years go by and they realize that nothing is farther from the inclination of either than any form of dalliance. Marriage is obviously the thing; Georgie remembers that he is a man and proposes it.

I was a fellow guest, at Highcliffe, with Mr E. F. Benson soon after Lucia had become Mayor of Tilling. We talked of her for hours and he said, 'What must she do now?' Alas, he died in the first year of the war; can we doubt that if he had lived Lucia would have become a General?

Sunday Times, April 23, 1967

Tam & Fritz: Carlyle and
Frederick the Great

Nancy Mitford to Lucy Norton September 11, 1967

'I'm slightly drowned in work. I can't really see how to manage – viz a long essay on Carlyle's Fred the G. I've been pegging away for three weeks & seem to be no further forward. Good for my soul I daresay.'

Nancy Mitford to Sir Hugh Jackson April 30, 1968

'I love Frederick. He is everything I like, brave, funny, no nonsense, marvellous taste, common sense, interested in everything.'

When Carlyle had finished with Cromwell in 1845, he looked about for another hero to worship; his choice fell upon Frederick the Great and the result is one of the oddest biographies ever written. It was published, volume by volume, from 1858 to 1865. The eighteenth century is the time in all history with which Carlyle was the least in sympathy and which he understood the least. 'Once we had a Barbarossa and a world all grandly true.' Unfortunately he found much that was not grandly true of Frederick; much that he would have liked, but was too honest, to ignore, and much that he failed to understand. He loved the King, the soldier, the administrator, the leader of Germans; he disliked the cynical pupil of Voltaire, the composer, the collector and the builder of baroque palaces. For this civilized, un-Barbarossa-like, side of Frederick he blamed, and rightly, the age in which he lived: 'the life-element, the epoch, though Friedrich took it kindly and never complained, was uncongenial to such a man.' Far more uncongenial, in fact, to Thomas Carlyle – besides which, complaining of one's epoch is a modern occupation; eighteenth-century characters never thought of such a thing. Many people nowadays would consider that Frederick, who was born three years before the death of Louis XIV and died six years before the

French Revolution, enjoyed what was, for a healthy member of the ruling classes, the most enviable span of life in the history of our civilization. But to Carlyle the arts of the eighteenth century were vacant oblivion, and its enlightenment eternal night. He can write at length about Augustus the Strong of Saxony, 'gay, eupeptic son of Belial', without mentioning ceramics or the fact that Dresden was one of the most beautiful, most civilized cities in the world. He never once names Watteau, a painter whom Frederick adored, buying anything of his that was on the market, including *l'Enseigne de Gersaint* and one of the two *Embarquements pour Cythère*. Carlyle's attitude to Frederick's artistic, musical and literary activities, when he does not pass them over in silence, is that of an indulgent father whose son is in most ways so satisfactory that he must be allowed a few queer hobbies. On the subject of his really queer hobby, the reader is honestly presented with the evidence and allowed to form his own conclusions – the worst; though Carlyle cannot stifle a few groans in the process.

As for France, the country where the eighteenth century came to its full flowering, ah, well, we know the French! Brave in battle, mischievous in politics. Louis XIV, 'Gallant Old Bankrupt', for whom both Carlyle and Frederick had a soft spot, is no longer on the scene; as for Louis XV and his unfortunate females, better to draw a veil. Belleisle is allowed to exist, and so is Voltaire, though his dreadful faults are exaggerated and his shining virtues minimized. All other Frenchmen are spoken of in a slightly condescending, if not contemptuous, tone. Ignoring the fact that Frederick himself hardly knew German, but wrote and thought and dreamed in French, Carlyle uses the most affected spelling for German names and place names: Prag, Beutelsbacher (for Wittelsbach), Els Sass (Alsace); Kaiser Karl; Teutsch; Preussen and so on; while French place names are spelt in the English way. Frederick, who always signed Féderic, is called Friedrich (rich in peace).

Carlyle was not only at odds with the epoch. His sources were a perpetual irritation to him; loud and vigorous are his complaints. 'Those dim dreary books, unindexed Sybilline farragos.' 'Heavy old printed German rubbish.' 'Books done by pedants and tenebrific persons under the name of men, dwelling not on things but, at endless length, on the outer husks of things.' He made much use of Voltaire's correspondence, with many a justified groan about 'the lazy French editors'; he also approved of the memoirs of Wilhelmina, Frederick's sister. He is fond of quoting, in small print, somebody described as 'a certain author whom we often follow' or 'one recent tourist' or 'my abstruse friend'. We are left to identify 'my abstruse friend' – Carlyle himself – from his style which is unmistakable.

The book begins with the story of Brandenburg – Henry the Fowler, Albert the Bear and so on – which resolves itself into a potted history of the 'Holy Romish Reich'. Carlyle's genius is immediately established; everything is alive and fascinating; he assists the reader's fancy. St Elizabeth, 'meandering about, capricious, melodious, weak . . .' Alfonso, King of Castile and 'Kaiser of the Holy Romish Reich' in the thirteenth century, 'said of the universe it seemed a crank machine – pity the Creator hadn't taken advice'. Comes the Reformation: 'will you obey the heavenly voice or will you not?' Since all world trends were formerly related to religion, just as now everything is seen in terms of economics, the nations who kept the Romish faith went rapidly downhill, while those who obeyed the heavenly voice prospered. In Prussia this prosperity was greatly assisted, after the Edict of Nantes, by some twenty thousand nimble French souls who fled there from the persecutions of the Gallant Old Bankrupt.

The Elector of Brandenburg became a King in 1701, with the title of Frederick I of Prussia. His son and heir, Frederick William, had been dropped by a nurse as a baby; and his nervous system ruined thereby; which Carlyle thinks may have been all to the good, as his crooked back and wish to be beautiful made him ambitious. He married the daughter of George I and their son was Frederick the Great. Frederick William was wonderfully eccentric; Carlyle is very fond of him and, indeed, he is God's gift to a writer, but as a father, even for those days, he was a bit rough. He is now chiefly remembered for his regiment of giants, which Carlyle sees as a poetic conception. His fellow sovereigns often gave him giants as presents – the Tsar sent a hundred men of seven to eight feet high every year; but Frederick William also helped himself, and no giant on the continent was safe from his kidnappers. If the wretched creatures tried to escape, their noses were cut off. Frederick William had a considerable talent for ruling, however, and was not nearly so mad as he looked. Prussia under his government became a highly solvent state with a first-class modern army. He had a collaborator in the Prince of Anhalt-Dessau (the old Dessauer), father of modern tactics, a favourite of Carlyle's and one of the chief characters in his book. In early life the Dessauer fell in love with an apothecary's daughter; murdered her fiancé ('one always tries to hope not'); married her and lived happily with her for about sixty years. He was a nephew of William of Orange – went to all his wars and most of Prince Eugene's. 'Not much of a reader, though he knows French; has a big horse-laugh in him where there is a fop to be roasted or the like.' Old Dessauer was much the most civilized of Frederick William's associates; even Carlyle is obliged to admit that the others were 'grim, hirsute, hyperborean figures, growling in guttural Teutsch what little of articulate meaning they had'.

The Crown Prince who was born into this still medieval court, really a glorified barracks, was not only a political and military genius but also a man of letters, artistic, witty, musical, cynical, agnostic and amoral. The life element took hold of him; and, whatever Carlyle may say, he swam with, and not against, the tide. As always in those days, his early childhood passed unnoticed, though Carlyle is quite embarrassing on the subject of the Princikin, beautifulest, hopefulest of little drummers, baby Colonel of a regiment of babes. It is worthy of note that he had a French nurse and a French tutor, before he was handed over to a German general; and that the sergeant of his regiment of small boys was an expert flautist. To begin with, Frederick William loved his little Fritz; he always took him on army manoeuvres and was proud of him. But, by degrees, the morning clouded over. Frederick preferred chatting with his mother and sisters to drilling his contemporaries; he did not care for hunting – would escape from sow-baiting to play his flute in woodland glades; he affected French modes and combed his hair like a cockatoo until his father had it shaved off; he wanted to learn Latin. 'I'll Golden Bull you!' Frederick William had caught Frederick and his tutor at work with Latin books – whack, whack, whack. But worst of all, the bright young soul began to consort with 'Lieutenants Katte and Keith [no relation of the Lord Marischal] and others of their stamp who led him on ways not pleasant to his father nor comformable to the laws of the universe.' He and his favourite sister, Wilhelmina, were both in love with the fascinating Katte. His father began to hate him, with the not unusual hatred of

186

Kings for their heirs, as a Francophile and as a homosexual. *'Tu es né faux et trompeur.'*

Frederick's mother had a long-cherished scheme whereby he should marry her niece, Princess Amelia of England, and Wilhelmina the Prince of Wales. The pros, the cons and the negotiations with regard to this double marriage take up nearly a volume of the *Life of Friedrich*. At one moment, Wilhelmina's affair seemed settled; and Queen Sophia Dorothea began calling her 'my dear Princess of Wales' and her lady in waiting 'Milady'. But Frederick William did not wish for an English marriage for Frederick; he was anxious to maintain his ties with the Empire; he suspected that England wanted to meddle more and more in European affairs, and thought that a rich English princess in Prussia would be well placed to use bribery to this end. He had no objection to Wilhelmina marrying the Prince of Wales; but George II, hoping to draw Prussia away from the Empire, said there must be both marriages or neither.

While the negotiations were going on in 1730, Frederick William made Frederick's life a misery. He knocked him about, roared at him; 'burst out at him like the Irish rebellion' for dropping a fork at dinner, and humiliated him in every way. Frederick began to think of escaping. He wrote to various German princes and to George II, begging for help; but they all said he must be patient, or he would find himself in a dangerous situation. Frederick's mind was made up, however; unfortunately he planned his flight with such ineptitude that the plot soon came out; he was caught in the act and so was his accomplice, Katte. Frederick William was only just stopped by the courtiers from running him through there and then. He half killed Princess Wilhelmina, shrieking at her that she had had a baby with Katte – she and Milady were shut up together for months and starved. Frederick and Katte lay in dungeons awaiting court-martial as deserters from the Prussian army. The double marriages were definitely cancelled; and there was a purge of all Frederick's friends at Court.

At the court-martial Katte was given a prison sentence, and Frederick condemned to death. Frederick William then ordered that Katte should be shot under the eyes of Frederick. Frederick's gaolers, who were all on his side, spared him the sight of the execution, but allowed his friend to say goodbye on his way to the firing squad. *'Pardonnez-moi, mon cher Katte.'* Katte, beaming all over, replied: *'la mort est douce pour un si aimable Prince.'* Frederick's turn seemed at hand. But the German Princes all begged Frederick William to show clemency, pointing out that his son was a Prince of the Empire as well as a Prussian colonel; the Emperor Charles VI wrote a letter in his own hand; and it was probably this that saved Frederick's life. He was kept under strict arrest for a year. In August 1731, Frederick William went to see him, saying sarcastically that, of course, he was only a rough German with no French wit. At the end of a long interview, Frederick was forgiven and kissed his father's feet: 'linen gaiters, not Day and Martin shoes.' Wilhelmina was set free, dusted down, given a few square meals and affianced to the Margrave of Bayreuth, a far more agreeable *parti* than poor English Fred. Frederick took his rightful place at Court for the wedding festivities, and everything returned to normal.

The upshot was that from now on Frederick and his father were on the best of terms. Frederick became perfectly dutiful. He longed to do the Grand Tour before settling down; he had always said he would rather be made *cocu* by an amusing wife than driven mad by a blockhead; nevertheless, he accepted an immediate marriage with an 'insipid Brunswick specimen' without raising any objections. The advantage was that he now had his own establishment. He was given a charming country house called Reinsberg where he and his wife 'kindled the sacred hearth'. (Carlyle knew perfectly well that they never slept together and that, in fact, Frederick was kindling other things, less sacred, with Chazot, the French deserter, Keyserling and the like.) In later life, both Frederick and his neglected specimen said that the nine years they spent at Reinsberg were the happiest they ever knew. He was at last able to lead a civilized existence, to surround himself with clever people and good talkers, mostly French refugees; the best of a rather poor lot was his librarian, Jordan. He did not quite dare to import real Frenchmen from Paris for fear of annoying his father; but in 1736 he wrote to Voltaire, and their famous relationship began in a series of mutually flattering letters. Indeed, there was not much to do at Reinsberg but to write and receive letters – those of Frederick to his father are very lively and funny.

In 1738 two members of what would now be called café society visited Frederick on their way from Russia. They were an older and a younger man. Lord Baltimore, aged thirty-eight, was in the household of the Prince of Wales, scandalously debauched (according to Lord Lyttelton who met him at Lunéville), frequenter of foreign courts; and with finances not in too good a state. His friend was the young Venetian Algarotti, the same age as Frederick, handsome, brilliant and seductive, with the Italian polish that operates so powerfully on Northerners: Algarotti was an intellectual; he wrote many books on philosophical subjects; Carlyle sees him as 'one of those half remembered men whose books seem to claim a reading and do not repay it when given . . .'. But he had 'a high style of breeding about him'; his tact and his discretion never failed. We should all have liked Algarotti. These were the first fashionable cosmopolitans to come Frederick's way; and he was entranced by them – especially, at first, by Baltimore. Then he and his sister both fell in love with Algarotti; provincial young Germans, they may have been easy game; but so did some of the most sophisticated people in Europe: Voltaire, Mme du Châtelet, Lord Hervey, Lady Mary Wortley Montagu. Algarotti and Frederick remained life-long friends; and, when he died, Frederick erected a tomb to him in the Campo Santo at Pisa.

In 1740 the happy, easy, dull life at Reinsberg came to an end. Frederick William, half senile at the age of fifty-one, lay dying. There were some touching scenes. The parson urged him to forgive his enemies, and he agreed; he would forgive George II whom he had always loathed, and who had been most disagreeable over the kidnapping of a few Hanoverian giants. He sat at his window while his horses were trotted out into the courtyard below, and told the Dessauer to choose one. Blinded by tears, Dessauer chose at random. 'But that's the very worst – you must have this one.' 'No Baresack of them, nor Odin's self, I think,' says Carlyle, 'was of truer human stuff.' Frederick was now of the same opinion. He considered that his upbringing had been perfect in every respect – as indeed in our heart of hearts we all do, since it has produced such splendid characters.

Frederick the Great began his reign with many a liberal reform, of which Voltaire approved more than Carlyle did. He abolishes torture: 'to applause in which we must join, though the *per contra* becoming visible to us, with less enthusiasm than formerly'. He institutes freedom of the press, his subjects to say what they like while he does what he likes. 'Will not answer very long among sane human creatures and indeed becomes impossible amazingly soon.' He resuscitates the Berlin Academy of Science to be presided over by Maupertuis – nobody could disapprove of that, or of putting a thousand indigent old ladies to spin in warm rooms, or of the disbanding of the giants; though they got no golden handshake, and the roads of Europe were soon covered with starving half-wits, trying to find their way home. Frederick's first meeting with Voltaire, in July 1751, was a success; it did not last long enough for disillusionment to set in, though it was rather spoilt by coinciding with one of Frederick's attacks of quartan ague from which he had suffered for years and which seemed incurable.

It was soon cured for good by the death of 'Kaiser Karl VI', who had saved Frederick's life at the time of his escape. He died happy in the knowledge that all interested parties had signed the Pragmatic Sanction which secured his daughter's succession to the Habsburg lands. Maria Theresa could hardly have lost her father at a more propitious time, since England and Spain were fully occupied with the war of Jenkins' Ear and all the other nations wanted peace. All except Frederick. Like a naughty boy who suddenly finds himself in possession of a weapon – Frederick William's army – he could not resist using it. Never hypocritical, he frankly admitted this, adding that he wanted to make people talk about him. Fame was the spur. Troop movements began in Prussia. When Uncle George's Ambassador, Dickens, ventured to ask what this meant, he was told to mind his own business. 'I find it is your notion in England to bring other sovereigns under your tutorage and lead them about.' On December 3rd, 1740, Frederick gave a masked ball and, having cooked up an ancient Prussian claim to fine, fertile, beautiful Austrian province of Silesia, he moved into it at the head of his army the next day.

There was paralysis in Vienna; the least paralyzed person there being 'High Maria', aged twenty-three and pregnant. In Silesia itself a few local governors put up as much resistance as they could, which was feeble, while the population, mostly Protestant, was quite pleased to see the Prussians. In a very short time, Frederick was in possession. He then proposed to Maria Theresa that he would ensure the election of her husband, Francis of Lorraine, to the Imperial throne and lend him a much needed

190

sum of money, in return for the cession to Prussia of Silesia. 'High Maria' furiously refused to consider any such deal; the result, says Carlyle, as if the whole thing had been her fault, was twenty years of bitter fighting, an agony to her and all the world. He adds: 'if, instead of the Pragmatic Sanction, with eleven potentates guaranteeing, Maria Theresa had at this time 100,000 soldiers and full treasury (as Prince Eugene used to advise the late Kaiser), how different it would have been with her.'

Frederick had hitherto seen little active service – only one or two minor campaigns with old Prince Eugene; but in April 1741 the Austrians sent an army to Silesia, and battle was joined at Mollwitz on the 10th. Frederick was nervous beforehand; he thought of death and wrote recommending to his brother the two people he loved the most: Keyserling and Jordan. At midday, the battle seemed to be lost and he fled the field. (Voltaire used to say that the only living creature to whom Frederick ever felt grateful was the horse that bore him from Mollwitz.) When finally, looking uncommonly foolish, he turned up again, he found that his army was victorious. The whole of Europe now enjoyed a good laugh, not only over the antics of war-like Frederick but over those of the President of his Academy, Maupertuis, whom he had taken campaigning to provide interesting conversation. This large, pompous man was chased up a tree by the Austrians, who dragged him out of it, undressed him and stole his clothes. Mollwitz was really Frederick William's battle, won by his officers with the tactics he would have employed. Frederick's own style was quite different; his physical courage was never again put in question.

The next country to turn against Austria was France. When the French had annexed Lorraine, and married its Duke to Maria Theresa, they had promised her father to respect the Pragmatic Sanction. Good, pacific Cardinal Fleury, who used to say that, since France had all the territory she wanted, she ought to watch the hunt go by without joining in, was now nearly ninety. Louis XV began to take the advice of Maréchal de Belleisle, the grandson of Fouquet: 'there are in this man the biggest projects any French head has carried since Louis XIV' – projects, in fact, for France to take the place of Austria in Europe. Louis XV recognized Maria Theresa as Queen of Hungary only; while Belleisle went round the German courts to arrange for the election of Charles Albert of Bavaria, a colourless figure who, had there been no Pragmatic Sanction, bore the best claim to the Empire. In a very short time, largely owing to Belleisle's power of persuasion, 'High Maria' was deserted by ten of the twelve countries who had sworn to support her; only Britain and Holland keeping their word. Carlyle, while fully approving Frederick's invasion of Silesia, blames the French for its consequences. He says it was Maria Theresa's plain duty to relinquish the province without any more fuss, and to make friends with Frederick; between them, they would soon have accounted for the French. As it was, Frederick and Louis XV formed an alliance against the Austrians, the British and the Dutch. Carlyle says it was at this point that Frederick got a bad press in England, from which his name has never recovered. 'Cause of liberty, one is amazed to find it means support of the House of Austria!' On April 24th, 1742, Charles Albert of Bavaria was elected Holy Roman Emperor.

Frederick now began to double-cross everybody; Carlyle observing that he was quite right not to be 'superstitiously veracious'. Having lured a French army into the Empire, he signed a secret protocol with the Austrians by which he and they were to pretend to go on fighting for the present until they could come to an agreement over Silesia. He gave away the French positions to the Austrians. In this clever way, Frederick took Neisse with a sham siege ('sublime playhouse thunder') and kept it ever after. Then he tore up the protocol, on the grounds that its clauses were the gossip of the London clubs and began the war again in good earnest. Frederick and the French were joined by the Saxons under Maurice de Saxe and his two half-brothers, all sons of 'the Saxon Man of Sin', Augustus the Strong. 'There, with his black arched eyebrows and black, swift, physically smiling eyes stands Mgr le Comte, one of the strongest bodied and most dissolute-minded men now living on our planet.' He made himself at home in various noblemen's houses and saw but little fighting; while the French, whose hearts were not in this war so far from home, did poorly under the incompetent Broglie.

On May 17th, 1742, Frederick at last had the chance to prove that he was a first-class general and a fearless soldier. In clouds of dust he won the battle of Chotusitz, some sixty miles east of Prague, against Maria Theresa's husband and brother-in-law, Francis and Charles of Lorraine. George II then persuaded her to sign the Peace of Breslau, which gave Silesia to Frederick. As soon as this was concluded, Frederick abandoned his French allies, who were being besieged in Prague, and went home. Voltaire now addressed his friend as Frederick the Great. The following December, while he was gaily opening an opera house at Berlin, Belleisle was forced to retreat from Prague. Of the three famous winter retreats of modern history – the other two being the Swedes from Norway after the death of Charles XII and Napoleon's from Moscow – Belleisle's was the only one in which the troops came away in perfect order with all their cannon.

During the next year or two, the Austrians were fairly successful against the French. Valori, French Ambassador to Prussia and one of Frederick's closest friends, said: 'very little cheers up the Austrians and nothing can crush them completely.' (Louis XIV used to say: 'It's not Leopold I fear but his miracles'.) In 1744 Frederick broke his treaty with Maria Theresa, whose army was safely in the West, and marched on Prague. Carlyle explains that he was upholding the true and legally elected Emperor, the Queen of Hungary's sovereign head whom she was flouting. The English newspapers, already furious with Frederick, saw the Cause of Liberty in danger again, and cried out that he was perfidious, capricious and a public menace. He was not as successful as usual, however. The Czech patriots, who loathed the heretical Prussians, took to guerilla warfare: 'an unspeakable, contemptible grief to an earnest leader of men'. In 1745 the muddled situation was clarified by the death of the Emperor Charles Albert. Frederick cleared the Austrians out of Silesia for good; the French won the battle of Fontenoy against the English; Maria Theresa's husband was elected Emperor at last; and on Christmas Day the Austrians and the Prussians signed the Peace of Dresden, which lasted for ten years.

The first five years of Frederick's reign had been taken up with warfare; he looked forward to the fruits of peace. He proved an excellent administrator. He reformed the laws, an achievement of which he was proud, and applied himself to the improvement of shipping, agriculture and trade. He was the 'reverse of a free trader and had never heard of unlimited competition, fair start and perfervid race by all the world towards the cheap and nasty'. His relaxations were building, collecting pictures; composing, playing and listening to music; and talk. He had a concert and a dinner party, consisting of men only, every day; there is no doubt that he himself was a brilliant conversationalist; Voltaire said so, as in later years did the prince de Ligne. Valori, who knew him intimately, said it was impossible to be more fascinating, but added that, as soon as somebody was under his spell, he was inclined to regard him as a slave, and to neglect or tease him.

'Well, Sire, your old Danae, poor malingering old wretch, is coming to her Jove.' In other words, Voltaire was on his way to Berlin in August 1750. *'Ici je suis sûr d'un sort à jamais tranquil'*, he wrote to Richelieu, and for a while everything seemed perfect. He sparkled at the dinners; the Royal family made a pet of him; he played chess with Frederick's brothers and kept them out of mischief. 'Ten years of a great King's life, ten busy years too; and nothing in them of main significance but a crash of author's quarrels and the crowning visit of Voltaire.' This crowning visit cannot be summarized; it must be given at length in all its details; and nobody has done this better than Carlyle. Of course, he takes Frederick's part; indeed, there is nothing to be said for Voltaire in his dealings with the Jew Hirsch – they were dishonest and clumsy, showed a total lack of knowledge of the world and culminated in the supreme idiocy of expecting that Frederick would order the judge to find against Hirsch. On the other hand, Voltaire's behaviour to his old friend Maupertuis, whom he tortured and goaded, probably hastening his end, was Frederick's fault. He set the two men at each other, like two fighting cocks, for his own amusement. If Voltaire was out of sorts and Maupertuis did most of the talking, Frederick would pretend to be utterly entranced, so that Voltaire would go to bed in a frenzy of jangled nerves. Very odd that he, himself the head tease of the universe, should not have seen Frederick's game; but he never failed to rise. The *sort à jamais tranquil* lasted almost exactly three years, counting the last dreadful weeks at Frankfurt. 'Poor Voltaire after all, lean, of no health, but melodious extremely (in a shallow way) and truly very lonely, old and weak. What an end to visit fifth; began in Olympus, terminates in the lock-up.' Danae and Jove never met again, though in 1757 they resumed their correspondence, which only ended with Voltaire's death. At first Frederick was bored without Voltaire, but soon he had other things on his hands.

'High Maria' had never ceased to mourn over Silesia, and was determined to take back the province sooner or later. Furthermore, she and her fellow rulers regarded the new Prussia with no good eye; they had noted Frederick's tortuous methods in diplomacy, his shameless treachery as an ally and his genius for war; they saw that he now had a full treasury and a first-class army, and they dreaded his next move. According to Carlyle, Frederick only wanted to live in peace. But the upsurge of Prussia had altered the European balance, and caused the *Renversement des Alliances* by which France and the Empire made up their age-old quarrel and were joined by the Tsarina Elizabeth, 'mainly a mass of esurient oil', Augustus of Saxony, King of Poland, and the Swedes. The Maritime Powers joined forces with Frederick – in other words, the British subsidized him while consolidating their Empire overseas. Seeing himself encircled, Frederick decided to attack and on September 9th, 1756, he marched into Dresden.

The Seven Years War is the most interesting period of Frederick's life – had it never taken place he would chiefly be remembered, like so many of his contemporaries, for his sparring matches with Voltaire. Carlyle devotes two of his eight volumes to the war; he visited all the battlefields and thoroughly understood the campaigns and battles. For many years, German students of military history used his *Frederick the Great* as a text book. Frederick stood at bay against the whole of Europe, assailed on every frontier by huge armies; it still seems incredible that he and his small country could have held fast for seven years. On his side he had his own military genius; several excellent generals; a unified command and the fact that he was fighting from his own base – Dresden much of the time, where Augustus III's picture gallery was a comfort to him; though Carlyle never mentions that. He was responsible to nobody; childless, ready at any moment to commit suicide, he could and did take enormous gambles. Sometimes it seemed as if he must be utterly defeated; but he always managed to recover and fight again. When he lost the battle of Hochkirch he quoted Racine: *Je suis vaincu; Pompée a saisi l'avantage* and went off to deliver Neisse. The sufferings of his people were appalling, especially from the Russian occupation; but they never wavered. In 1762 he was at his last gasp, 'the inflexible heart of him like to break', when the situation was suddenly changed by the death of the Tsarina Elizabeth. Peter III, whose hero Frederick was, immediately withdrew from the war. Frederick's other enemies had had enough; except for Maria Theresa, they had really forgotten what it was all about; none had distinguished himself. On February 10th, 1763, the Peace of Hubertsburg was signed on a basis of *status quo ante*. 'High Maria' had lost Silesia for good; German nationalism was born and, with it, the German culture of the nineteenth century and the German wars of the twentieth. Europe was radically changed from now on.

Carlyle finds the first partition of Poland in 1771 a wearisome subject and prefers not to linger on it, merely remarking that 'deliverance from anarchy, pestilence, famine and pigs eating your dead body was a manifest advantage for Poland and the one way of saving Europe from war'. But 'High Maria', old, and over-ruled in this matter, saw it in a different light. '*Placet*, since so many great and learned men will have it so; but long after I am dead it will be known what this violating of all that was hitherto held sacred and just will give rise to.'

So the King came to old age. Most of his great friends were dead; but he still liked to see clever young foreigners, especially Frenchmen, and their accounts of him show that the charm was as irresistible as ever, while he seems considerably to have mellowed. One feels he would not have teased Voltaire so cruelly if they had met later in life. Always an excellent ruler, he was now the idol of his people.

Nothing more of world interest was to happen until the French Revolution. Carlyle remarks how odd it was that neither Voltaire nor Frederick saw any danger signals in France, though 'Voltaire stood at last only fifteen years from the Fact and Friedrich lived almost to see the Fact beginning'. Indeed, in 1786, Paris was buzzing with gossip about the diamond necklace when a pouring wet day at army manoeuvres brought on a fever that killed Frederick the Great. His last words were to tell his servants to throw a quilt over his dog, which was trembling with cold. 'Adieu good readers; bad also, adieu.'

It must be said that one puts down this extraordinary book having become very fond of Frederick; but perhaps in spite, rather than because of Thomas Carlyle.

History Today, January 1968

Views

Rip van Winkle was away for twenty years; when he returned he found that he was no longer governed by Good King George III but was an American subject; the world had completely changed and his friends were all gone. I have been away twenty-three years; when I return I am no longer governed by Good King George VI; I realize that I am an American subject and that the world has completely changed; but my friends are all prominent. Admittedly some are only prominent as failures or traitors, but very few have sunk into oblivion. My generation, which got off to such a poor start in the Twenties, has finished quite honourably. Who would ever have suspected it? Certainly not the grown-ups, who loathed our short skirts, painted faces, drugging friends, wild parties and general bloody-mindedness. I well remember my father turning a now respected old Tory squire out of the house for saying that, in his view, Nurse Cavell was a spy. Our contempt for anybody over 30 and for their heroes knew no bounds; our laughter crackled like thorns beneath the pot at the mere thought of such fashionable writers as Kipling, Masefield, Galsworthy and Barrie; in the world of art our favourite butt was Munnings. Had we known that posterity was to crown him with thousands of guineas in the sale-room we would have been suprised indeed.

The vernacular has changed considerably during the last twenty-three years. One might suppose that this is due to a desire to commune even more deeply with our overlords but, although I am not very conversant with American, it seems to me that there is a certain native wildness about the changes and that they do not all come from the West. Pronunciation has always varied from one generation to another and the Victorians talked differently from us. For instance, they often put an 'i' before 'a'. 'He is not a miarrying mian, I believe?' was a phrase pregnant with meaning in the days before one called a spade a spade. On the whole, people of my age pronounce words as the Oxford Dictionary suggests. The speech of the present generation is very fanciful; neither spelling nor tradition is taken into account. 'Dad' and 'dud' are pronounced the same (and are no doubt considered to be so). 'He is mud, bud and dangerous to know.' 'Pretty' and 'poetry' have changed for the second time in my life; my parents said 'prooey' and 'poytry'; we said them as they are spelt, and now I hear 'prettee' and 'poetree'. Other innovations I notice are: 'cabinut', 'officers' for 'offices', 'lornch' for 'launch', 'INcrease', 'West-MINster', 'hostESS', 'actOR',. 'Azian' for 'Asiatic' sounds odd, and I notice that Sir Alec Douglas-Home still says 'Asiatic' and also 'Kenya' instead of the fashionable 'Kennya'. Most of the BBC announcers use the new pronunciations, but they sound like Englishmen and their voices bear no relationship to the gargling and gurgling of the Voice of America. Mr Alvarly Dell (this is how I always thought it was spelt until I received my galleys from the editor) speaks English as I have been used to hearing it.

If pronunciation does not matter very much, words used in a wrong context and faults of syntax do. G. M. Young used to say, let the English language take care of itself, by which I think he meant: don't fuss, the easy, simple way of saying something is the right way. Too often one hears people on the wireless beginning an elaborate sentence – they flounder about for a bit and then break off with: 'you know'. There is too much fuss and too much overemphasis. 'Nobody has a good word for the PM' is blown up into 'The PM is undergoing character assassination'; 'nowadays' is 'this day and age'; people don't say any more, they claim; a book is a book – length work. 'This' has a horrid new role; it is nearly always used instead of 'that' and often instead of 'it' or 'so'. It creeps in everywhere, giving our language a curious hissing sound; it also serves the cause of overemphasis: 'This I believe to be true' instead of 'I think so.' What is that little word 'up' up to? People don't meet, they meet up; they also think up, cook up, read up. 'Personal' is another intruder: 'Mr Wilson's personal dog', 'I wrote him a personal letter,' 'Liz Burton's personal friend'. 'In fact' has its uses but not as a prelude to every sentence, and I can't see that 'well now' adds very much: 'Well now, we have with us in the studio . . .' 'Contact' – an undergraduate wrote to the head of his college: 'I have arrived in Oxford and been advised to contact you.' Reply: 'You may have arrived but the verb *to contact* has not.' By the way, why are undergraduates always called students? To me a student is somebody in a Russian play or a revolting foreigner, not a young Englishman up at Oxford. Mr Roy Jenkins speaks attractive English and I was sorry to hear him saying 'we don't have' for 'we haven't got'. I first heard this usage about ten years ago at Manchester airport: 'We don't have *The Times*.' In any case it doesn't mean the same thing: 'We don't have *The Times*, it's so horrid about Aunt Sally.' The girl at Manchester meant *The Times* was sold out.

The 'basic' mentality is a real danger to our language. For some reason, Sir Winston Churchill took an interest in basic English and he once asked the late Duke of Devonshire to help him to popularize it. The Duke said: 'What is "to hell with the Pope" in basic?' They looked in the glossary: 'The Holy Father must go to a hot spot.' The Duke said that was not good enough. Of course it's not good enough, but basic is spreading like a spot of oil. No word not in current kindergarten use may be introduced into the dialogue of a film. When working on a script I once wrote 'ineluctable'; I was told to take it out at once as nobody would know what it meant. I protested that people are educated now – we know they are – the papers are full of schools, their buildings, their milk, their levels and their leaving age; if the scholars don't know what 'ineluctable' means, I said furiously, they can go home and look in a dictionary. Nobody listened to me. The Bible and Prayer Book used not to be too difficult or too immodest for Scotch shepherds or maiden ladies or workers who left school, if they ever went to one, at the age of ten, but now these great English classics must be watered down and bowdlerized for the educated men and women of today who are supposed not to know what a wilderness is and to be embarrassed at the idea of worshipping with their bodies. It is all great nonsense. So far the basic-mongers have left Shakespeare alone, and yet people flock to his plays. If they do not understand every single word, who cares?

A young man said to me: 'I am twenty-five; in the olden times one was famous at twenty-five.' I said: 'Yes, but in the olden times there were only about ten people, so of course they were all famous.' I think young men of parts suffer very much from a feeling that they are like ants on an ant-heap in a forest full of ant-heaps. They have to compete with countless other men, from all over the world; the younger generation knocks louder and sooner than ever before. How many individuals can hope to make their mark? Everybody who delves into eighteenth-century letters knows the name of M. de Gisors. Now Gisors was good and virtuous, charmingly conversable, a first-class officer. He was full of promise, but at twenty-five he was killed fighting against Frederick the Great at Crefeld. Paris and Versailles were plunged into desolation at the news of his death; he was mourned in Vienna and London; Frederick said he could forgive the French anything for having produced Gisors. A hundred years later his life was written. Today, Gisors would be killed on the road, the modern equivalent of the battlefield, and in ten years' time would be forgotten except by his parents – posterity not even according him the passing tribute of a sigh since tombstones are out of fashion. And what of the Eugenes, who roam the streets with other naughty boys, as he did, upsetting honest citizens? Aware of their own possibilities, such young men must suffer when they think that, however much they may protest as students, their future is bounded by office walls, that fame spurs them in vain while the laurels go to pop singers. No wonder the youth of today is in ferment.

I have always been squeamish about torture. I can't read about it or see the films and plays in which it occurs. When I was little, I was told that it is now over: Tyburn is only dear old Marble Arch, the rack a museum piece, and the grid a subject for religious pictures. When I first grew up, this still seemed to be the case and only during the war did one realize that torture is far from being over; now it appears to be universally employed. I don't worry about human beings as much as I used to: if they are so stupid as to torment each other, good luck to them. The public is not averse from such practices and nothing succeeds in literature and at the theatre like infliction of pain. But the fate of animals is a nagging source of disquiet. Certain creatures such as wolves, rats and bluebottles seem to be regarded as inherently wicked, deserving the worst agonies, while others, such as rabbits, guinea-pigs, hens and pigs, are non-creatures, presumably insentient, to whom any treatment can justifiably be handed out.

I was horrified to read in an English paper an account of an interesting experiment carried out on six white hens and six brown ones to see which would die of thirst more quickly. Now death by thirst is an appalling thing: how could anybody, even a scientist, inflict it on these creatures for such a frivolous reason? I didn't write to the editor of the paper because I thought he would receive a deluge of letters; if he did, none was published. One has to be pious in science, as formerly in religion, and accept everything done in its name. Then we come to dogs. You don't have to be a sentimental old lady to know that dogs, having lived for so long with human beings, are more anthropomorphic than other creatures, so that they suffer mentally to a greater degree. They suffer terribly from boredom, for instance. Granted that so many experiments on dogs are necessary (we must try to be pious), I worry about the lives they lead while waiting for the worst. Unfortunately nobody is ever kind to an animal which is doomed – one sees that over and over again in the treatment of beasts on their way to the slaughterhouse. Presumably these dogs bark away their sad lives in prison until their heads are sawn off and sewn onto the bodies of other dogs so that, eventually, old businessmen will be able to have the limbs of young athletes.

Thoughts of a pedestrian trying to cross the road: young men won't stop; women can't stop (no control of the machine and thinking about their lovers); and old men, who might stop, are always driven by women or young chauffeurs.

The Listener, May 16, 1968

France, May 1968: A Revolution Diary

Nancy Mitford to Diana Mosley May 17, 1968

'I suppose there is going to be a general paralysis here . . . Can't help slightly enjoying the excitement though I know it's wrong.'

Nancy Mitford's Diary June 4, 1968

'I've sent up to now (June 3rd) to the *Spectator*, reading it over the telephone v. tiring. Don't know whether I'll go on or not. I don't think I've got the temperament of a diarist.'

Versailles, 16 May   We have heard the young leaders on TV for three quarters of an hour. It was very tiring. There is a fat boy whose name I didn't hear; the other two are suitably named Sauvageot and Cohn-Bandit. People's names are so often suitable: Montgomery, Alexander, de Gaulle, Wilson, Brown and so on. Sauvageot apes Robespierre, cold and quiet, hoping to be creepy no doubt and not quite succeeding. Bandit very reminiscent of Esmond Romilly – a bounding, energetic little anarchist, giggling from time to time but not making jokes which one might have liked. The fat boy seems the most human of the three.

Having said how much they despised everything in life, especially money, they keenly gave the numbers of their postal accounts so that we could hurry out and send them some. There was a great deal of wailing about their treatment by the police. I despise them for it. They were out for a rough-up and they got it. Nobody was killed and now they are behaving like babies who have been slapped. It's not very dignified.

The postman has made our blood run cold by saying *'tout va changer.'* He comes an hour late and dumps the neighbour's letters, and I must say mine, in my box. Madame Pines said to Marie, my old servant, 'What is the General waiting for? As soon

202

as he has gone everything will be all right.' I told Marie to remember that this lady is a most fearful idiot. She is the only person I know down here who is against the General. But then to be quite honest she is the only real have-not that I know. Even so her little flat is adorable and with her work and her late husband's pension she is absolutely comfortable.

Frank and Kitty came from Paris to see me at eleven. Very friendly of them. Frank thinks we are having one of those periodic student upsets which France has always known. He doesn't think it's serious. He is a clever man, knows France and French history, but I well remember that in May 1958 he never expected the return of the General. I said to him at that time 'Frank, surely after the press conference you must have realized that it was inevitable?' and he said (very honestly), 'No.'

Miss Sweeney came to tea. She had been to the Château. She says it beats Chatsworth.

17 May Thierry came to lunch, full of Paris gossip and bringing brochures and so on from Germany where he has just been and where I am going in August in search of Frederick the Great. No political talk except he said, 'If the workers come out seriously it will be a nuisance.'

Bertrand says that there is no revolutionary spirit. But I say there never is at the beginning. All is bonhomie at first. Tough stuff comes later. I have a feeling we may be at one of those moments in history when the authorities can't do right.

18 May Lucy rang up. She has put on the Phrygian bonnet. Went to the Sorbonne dressed as a student. As she is my age she must have looked odd. Said they were all so beautiful and so polite. The Sorbonne seems to have become a tourist attraction.

19 May General strike so as I haven't got a car I am stuck here. Very good for work. The wireless has been taken over and the announcers who used to seem such dears have suddenly become extremely frightening. They rattle out bad news like machine guns. The French seem to have turned into Gadarene swine.

I've got a great friend in the town who is a workman at Renault's where the strike began. I have dined with him and his wife and they have dined here. I went along to see them. Both very Gaullist. According to them nobody wants to strike, but what can one do? *They* say one has got to, and that's that. It seems Renault are having trouble keeping up the pickets because the workmen, who have all got cars, want to go away for the weekend.

20 May The Canfields were to have come for luncheon. I waited until two. They must have forgotten or they would have telephoned. Oh well, never mind.

At three Nicholas Lawford came to talk about Frederick the Great and we had a very enjoyable historical gossip. He says the R——s are as red as can be. I am not at all surprised. A good deal of bandwagoning in progress, I note. He says Paris is intolerable and he is off to Germany – back in ten days.

Dear M. Dubois came to do some odd jobs. He is very depressing. He says the workers have all got over-excited and thinks the Communists will soon be in power. His colleagues will probably strike on Wednesday. Like my Renault workers, he is entirely against but what can one do? He installed a Calor gas cooker for us for when the current fails. Very sweet with old Marie who is beginning to be frightened.

The wireless is terrifying. If the BBC were not always so utterly wrong about French affairs I would listen to it, but what is the good? They understand nothing. The *Figaro* still appears, screaming 'do something' to the government like a hysterical women whose house is on fire.

Marie tells her beads whenever there's nothing else to do. I am afraid that I think like Frederick the Great that God exists but leaves us pretty well alone to make our muddles while we are here. No good bothering Him, I'm afraid. 'Mrs Rodd is on the line again, Almighty.' 'Tell her to get on with her work.'

21 May That ghastly old windbag François-Poncet and Daninos provide the two leaders in this morning's *Figaro*. How inspiring.

The bourse, quite good yesterday, has shut up shop now and so have the banks. I can live on Marie's savings so don't need to worry.

I rang up Henry. He says that last night some youths dumped a lot of arms in his courtyard saying they would come back for them later. 'Frankly Nancy one blow with that iron bar would finish one off.' Rang up and told Bodley. Both screaming and she rang up Henry about an hour after I'd spoken but he'd already left for Belgium. Bodley and I think we'll dress up as students like Lucy and go to his flat and take away the Sèvres.

The garden is full of baby pigs shivering with cold, poor little things.

Bertrand thinks a way will be found but that it will be a very long business. I tell about Henry. Bertrand: 'One can't be too careful.' I said 'Yes, he took one look at the iron bar.' Bertrand: 'Iron bars do not a prison make, am I not brilliant?'

No butter in the rue de Montreuil so I went to the market where there is masses. The Tricolour is still flying over the Lycée Hoche and all the boys seem to be there but discussing instead of doing their lessons. What a bore it must be. Some of the ones hanging about outside are wearing armbands and pansies in their buttonholes. On the way back I met Monsieur, Madame and Mademoiselle Saclay and we walked home together. They say everybody has gone mad. Mademoiselle, who is studying to be a chemist, is striking. The third striker that I have met – all unwilling.

I went to see the Lebruns. Madame Dupont, Madame Lebrun's sister and her husband were there. Madame Lebrun looking too lovely and about sixteen. She's got five or six good little children wandering in and out. How awful to think that very soon they will be students. A great deal of talk, pro-Gaullist and Catholic, getting nowhere except M. Lebrun said it would be better if the *motion de censure* were voted as then there would be general elections and we'd know where we stand. I said the minimum wage here is far too small. Madame Dupont said, 'Yes, but when you come to look into the facts every family has some other undeclared source of income. The wife takes in sewing or goes out cleaning. The husband goes out as a waiter and so on.' I said 'Yes, here in Versailles, but probably not in the big working class conglomeration because who would give them extra work to do there?' *La Croix* has been saying for years you must not segregate the workers and the bourgeoisie and that seems elementary, and yet the segregation goes on happening.

I came back here and saw the debate in the Chambre on television. Two excellent speeches by Poujade, who seems quite remarkable, and Duhamel. Billères not bad but far too long. At one moment after the end of his speech he got up to answer Pompidou's observations and Marie said *'Mince alors, il revient.'* It looks as though the government will win comfortably but the wireless says the General won't be allowed to organise a referendum.

22 May Moscow says the French workmen are trying to go too far. Of course the wireless doesn't relay that. *Figaro* drearier and more annoying than ever. I wish there was a reasonable morning paper but there isn't. I've tried them all. *Le Monde* is first class but I never want to read newspapers in the afternoon.

Marie, who has become rather bold, said this morning in the dairy, 'All these strikes are organized and the men have to come out whether they like it or not.' A young woman with a baby said 'You are quite right. There's a little factory here where nobody was on strike. *They* came and told the men to come out. The men went to the *patron* and said, "We've got nothing against you but we've got to come out".'

Bodley has gone to Paris to see the fun – partly, too, because of the cold. The English wireless says the temperature today won't rise above eleven degrees. Our meteorological office is on strike. No great loss. Bodley says a few days ago Henry said, 'So how is Bertrand taking it?' 'Oh, Nancy says he's shrieking with laughter as usual.' Henry: 'Frankly, Bodley, I wonder if he is. I believe if Nancy saw you and me in a tumbril she would say "Oh, they were shrieking with laughter".' I said well probably you would be. There's always something to laugh at.

I'm still living on the Canfields' *pot au feu* at every meal. Rang up the Catescos, a Rumanian couple who managed to get out a year or two ago, to see if they're all right. No answer. I expect they've buggered back to the now soaring Rumania. Don't blame them.

The mother tit has taken the family off. Quite right. They were being hunted by three cats. But we are deprived of a great amusement. The excellent *Société d'Assistance aux Bêtes d'Abattoir* to which I subscribe has rescued all the livestock out of the immobile trains so that's a weight off one's mind.

23 May I went yesterday afternoon to the Château half expecting to see Florence van der Kemp on the balcony. But the situation there is more like that of the days after the royal family had left. The Château empty and shut up, not a soul on the terrace, only the gardeners still working. Cold like winter. The orange trees looked miserable. Before going up there I saw Pompidou making his speech to the Assembly on the television – perfectly excellent, spoke for over an hout without notes. Nearly all the deputies read their speeches and the effect is very dull. Pisani has ratted. He hasn't got a beard for nothing.

Peter de Polnay telephoned. They live in an hotel at St Germain-des-Prés. He says they are all right and he feels everything will be.

Emmanuel de la Taille reappeared on the television looking rather ruffled I thought. Perhaps he has had a day or two in the cooler. Léon Zitrone, whom Dolly used to be in love with, hasn't been seen of late. All the nasty-looking men who rap out the news like machine funs are fairly new. They don't seem to shave as well as they used to. But at luncheon-time we had the charming Jacqueline Baudrier who reports parliamentary proceedings. She looks worried but not a pin out of place.

The *Figaro* hardly gives any space to last night's speeches but yatters on about *la fête des mères* – will it or won't it be put off? – and one of the leaders is an article on the little snatches of song to which Napoleon was addicted. What an awful paper it is.

The new Archbishop of Paris speaks of much misery. It's so strange – where is this misery? One sentence recurs among all my modest friends here: '*La France a été trop heureuse.*' My impression for several years now has been that France is almost entirely bourgeoise. Marie's father was a very poor peasant and his children were brought up almost hungry. But her nephews and nieces are more than well off. All with motor-cars and little weekend houses.

The Saclays came for a glass of champagne before dinner. They are very optimistic, say that the workers see the holidays approaching and also pay day. He says the first few days people stayed at home and there was hardly anybody in his shop. Now they are used to the situation and come as usual but he is beginning to lack certain things. The deliverers were leaving to make their rounds when some men from St Cyr came and told them to strike.

The dustmen still come here to take away our rubbish. Something to remember when giving Christmas boxes.

24 May More trouble with the students last night. Cohn-Bandit is not being allowed back from Germany. A move which seems to me fatal but is wildly applauded by everybody here. I can just imagine the fun he'll have getting in – which of course he will. Lovely cloak and dagger stuff, and then how will they ever dig him out of the Sorbonne?

All night a pitched battle raged around Jean de Gaigneron's house. I hope he's gone away. These battles are a nightmare for those in nearby houses because of the tear gas which seeps in and can't be got out for ages. Marie says all these young people seem very *mal élevé*. Tony Gandarillas rang. He says Jean had an awful night and the streets are still full of gas.

Went to the market. Never saw so much food. Bought chicory for Marie who can't find it here and craves it. How can she? Things seem a shade more hopeful, I should say.

25 May The General was perfect last night. After the flood of words we've been treated to of late, it was a relief to hear something short, sharp and to the point. But I've got a feeling that he is fed up. Though he will do his duty of course for as long as he can.

I've just turned on the wireless. It seems they had another sick night in Paris. Fouchet made a statement. He says the *pègres* have crept out from under the stones. I remember Bodley once talking to a French friend about the Commune and saying, 'What can have happened to all those savages who, such a little time ago, set fire to everything and skinned live horses in the streets?' 'They are still there,' he replied. The men of General Leclerc's division have issued a statement to say that they didn't liberate Paris in order to see it destroyed from within and are ready at any time to come and keep order. Mendès-France, gloating over the riots from a balcony, said the police have got an unfair advantage. Thank God. Bertrand says the problem is democratic. There are too many young people and they are turning against the old everywhere.

I note that the *fête des mères* is to take place tomorrow, which seems inappropriate as the whole thing is the fault of these wretched mothers for having such vast families and for bringing them up so badly. I'd love to have a few words with Cohn-Bandit's mother. Bodley says she saw two people beating dogs yesterday. Unheard of here. Can this mean a return to discipline and might it extend to children? I simply long to see somebody frowning at a child. I often think the worst part of being a child nowadays must be the silly smiles on everybody's faces.

Pompidou was marvellous on the telly at lunchtime. He is more impressive every time one sees him.

I've got masses of champagne and no mineral water, so if the tap gives out Marie and I will be permanently drunk. What a picture. Spent the afternoon deadheading buttercups. I'm reading Lady Cynthia Asquith – don't think her as bad as I believe the reviewers did though I dislike the person who emerges. I haven't seen an English paper for a fortnight, though Bodley managed to get the Sundays and is keeping Nigel Dennis for me.

26 May   Léon Zitrone reappeared on the television last night smiling and *pimpant*. But this morning all the RTF journalists are on strike, saying the news they have to give is not objective. That beats me – there has been a running river of communist propaganda for a week. Perhaps they want to keep Pompidou off the air.

The General told the new American ambassador that the future belongs to God, but the Archbishop who broadcast last night never mentioned God. He only spoke of material things like wages. Though at the end he said that Christians could pray. Marie didn't notice the oddity of this and I didn't point it out. Madame Saclay says it's the new style in the Church. The accent is no longer on God but on living conditions. I got her on her own and asked if Suzanne (the daughter) had been surprised by the revolt of her fellow students. She says Suzanne is deeply religious and takes everything calmly but she has been saying for a long time now that the boys – though not the girls – have been spoiling for a fight. Madame Saclay, like many people here, thinks the unrest comes from a physical desire for violence. Young friends of ours from the Argentine who until recently had been living in the *Cité des Arts*, an annexe of the university, and who still go about with students, told Bodley that so far from foreseeing events they were astounded by them. They had a horrid frightening time when lunatics surged into their street and set fire to the dustbins. Our faithful dustman still comes, by the way.

Marie dreamed all night of the General. She worries about him. I wonder if he knows how much people like her love him.

I went to see my friend from Renault's. His wife has shut up her little postcard kiosk as there is no trade. An *Institutaire* and his wife were there. The usual talk of what is it all about.

Christien, the black man who sells vegetables and is the pet of the whole street, says de Gaulle must go. Although pitch he was a French *colon* in Algeria, and, of course, they are out for revenge.

I have done a bit of telephoning. *Les gens du monde* seem quite philosophical, saying 'Very well; we must now make up our minds to live as the Swedes do – much more simply and do our own cooking.' In that case I shall starve to death as I can't cook – who cares?

Poujade has won his municipal election at Dijon getting 6,800 votes more than he got last Sunday. Nobody that I have seen has the slightest doubt that the General will win his referendum.

What a volcano this country is! Of course one knows it may erupt at any moment; but as with real volcanoes the soil is so rich and so fertile in every way that having once lived here any alternative seems unthinkable.

Spectator, May 31, 1968

A French Revolution Diary:
Part Two

27 May   Today I gave the whole thing a rest and only listened to the news at dinner-time. The strikers have not accepted the government's protocol. They say if they do, in a few months the country will be ruined and they will be blamed. Good joke – but where do we go from here? The students are upset because they have lost the limelight, reminding me of a little girl I could name who has to be the centre of all attention or else. The fat boy has resigned from the students' union to devote himself to politics. We certainly need more like him in public life.

It now seems they think that everybody over thirty ought to be dead. Marie-Antoinette, when she became Queen, said she didn't know how people over thirty dared show their faces at court. She called them *les siècles*. Poor dear, she was soon over thirty herself and didn't end too well. The political associates of the Sorbonne gerontophobes are Waldeck-Rochet, who looks like the father of Yul Brynner, Mendès-France, aged sixty-one, and the *taureau de la Nièvre* (Mitterrand), who at fifty-two is no lad. Perhaps they count as being in their second childhood.

The chemists in Paris are out of stock but tons of medicaments are said to have been squirrelled away at the Sorbonne. I do hope our future rulers are not a bunch of hypochondriacs.

28 May   Lucy rang up – she abandoned the red bonnet when the young Delacroix of the Sorbonne, so beautiful and so polite, took to incendiarism. She has been back there and I gather that its denizens are beginning to look less like Delacroix and more like Van Gogh. She says she can't go on living in a town where the hairdresser takes £4 and the doctor takes £5 – I told her not to worry a bit, very soon there will be no hairdressers or doctors. All very well for you, she said, with your wiry hair and perfect health. She's off to London, so my link with the Sorbonne has gone.

The French wireless has asked anybody who knows of a full petrol pump to report it. I am fairly public-spirited but if I knew of a full petrol pump I should tell my friends and not the French wireless in its present mood.

Went to the town and bought a few things to hoard, a practice to which so far I have not lent myself, but I only took as much as I could carry and only things abhorred by the French like Quaker Oats.

Madame Denis told Marie that she knows somebody who has hoarded £40 worth of food and added darkly, 'So if things turn out badly we know where to go'; but on Saturday she touched my heart by saying I mustn't give her her week's wages if it was awkward for me.

On my way home from the park two boys on a motor-bike pretended they were trying to kill me, following me up on to the wide footpath; but I must say when I laughed so did they, and went away with friendly waves. I do hope the over-thirties are going to be killed mercifully and quickly and not starved to death in camps.

K rang up to say she has got some petrol and can she take me anywhere – what an angel she is. I said, 'No, but I would love to see you.' Like Marie, she worries about the General. Evidently the people in Chatou where she lives are thinking and saying the same things as my neighbours. The same words, 'France has been too happy,' seem to recur as they do here.

Mitterrand on the tele – Marie kept up a running commentary and I was laughing so much at it that perhaps I didn't get his message correctly, but the impression was that he is claiming a *coup d'état*. Then we had Pompidou, whose calm reasonable manner inspires optimism every time that he appears. He asked for a secret ballot in the factories. What a hope! I also heard William Pickles from London, who said that Mendès-France is every Englishman's favourite French prime minister, but not every Frenchman's. This is true. I wish the BBC correspondents here were as well informed as Mr Pickles – but they seem to hate France and to predict a worst for which they long. The worst will probably occur but one can't be certain that it will.

29 May   The French architects are demanding liberty – in other words, anarchy – in other words, a free hand to pull down Paris and put up New York.

I saw a young man selling *L'Action Française* – how typical of Versailles. I had a look at it. It is almost too silly and, readers of this diary will be surprised to hear, even more right wing than I am. De Gaulle and Waldeck-Rochet are put in the same basket and Cohn-Bandit is chiefly reproached for being a German Jew. The only thing I have liked about the students is their slogan – 'We are all German Jews.' If I am a conservative it is because I see so much worth conserving in French society. It seems a pity that all should have to go up in flames for the sake of a few reforms.

I hear that the Embassy Rolls-Royce has been all round Paris delivering cards for the garden party – that's the spirit – up the old land.

At luncheon-time the wireless announced that the General has left for Colombey. Marie and I looked at each other in terror and despair, but it seems he has only gone to ponder and will be back tomorrow. There is now a rush of politicians to the microphones – all kindly say they are ready to take over. God preserve us from any of them: even the students might be better than those old hacks. What do the students really want? We know so little about them; when they appeared on the tele their only cry was 'Down with everything.' Fouchet said rather impatiently the other day they've got ideals – everybody has at that age, but what ideals! People over thirty must go, nobody need learn anything or pass any exams (as an autodidact myself I see the point – though as a taxpayer I can't quite see in that case what the schools and universities are for). People who don't agree with them must keep their mouths shut. They enjoy lighting fires and desecrating war memorials. They have also said down with concrete – hear hear, but where will everybody live? In tents? None of this constitutes a positive programme. They now say they will go from house to house and explain their policy. I can't wait. Marie thinks if we let them in they will be laying plans for future burglary. Never mind, I must see them.

In the grocer's shop a woman said, 'Is the post office open?' 'Of course it is, it's occupied.' General laughter.

30 May   I hadn't quite realized what a hermit I am by nature – the days go by and I have no desire to move from my house and garden. I haven't done so for three weeks now. Of course one is virtually kept going by the excitement. We live in a thrilling serial story and the next instalment will be the General's statement this afternoon. *(Later.)* I waited for it feeling quite sick but as soon as he opened his mouth one knew everything would be all right. France is not going to be handed over like a parcel to a regime which she may or may not want without being allowed to say 'Yes' or 'No.'

I went to the market and thought the shoppers in the streets were looking more cheerful already. Then the demonstration in the Champs Elysées, reported in full and with enthusiasm on the wireless, showed that the General has not lost his magic. I'd have given anything to leave my house and garden for that.

The eight o'clock news on television was a real muddle –. perhaps Lady Asquith had got into the building. But we were shown a lovely photograph of Mendès-France and Mitterrand looking like two vampires who had seen a piece of garlic.

31 May   Woke up feeling as though I had come out of a nightmare. People who went to the Étoile yesterday say it was like the Liberation. The General's ADC, hearing the noise from the Elysée, said, 'That's all for you, *mon Général.*' To which de Gaulle replied, 'If it were only me.' The Parisians have been bottled up for about a fortnight but it seemed much longer and the sky looked black indeed. Now they have exploded.

Some hours after the demonstration the *taureau de la Nièvre* was caught between two groups of students, Gaullists and anti-Gaullists, in the Boulevard Saint-Germain. They stopped arguing with each other and all rounded on him and a corrida began from which the poor old bull, puffing and blowing, had to be rescued by those very police about whom he has been so insulting.

The BBC, at it again, says it is evident that the ORTF is back in the hands of the General because no opposition reaction to his speech has been broadcast. Untrue. We have had statements in all the news bulletins from every leader except Mendès-France, who has so far refused to comment. As a matter of fact, a child of six could have written these statements – they are so predictable and so dull.

I wonder if habitués of the television find the lack of it as much a relief as I find the lack of letters? I used to think I lived for the post, now I don't know how I shall bear the sight of it. The joy of letters from various cherished correspondents is outweighed by all the requests, demands and statements from strangers. Plans to remember, forms to fill in, and so on, which often occupy my whole morning. I haven't got a secretary and wouldn't care for the physical presence of one. I see that the post office workers are on their way back, so I am doubtless enjoying a last few days of peace.

The television comes on for the eight o'clock news only, but the news bulletins on the wireless are as usual. The sale of books has trebled since the strike began. *(Later.)* Horrors! The beautiful, the brilliant Emmanuel de la Taille, who looks so English and reliable and who reports Common Market and other diplomatic proceedings on the television, is one of the strikers. We have all been anxious over his fate. One thought he was in some dreadful torture chamber of the ORTF, bravely enduring, like the boy in the *Bengal Lancer* film without an American mother and a yellow streak; and all the time he was agitating at the Sorbonne. My faith in human nature is not shaken – it is destroyed. It will be most interesting to see what does happen to the ORTF. Reforms have been promised and I suppose much will depend on whether some Lord Reith (*Ah oui, Monsieur le Baron*) can be found to organize it on the lines of the BBC. Some of the striking journalists say they want to run it themselves like a private company or a newspaper. Others say the source of power must be the nation, whatever that means. I hope it won't lose its own special lively character. I feel doubtful about the entertainment value of anything run by the people for the people.

1 June I took the local bus and went over to Orsay. This little bus, which has been faithfully running all through the troubles, is very symptomatic of the modern world. As every soul in this country except me has got a motor-car it only caters for Arabs and children. I have never seen a fellow-bourgeois in it. The journey is most beautiful, through Jouy-en-Josas which, buried in deep woods and composed of seventeenth-century cottages, must look

215

almost exactly as it did when the duc de Luynes saw Louis XV galloping quite alone down the village street, having lost the hunt. Then one goes through the woods on to a great plain of cornfields and huge farmhouses – the atomic centre in the middle of it is not ugly or out of scale and is discreetly hideen by poplar trees. Down again into the valley of the Chevreuse and here the spoiling begins. Orsay, which used to be such a dear little market town, is now part of the Sorbonne, covered with university buildings in the modern taste. The inhabitants are furious with the students – they say everything has been done for them – huge swimming pools and sports grounds, free holidays in the mountains and so on, and this is how they show their gratitude.

I got hold of some English papers of the last week or two. My goodness, they were alarming – no wonder people rang up from London offering blankets and tea. One felt frightened here, but it was for the future – the possible ruin of this beautiful land. The bang on the door and the commissaire telling one to pack up a change of linen and go. There was a letter in one of the papers from a woman whose hedgehog speaks to her – I am jealous. My hedgehogs never address a word to me and I am rather anxious to know their demographic plan.

I listened to *A Word in Edgeways* on the BBC, as I believe it is supposed to be typical of the conversations people are having at home. I was surprized to find that no distinction seemed to be made between Russian and Chinese forms of communism. It is the latter we are threatened with here, and nothing was said of the demographic aspect of the revolt: the young against the old. A lady speaker said she had met Mendès-France and he is a very democratic sort of chap. He may seem so at a dinner party but his behaviour last week was not democratic at all.

There are many more swallows this year than last. I wonder if this is also true of swifts – I was afraid they were beginning to feel the effects of insecticides.

2 July (Sunday). People are flocking to church. Marie had to wait in a queue for two hours yesterday to confess her saintly sins. Our beautiful Saint Symphorien was overflowing this morning. They collected for the foreigners who have suffered from the strike: not stranded Britons so much as Portuguese workmen.

Lucy is yearning over the students again. She says they are out in the streets again this morning, beautiful and polite, collecting money for the old – to give a Molotov cocktail party for them, I expect, said I. 'Oh Nancy, you're so cynical.' The fact is these students are like a chicken whose head has been cut off – they are running round in circles with nobody paying much attention to them and with nothing to do. They held a demonstration yesterday, but instead of the hundreds of thousands of a week ago they mustered only about 20,000 people.

Cohn-Bandit's locks are now dyed black – he'll soon look very odd unless he forks out £4 to a hairdresser to have them retinted.

3 June The deepest holiday sleep outside – the streets are far quieter than yesterday, when there was much activity round the church. The public opinion polls show that Mitterrand has lost ground. However, he won't notice that and Frossard said in the *Figaro* he will probably soon announce his readiness to be Archbishop of Paris. Nothing on the student front except that, fighting having broken out between Jews and Arabs in Belleville, they seized their red flag and sallied forth to join in. Unfortunately they arrived when all was over. They had much better start their lessons again.

I went to see my friend from Renault's. He spoke as if everything had already returned to normal, though in fact the strike is still going on: *'Oh là, on a eu chaud.'* That's what they always say when France has seemed to be losing a big football match and then wins it. But what will happen to us when *le Grand* has gone? I said, 'France explodes like this about once in a generation. Thank God this blowup happened while the General is still here to cope with it. With any luck at all you and I won't be alive to see the next time.'

Spectator, June 7, 1968